INTRODUCTION TO BUSINESS MANAGEMENT

TEXT BOOK

BY

Abebe Ejigu Alemu, PhD

Professor of Marketing and Supply Chain Management College
of Business and Economics School of Management-Mekelle University
Department of Logistics Management
International Maritime College Oman
abebe@imco.edu.om

Abdelsalam Adam Hamid, PhD

Assistant Professor
Department of Logistics Management
International Maritime College Oman
abdelsalam@imco.edu.om

First Published by Notion Press 2021

ISBN 979-8-88521-233-5

Acknowledgment

First of all, I would like to thank the Almighty God for helping me in every aspect of my life. I am grateful to my wife Tsige G/silassie, my sons Abenezer Abebe & Eyoas Abebe and my daughter Ruth Abebe for giving me their love and time while preparing this textbook. My mother W/ro Yalga Shiferaw, my brothers Molla, Mesafint, Aderajew & Adino Ejigu; and my sisters Askal & Elsabet; are always on my side to encourage me to add value on my career.

My colleagues at the School of management of Mekelle University where I have been serving more than twenty years, have to be credited for commenting and enriching the contents of the textbook. My appreciation goes to Mekelle University, College of Business and Economics and School of Management which has provided me opportunities to further my education and conduct research in the field of management. The Late Professors Dr. Yassin Ibrahim and Asst. Prof. Gebremedhin Yihdego who were my close friends in the School of Managements are in my thoughts with their loved ones as their contribution was immense in commenting the textbook.

I am grateful to my students at undergraduate and graduate level who attended several management courses at Mekelle University and International Maritime college Oman who has persuaded me to prepare the textbook.

International Maritime college Oman, Department of Logistics Staff members also deserve my appreciation for their encouragement and support.

Finally, I want to dedicate this book to my late father Ato Ejigu Alemu; my late sisters Birhanua and Abaynesh ; and to my late Mother In-law W/ro Tsadikan Asgedom.

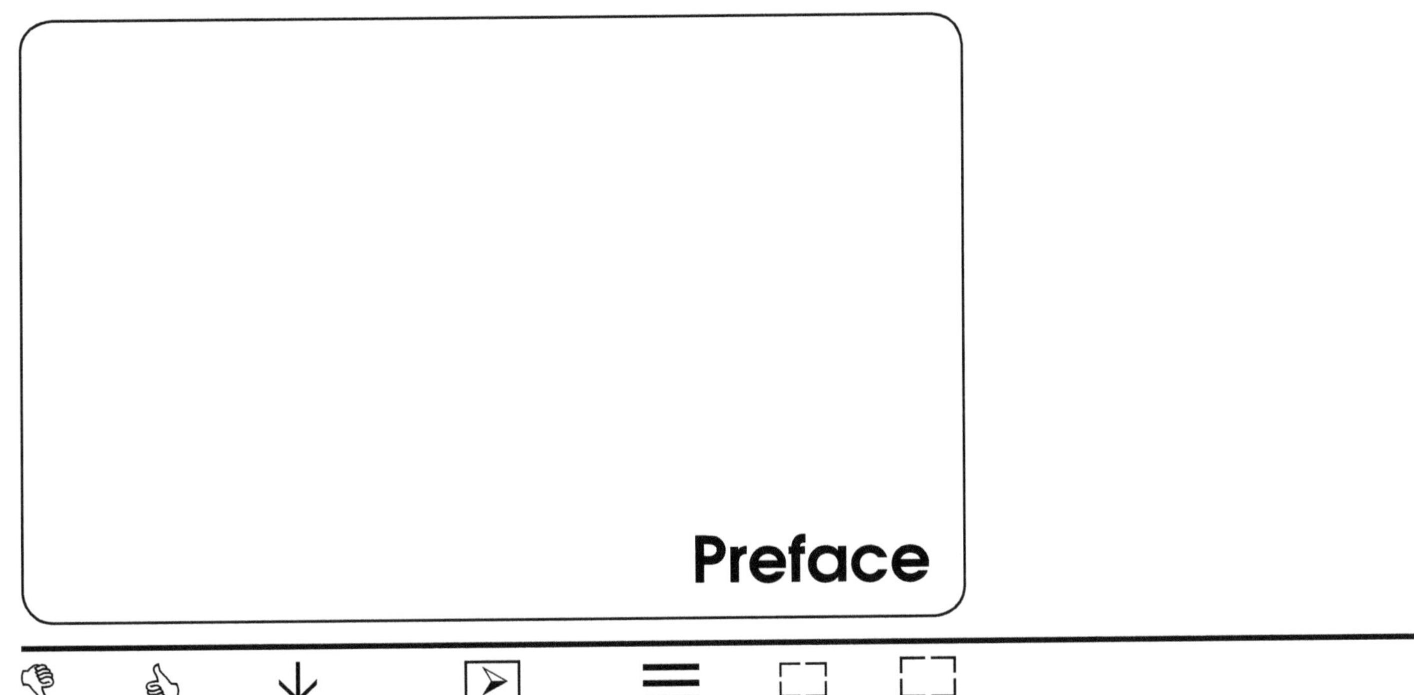

This book aims to introduce the reader to the broad concept of management from the content of this chapter the reader will understand different aspects, such as management functions, skills and problems, environment, and levels of management, but all the sub-topics are related and interconnected since it supports the core concept of the management. In addition to the ideas of the pioneers' scholars of management-initiated principles for managers, and those principles became as main guidelines for the late scholars and practitioners, From the practices and observation of the early management scientist, the principles were developed and introduced as the first organized and theoretical nucleus for management science. Moreover, the book comprehensively covered the area of management functions; planning, organizing, staffing and leading However, planning is surrounded by many factors constraining and affecting the plan performance; these factors have been considered in this book, also Organizing is a function of smoothing the organization well established principles and systems, beside theories associated with human resource staffing, and leading staff as one of most important topics in management. The book discusses the core concepts of leading, elements of leading, motivational factors, theories of Motivation and how leaders motivate their subordinates. Lastly the book highlighted the contemporary issues in management.

Chapter One: Chapter one focuses on the general overview of management, nature, This chapter aims to introduce the reader to the broad concept of management from the content of this chapter the reader will understand different aspects, such as management functions, skills and problems, environment and levels of management, But, all the sub-topics are related and interconnected since it supports the core concept of the management.

Chapter Two: Development of Management Thought

The pioneers' scholars of management initiated principles for managers, and those principles became as main guidelines for the late scholars and practitioners. When educated, workers and employees were few, and most of the tasks were manual; therefore, most of the jobs were performed in a classical way with a low level of innovation and change.

From the practices and observation of the early management scientist, the principles were developed and introduced as the first organized and theoretical nucleus for management science; this chapter cover pre-scientific, scientific school, Bureaucracy, Behavioural, Human Relations school.

Chapter Three: Planning

This chapter will discuss the planning concept, process (steps), components, approaches and the role each planning stage plays in developing a successful plan. However, planning is surrounded by many factors constraining and affecting the plan performance; these factors have been considered in this chapter. Furthermore, planning mainly relies on forecasting the future; therefore, this chapter covers the forecasting process and types.

Chapter Four: Organizing

This chapter the discuss the concept of organizing and fundamental features of organizing, such as work specialization, chain of command, span of management, and the process of organizing, formal organization, informal organization. Organizing is a function For smoothing the functioning of organization well established principles of organizing need to be followed.

This chapter also discussed organization structures implanted by business firms. Each type of structure has its own advantages and disadvantages, Organizational Relationships and Behaviour.

Chapter Five: Staffing

This chapter covers the concepts and theories associated with human resource staffing. The chapter is exploring the recruitment, selection, training, the steps in the staffing process, employee training you, staffing strategy plan, all these topics to enable the readers to have a comprehensive idea and understanding.

Chapter Six: Directing (Leading)

This chapter explores the topic of directing (leading) as one of most important topics in management. The chapter discuss the core concepts of directing, elements of directing, motivational factors, theories of Motivation, leadership styles characteristics, advantages of each style and disadvantages and consider how leaders influence others to get things done. also, this chapter discusses servant leadership and moral leadership.

Chapter Seven: Controlling

The objectives of this lesson are to enable to define management; to describe the nature and scope of management; to know the difference between management and administration; to understand various levels of management; and to describe the various skills that are necessary for successful managers.

Chapter Eight: Chapter Eight Contemporary Issues

this chapter discussed the new issues in management which are emerged because of business environment changes and the development of the business practices and theories

Table of Contents

     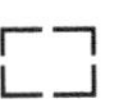 

List of Figures

Introduction

The existence of organisations in society is essential in order to meet the purposes and needs of society. Regardless of the types and sizes, all firms must be committed to goals and objectives and principles and values common to all their parties. Management objectives and principles are a guide that makes the existence of the firm meaningful. The management's mission is to improve the organisation's work and develop its ability to seize opportunities and help people through training, learning and community service. Because management deals with business activities and practices, the final output is measured by the outcomes achieved for all parties. Drucker argued that management is considered as a liberating art because it deals with wisdom, science and leadership, where managers need various human and social sciences - such as economics, sociology, psychology and philosophy along with other applied sciences, so these sciences help achieve the overall goals of institutions and management As for it as an art It is related to practice and application.

There is no doubt that management differs from one organisation to another. The organisation's main task is to determine the method, systems and procedures of work, and these systems and methods, in turn, affect the outputs. The failure of management to find solutions to stakeholders' problems puts the firm in danger of collapse. Therefore, organisations from various fields and sizes need management to help them achieve sustainability by fulfilling their goals.

Management as a practice existed for a long time before it was transformed into a written theory for people to learn and benefit from organisations' experiences and success stories. The twentieth century witnessed a significant development in management as a science that can be studied, and its results can be projected as principles and theories. As an application also management various experiences can be shared as lessons from previous practices, especially after the second world war. As business and innovation grew in the field of industry, the world witnessed economic and political openness, which increased the need for specialists in the field of management, and this, in turn, increased the demand for studies and research in administrative problems and their solutions. In its development and growth, the administration passed through stages of experience and theorising that produced several different schools with different philosophies and distinguished curricula that are often linked to each other. Management philosophies, approaches, and schools were helping to meet the growing needs and problems of the industry and the market as a result of international trade and economic globalisation.

Today's business firms need management as an essential tool to carry out the tasks of planning, leading, organising and controlling their complicated business and projects to attain the business objectives efficiently and effectively as the nature and dynamism of today's business environment requires organisations with capabilities matching the level of complexity today. Management is a powerful tool that enables organisations to survive and continue in today's world based on rapid movement, continuous development, power of customers, the multiplicity of alternatives, the openness of markets and the removal of trade barriers.

In the past, companies used to work traditionally were authoritarian or controlling management methods on people and restricted them by following strict rules, regulations, and work systems to show that they work efficiently. However, the management abused the hierarchical authority that obliged individuals to obey by following the autocratic system. Though, organisations need to innovate, renew, and motivate staff to achieve high performance. These conditions require managers to possess new skills that fit today's business requirements, such as focusing on change and strategic leaders for change, motivating people to innovate and create, developing common interests and shared visions, and delegating authority and power. In addition, because of the complexities of the business environment and changing jobs and employees, managers have to focus more on learning and training staff to increase their capacity and flexibility to adapt.

The only way of sustainability and survivance for Companies is to create a flexible, adaptable system that fit today's business environment.

THE NATURE SCOPE OF MANAGEMENT

      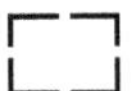

LEARNING OBJECTIVES

Reading this chapter will help you do the following:

1. Develop an Understanding of the nature of the management work.
2. Know the management concept and objectives
4. Outline management skills, roles, of the management and the challenges of the management.
5. Understand what the meaning of leading individual and group.

Overview

Chapter one focuses on the general overview of management, nature, This chapter aims to introduce the reader to the broad concept of management from the content of this chapter the reader will understand different aspects, such as management functions, skills and problems, environment and levels of management, But, all the sub-topics are related and interconnected since it supports the core concept of the management.

THE NATURE AND SCOPE OF MANAGEMENT

One of the most important human activities is *managing*. Ever since people began forming groups to accomplish aims they could not achieve as individuals, managing has been essential to ensure the co-ordination of individual efforts. As society has come to rely increasingly on group effort, and as many organised groups have become large, the task of managers has been rising in importance.

1.1 What is Management?

The term management has been defined in many different ways by different scholars. Because of its recent origin and extensiveness to give a comprehensive definition of it involves certain difficulties. Management is that, and more so much more, in fact, that no one simple definition has been universally accepted. Moreover, existing definitions change as the environments of organisations continue to change (Manson., Talya, and Berrin., 2012).

There are many definitions given by different scholars of management. Some of them to mention:

1. Management is the process of planning organising, leading and controlling the efforts of organisation members and of using all other organisational resources to achieve stated organisational goals (Mescon, et al,).

A process is a systematic way of doing things. Here they defined management as a process because all managers regardless of their particular aptitudes or skills engage in certain interrelated activities in order to achieve their desired goals. The process of management includes:

   i. Planning implies that managers think through their goals and actions in advance. Their actions are usually based on some method, plan, or logic, rather than on a hunch.
   ii. Organising means that managers co-ordinate the human and material resources of the organisation. The effectiveness of an organisation depends on its ability to marshal its resources to attain its goals. Obviously, the more integrated and co-ordinated the work of an organisation, the more effective it will be. Achieving this co-ordination is part of the manager's job.
   iii. Leading describes how managers direct and influence subordinates, getting others to perform essential tasks. By establishing the proper atmosphere, they help their subordinates do their best.
   iv. Controlling means that management's attempt to assure that the organisation is moving towards its goals. If some part of their organisation is on the wrong track - if it is not working toward stated goals or is not doing so effectively managers try to find out why and set things right.

The above definition stresses that management involves achieving the organisation's "stated goals." This means that managers of any organisation a university, the Internal Revenue Service, etc. try to attain specific ends. E.g., the stated goals of a university might be to give students a well-rounded education in an academic community.

2. Management is the process of designing and maintaining an environment in which individuals, working to gather in groups, accomplish efficiently selected aims. (Koontz and Weihrich, 1988). When the definition is expanded.

   i. As manager's, people carry out the managerial functions of planning, organising, staffing, leading and controlling.
   ii. Management applies to any kind of organisation
   iii. It applies to managers at all organisational levels
   iv. The aim of all managers is the same to create a surplus.
   v. Managing is concerned with productivity that implies effectiveness and efficiency

3. Management may be defined in many different ways. The most generic of its meaning is concerned with **process**, a series of co-ordinated, goal-directed actions. From this perspective, *management* is the process of utilising organisational resources (human, financial, physical and technological) to achieve specific objectives through the functions of planning, organising, leading and controlling.

4. Management is the effective and efficient integration and co-ordination of resources to achieve desired objectives. Now let's look at each key part of this definition

---

Objectives: All organisations have some mission that includes their reasons for existence. To be effective in this mission, the organization must have targets, the *objectives*[11] that managers hope to achieve.

- **Effectiveness and efficiency:** Effective management is at the heart of all managerial activities. *Effectiveness* refers to how well on organization reaches its objectives over a period of time and stresses the long range, continuing nature

1 Objective: the targets toward which managers move in order to fulfil organization's mission.

of management. *Efficiency* measures frequently are used to determine whether the organisation is meeting its short-term targets. For example, if Mesfin Industrial engineering were to use two tons of steel to build a Afrotruck, a lot of steel would probably be wasted. In other words, if we compared the inputs of steel to the output of one car, we would see that MIE was not using its resources efficiently. Thus efficiency is a short-term measure; it compares the inputs or costs directly to the out puts or benefits.

Effectiveness pertains to a longer period of time. To be effective, for instance a University must design curriculum that make graduates solve country or organizational problems. If it introduces curricula that doesn't satisfy the need of the country or organizations, the university will not meet its objectives effectively. An action that improves efficiency may not be effective in the long run.

- **Resources**: An organisation's people, capital, technology, clients, and time, all of which managers must use efficiently and effectively.

We can illustrate the nature of each resource by looking at university. The ***people*** resource includes the number of faculty and staff needed and the skills they must have. The ***capital*** resource involves the acquisition and use of money, including how much state funding is needed, how much tuition to charge, and how much each part of the university should be given. ***Technology*** includes the type of computer to buy the registration procedures to use, the buildings needed (class-room, offices, library and laboratories) and the maintenance of the grounds. ***Clients*** are those served by the University, including alumni, students and the community. Attracting students and "marketing" them to employers are also concerns. Finally, ***time*** is a limiting resource.

- **Co-ordination and Integration:** by co-ordinating people, capital, technology and time, an organisation hopes to serve its clients in such a way that it moves toward its objectives.

5. Management is a distinct process consisting the managerial functions of planning, organising, actuating and controlling performed to determine and accomplish stated objectives with the use of human beings and other resources.

Graphically

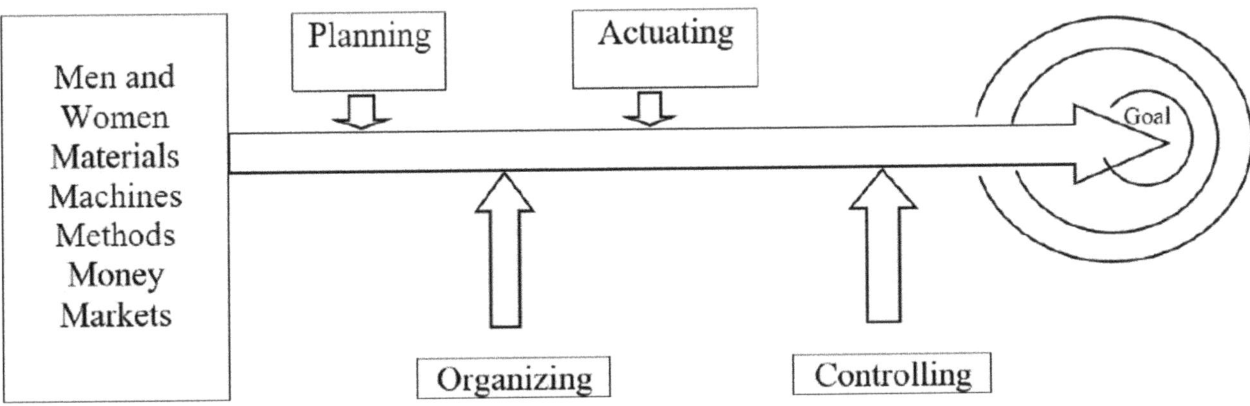

Figure 1.1 Management process.
Source: adopted from: Bose, D.C., 2012. Principles of management and administration. PHI Learning Pvt. Ltd..

6. Management is the art of getting things done through the efforts of other people.
7. Management is that function of an enterprise, which concerns itself with the direction and control of the various activities to attain business objectives.
8. Management is the art of securing maximum result with a minimum of effort so as to secure maximum prosperity for the employer and employee and give the public the best possible service.
9. Management is the creation and maintenance of an internal environment in an enterprise where individuals working in-group can perform efficiently and effectively toward the attainment of group goals.

10. Management is the process of co-ordinating all the resources of an organisation to achieve the organisational objectives
11. Management is the process of designing and maintaining an environment in which individuals, working together in groups, accomplish efficiently selected aims.
12. Management may be defined as a technique by means of which the purpose and objectives of a particular human group are determined, clarified and effectuated.
13. To manage is to forecast and plan, to organise, to command, to co-ordinate, and to control.

From the definitions mentioned, we can derive the following important points.

a) Management refers to the managerial functions planning, organising, staffing, leading and controlling.
b) Management co-ordinates both human and non-human resources- land, labour and capital for the accomplishment of group objectives.
c) Management applies to all types of organisations and all levels regardless to the size of the organization, profit or non-profit making, manufacturing or service giving; management is needed where ever people work together to try to reach a common goal.
d) Management is concerned with creating and maintaining an internal environment with due regard to the external environment.

Although it is emphasised that a manager's task is in designing an internal environment for performance, it must be understood that managers must operate in the external environment of an enterprise as well as in the internal environment of the various departments within the organisation. Managers operate in an open system and they depend on external environment for the inputs and outputs of their enterprise. In this case they have to understand and respond to the many variables of the external environment- economic, technological, social, political and ethical factors that affect their areas of operations.

For the sake of convenience, we can define management as the distinct process consisting the managerial functions of Planning, Organising, Staffing, Leading and Controlling so as to design and maintain a conducive environment in order to achieve common group goals or organisational objectives.

From the above discussions we can arrive at the following deductions:

1. Management is a continuous process - wherever there is group effort.
2. Management is viewed in terms of the managerial functions a manager does.
3. Management deals with the co-ordination of human and physical resources
4. Management is applied wherever there is an organisation with an objective to be achieved.
5. Since an organisation exists in an open system, management creates a favourable environment in order to achieve organisational goals.
6. The target of managerial process is to achieve organisational objectives- i.e. reasons for the existence of the organisation

1.2 The Nature of Management

1. **Universal Application:-** Management is applied in any organization (large, small in size, or service or manufacturing or for-profit or not-for-profit) and its functions are practiced in any level of management.
2. **Goal Oriented:** - Any organization is established to achieve objectives, and management is important for any organization to achieve its pre-stated objectives efficiently and effectively.
3. **Guidance:-** The main task of management is guidance in the utilization of material and human resources in the best possible manner. Without the involvement of management, resources might be misused and wasted. Through the optimum utilization of resources, it is to ensure that the objectives are attained.
4. **Divorced/Separated from proprietorship**:- Management does not signify proprietorship/ownership. Managers work for the attainment of organizational goals and objectives.

5. **Management is a human activity:-** Management functions are discharged by individuals not by machines such a computers. However, it can be aided by such instruments as computers.
6. **Management signifies Authority:-** Since the significance of management is to direct, to guide and to control, it has to have authority. Authority is the power to compel others to work and behave in a particular manner.
7. **Leadership**:- The manager has to lead a team of workers. He/she must be capable of inspiring, motivating and winning their confidence.
8. **Management is Multidisciplinary:-** It has grown as a body of discipline taking the help of so many social sciences like sociology, psychology, economics, etc.

1.3 Is Management a Science or an Art?

Science is a systematised body of knowledge consisting concepts, theory and principles concerning a particular field of study. Science is systematised in the sense that relationships between variables and limits have been ascertained and underlying principles have been discovered. The essential feature of science is that knowledge has been discovered and systematised through the application of scientific method. Scientific method involves determining facts through observation of events of things and verifying the accuracy of these facts through continued observation. After classifying and analysing the facts, scientists look for and find some causal relationships, which they believe to be true. Such generalisations, called "hypothesis", are then tested for their accuracy. When hypothesis are found to be supported, to reflect or explain reality and therefore to have value in predicting what will happen in similar circumstances, they are called "principles." (J. Timms., 2011)

Application of scientific method (approach) to the development of principles doesn't totally eliminate doubt. Every generalisation, however proved, may be subject to further research and analysis.

As science management is a systematic body of knowledge representing a core of principles or fundamental truths that tend to be true in most managerial situations. It is also assumed that if a manager understand this body (organised) knowledge and knows how to apply it to given situations, they should be able to perform the managerial functions both efficiently and effectively,

As an emerging science, management has certain basic principles, which are universally applicable in any organisation regardless of its size and nature. Effective managers use the scientific approach in making decisions.

However, management is not comparable to exact sciences like physics, chemistry and so on because it deals with human behaviour, which is the most unpredictable and ever changing.

Management is an inexact science. Therefore, to achieve the desired goal managers should blend the principles of management with realities. These principles explain relationships between two or more variables. To conclude, management is categorised as a science for the following reasons:

1. Its principles[2] are a systematised body of knowledge and universally applicable
2. They are based on scientific enquiry and observation
3. They explain cause and effect relationships between various variables
4. Their validity can be verified and they can serve as a reliable basis for predicting future events.

Art may be defined as a skill which can be modified or know how to accomplish a desired concrete result. As a practising art, management is know how or doing things in the realities of a situation.

Thus managing as practice is an art; the organised knowledge underlying the practice may be referred to as a science. In this context science and art are not mutually exclusive but are complementary. As science improves so should art. Art is concerned with the application of knowhow and skill to the specific time, place and condition tactfully, creatively and wisely. Generally art is based on judgement, feeling and intuition. Art in management has a great role in creating new

2 Principles: Fundamental truths, which explain relationship between two or more sets of variables.
Theory: Systematic grouping of interrelated principles. Its task is to tie together significant knowledge, to give it a framework.

idea, innovating, initiating and to implement and to integrate the skill or know how in relation with the resources, goals of the organisation.

Art helps to create new idea and effective methods to use from the underlying knowledge and skill. As an art management requires different approaches and methods to achieve the predetermined objectives. To conclude, management is considered as a creative art for the following reasons:

1. It requires practical know-how of the theories, principles and techniques of management in order to perform a specific job efficiently and effectively.
2. It depends on the personal skill and effective use of one's knowledge and proficiency to ensure maximum result at possible minimum costs.
3. It follows result-oriented course of action or depends specific objectives to be reached.
4. Management calls for creative ability to introduce new ideas, new products and new techniques to yield higher returns to an organisation.
5. Continuous practice of management theories and principles results in better performance.

1.4 Management as a profession

The essence of any profession involves elements of art and science plus something more. Being a manager clearly satisfies some but not all of the basic criteria of professionalism. Even though the field of management may not represent a true profession, the practice of management is a career path of high social importance. Managers are in a position to have a positive impact on the society in which we live. To be good as a manager, whether a true professional or not, is something to be proud about.

The professional character of management is enhanced by the presence of a basic body of knowledge, or scientific foundation, from which you and other can draw insight.

Some aspects of management are scientific while others are artistic.

If a profession is defined as an occupation that serves others, management may be so classified as a profession. However, if a profession is a vocation requiring licensing and graduate study, such as medicine and law, then management is not a profession.

One fact usually considered when referring to management as a profession is that the field does possess a *unique body of knowledge*. Over the years, certain general concepts of management have developed along with technical information in special fields such as production, marketing, financial and, human resource management. Thus, management is a technical discipline that requires mastery. But neither a license nor a degree is required in order to practice management. Given the variation in the situation demands on managers, possession of a license or degree wouldn't guarantee effectiveness nor would their absence necessarily lead to failure. So access to the field of management shouldn't be limited to those who have completed a prescribed course of study. Nonetheless, formal training and broad education usually improve managerial performance, particularly in a complex industrial society, and a bachelor's degree is required to gain entrance to the ranks of management in most organisations (Darr, 2011).

Entrepreneurship (owning and operating one's own business), is rapidly becoming the only means of entry in to management for persons with out that back ground.

A profession can be defined as a vocation requiring

1. Specialised knowledge and Technical proficiency
2. Formal training
3. Social responsibility
4. Code of conduct.

1. Specialised body of knowledge and Technical Proficiency

Management is a recent field of science requiring intellectual preparation or graduate study to ensure rational and scientific decision-making. The other way round, it is based on a systematic body of knowledge, which comprises managerial concepts, theories and generally accepted principles that require intensive academic preparation. However, it shouldn't be ignored that all managers do not have the managerial concepts and principles or the managerial graduate study as a whole. Because, they may acquire it through an intense devotion and involvement to acquire expertise in the art and science of management.

2. **Formal Education and Training Controlled by the Profession**

   There are universities and institutions specialised to provide formal teaching of the principles and practice of management, and engaged in a continuous search for new ideas and information. Of the institutions, which provide formal education our previous many Ethiopian European, American and Asian universities offer management and were/are producing and will produce graduates of management in degree level.

3. **Social Responsibility**

   Even though the primary objective of any organisation (either for profit or non-profit) is to generate surplus, it has to take in to consideration the social factors it has to fulfil. In order to achieve its objective it should have to see the obligations it has to give service to the society and adhere to the prescribed moral, social and legal conduct because its existence depends on the services, it provides to the society in general.

   Usually socially responsible managers have become trustees of the public welfare. That is, beyond the object of economic gain, a profession should exhibit a sense of social responsibility. Consequently, the desire of being useful to the society in general is always uppermost in the mind of professional managers.

4. **Code of Conduct**

   Entry in to a profession is subject to the fulfilment of strict standards, rules, and regulations providing the norms of honesty, integrity and professional morality to be adhered by the members.

   Many professional and trade organisations have formally written codes of ethics and conduct for managers. But unlike the traditional professions of law and medicine, not all managers have or adhere to common code of ethics. To enforce the code of conduct of management, Ethiopian management professionals' Association is established in the last few years.

1.5 The Universality of Management

The process of management is universal because it is significant in any group or organisation that have a specific goal to attain. The basic applications of management are the same whether the organisation to be managed is small or complex, business or non-business. However the style and approach any organisation uses may differ to achieve their goals and objectives effectively.

The universality concept of management is also applicable to all levels of management within the organisation, i.e it is not limited to a certain level in the organisation. But the scope of the authority held the responsibility assigned and the type of problems dealt vary from one level to another.

1.6 The Need for Management

Some form of management exists in every form of human organisation where it seeks for the attainment of a common purpose. Even in family to have good co-ordination, unity and co-operative family management is essential. Management is pervasive or universal.

Management is important, such as making a better economic life possible, improving social standards, and achieving more efficient and effective government are challenges to modern managerial ability.

Management makes human efforts more productive. It brings better equipment- plants, offices, products, services and human relations to our society. Improvements and progress are its constant watch words.

We are all affected by good or bad management practices, and we should therefore learn to recognise and influence the quality of management that affects our lives. Management brings order to endeavours by combining isolated events and disjointed information in to meaningful relationships. These relationships then work to solve problems and accomplish goals.

Organisations that have goals to be achieved do not run themselves- individuals run them. Individuals who run organisations or parts of them are called managers.

Managers run plants, recruit, select, direct and reward employees; coordinate the making of goods and services; accounts for revenues and expenses and facilitate the research and engineering of products. Managers are involved in most of the activities performed in an organisation:

Complex-Environment

Managers are becoming more important because organizations and their external environment are becoming more complex. Today's turbulent environment requires managers to anticipate and manage more change than in the past. As a result most managerial jobs are becoming more complex, that is, managers are charged (in a position) with the responsibility for ensuring the future of the organization.

Changing Nature of Work Force

The nature of the work force has been changing in several ways in recent years. For instance if we take our country (Ethiopia), the composition of work force is changing as increasing numbers of women enter to an organisation. Additionally, some numbers of women are entering professional and managerial jobs. In the coming future, women will hold more executive positions.

Increasing computerisation is affecting the work force in several ways. The nature of jobs has changed in that many jobs entail the use of microcomputers. Also, computerised robots are being used in assembly line manufacturing, replacing some workers. In addition, increasing development of computerization allows-analysis of mass amounts of data for managerial decision making.

Managerial Problems

Managers face a number of problems, including a turbulent economy, fluctuating government economic policies, government regulations, resource shortages, employee and union demands, productivity lapses, and so on. To deal with these problems effectively, managers must be open and frank about problems and opportunities, be prepared to change their own and others' attitudes, motivate employees to increase their organisational commitment, plan for larger (world) markets, and be prepared to introduce new technology a head of competitors.

Managers are also becoming more important because of a growing international interdependence on resources. Developed countries are experiencing shortages of certain natural resources for raw materials. Organisations in these countries are therefore seeking natural resources and human resources (labour) from developing countries. Managers are responsible for matching the natural resources and labour of developing countries with the resources of their organisation (for e.g. advanced technology, market, purchasing power, and managerial skills).

Because organisations of all kinds -- business, governmental, educational, religious, service- are run by managers, they are among the best paid and most respected members of society. Since managers are the leaders through whom organisational purposes are achieved, their activities are by definition important – at least to their organisation's owners and members. Because managers influence productivity and establish organisational policies and goals, they collectively influence a nation's standard of living and quality of life. Effective managers are a critical resource of developed countries and one of the most needed resources in countries that are struggling to develop.

1.7 Management levels, skills and Roles

Managers at every level plan, organise, lead and control. But they differ in the amount of time devoted to each of these activities. Some of these differences depend on the kind of organisation in which the manager works, some on the type of the job the manager holds.

Other differences in the ways managers spend their time depend upon their levels in the organisational hierarchy. The number of levels of management in an organisation varies upon the size, technology and diversification of the organization. Traditionally, management is divided in to three levels:

1. Top level management
2. Middle level management
3. First level (line) or supervisory management.

Unnecessary increase in the number of levels of management results in increase in costs, and creates problem of communication between various levels thus making effective co-ordination and control a difficult task. Also luck of effective communication results in misunderstanding which in turn makes efficiency and effectiveness less.

The skill required for the managers at different level is different. Although all managers need similar skills, managers at different levels need different mixtures of these skills (managerial skills).

1.7.1 Managerial skills

A skill: is an ability to translate knowledge in to action that results in the desired performance. Truly important skills for managers are those that help them to help others become productive in their work. The field of management offers a knowledge base for the initial development of these managerial skills.

The essential skills: Robert L. Katz classified the essential skills of managers in three categories: technical, human, and conceptual (planning related skills).

Technical skill: is the ability to use, the procedures, techniques, and knowledge of a specialised field. Surgeons, engineers, musicians and accountants all have technical skills in their respective fields. Or it is an ability to use tools, techniques, and specialised knowledge. For example, accountant doing audit, engineer designing a machine.

Human skill: To work with and understand communication attitudes and motivation in order to achieve co-operation. It is the ability to work with, understand, and motivate other people as individuals or in group, or ability to work effectively in interpersonal relationships. E.g an accounting manager supervising a group of accountants during an audit[2],i.e.,it is the ability to work with others and to win co-operation from the people in the work group.

Conceptual skill: is the ability to co-ordinate and integrate all of the organisations interest and activities. It involves the managers' ability to see the origination as a whole, to understand how its parts depend on one another, and to anticipate how a change in any of its parts will affect the whole. It is used for abstract, reflective thinking and for the concept development involved in planning and creative strategy formulation such as, analysis of a possible merger with another firm, new product line strategy.

To make it clear about the skills let's say some more:

A Technical skill: is the ability to use a special proficiency or expertise relating to a method, process, or procedure. Accountants, engineers, and attorneys, for example, possess technical skills acquired through formal education.

Human skill: is the ability to work well in co-operation with others persons. It emerges as a spirit of trust, enthusiasm and genuine involvement in interpersonal relationships. A person with good human skills will have a high degree of self-awareness and a capacity to understand or empathise (sharing another person's feelings) with the feelings of others

Conceptual skill: ability to view the organisation or situation as a whole and solve problems to the benefit of everyone concerned. Or one's mental capacities to identify problems and opportunities, gather and interpret relevant information and make good problem solving decisions that serve the organisation's purpose.

Although all the three skills are essential at each managerial level, their relative importance tends to vary across levels.

1.7.2 Levels of Management

1. **Top Management level (Executive management or top executive)**

   As the name implies, this group consists of the organisation's top policy and decision makers; the managers who assume responsibility for the entire origination. Characteristic position titles are president, Chief Executive Officer

(CEO), Chief Operating Officer (COO) and senior or executive vice president(s). The tittles and levels within top management vary across organisations. In some companies, top managers are called executives, but in others the term also includes middle managers[4]. In some firms, such as a small restaurant, the title of "owner" serves to identify the top executive· Top management need to have more of general knowledge or conceptual skill to enable them view the organisation as a whole.

Top managers deal with broad organisational matters and major projects such as long-range planning and development. They are commonly responsible for co-ordinating the overall direction of the organisation and the activities of major organisational units. Top managers (executives) serve as the visible symbol of the organisation to the public. They also have external duties, including such widely varied ones as testifying at legislative hearings, greeting important customers, serving on the broad directors of agencies (jones., Gareth, and Jennifer, 2006).

It is the conceptual skill that enables an executive to recognise the interrelationships and relative values of the various factors intertwined in a managerial problem (to conceptualise requires imagination, broad knowledge, and the mental capacity to conceive abstract ideas), applying this requirement may involve suggesting a new product line for a company, entering the international market or introducing computer technology to the organisation's operations.

Once the objectives and broad policy guidelines are set by the top (board of directors) management, the top management has to give a clear cut instructions to sectoral or departmental heads to ensure that the policies laid down by the top management are carried out efficiently.

Other functions of the chief executive (manager) include to co-ordinate the work at different levels, to perform the function of review and control. Human skill is important for managers at every level.

2. **Middle-level Management**

All managers between first-line supervisors and top executives are middle-managers, regardless of the number of levels. Middle-level managers are somewhat more difficult to identify than other managers. One sign of a middle manager is in their specific reporting relationships. Many middle level managers have first level supervisors who report directly to them.

Middle level management usually refers to department heads, deputy department heads, branch managers, work managers and so on. They perform their duties within the frame work of objectives and policies set by the top management level. They concentrate on the short term plans, monthly, quarterly other than long term plans of the organisation. They change the long range plan in to intermediate plan.

Middle level managers set targets and re-range priorities depending on the guidelines laid down by the top management and on the needs of a given situation.

Middle level managers calls for human knowledge and skill that involve the ability to work with others and to win co-operation, i.e., knowing what to do and being able to communicate ideas and beliefs to others, understanding what thoughts others are trying to convey to you and what adjustments or changes in these views might be made (Lee and David, 213).

Middle level managers are likely to spend much less time directly supervising their subordinates than are supervisors. Instead, they usually spend more time on activities such as planning, information, processing, and monitoring.

3. **Supervisory level management (first-line managers)**

The easiest group to identify is first-line managers because they supervise only operating employees. First-line managers are often called supervisors[4]. Supervisors are responsible for co-ordinating the work of non-managerial employees and for dealing with directions and instructions from their superiors. They generally do not actually perform tasks of the non-managerial employees, but they must understand those tasks in order to assist their subordinates when necessary. The first level managers are responsible for seeing the tasks are done.

For example, the cashier and host at a restaurant seldom serves food to customers but is responsible for overseeing the tasks done by waiters and waitresses.[1]

Supervisory management level includes office managers, super intendents foremen, chief clerks, supervisors. The supervising staff is mainly concerned with the following.

a) Planning of day to day work
b) Assignment of jobs
c) Keeping a watch on workers' performance
d) Sending reports and statements to superiors
e) Maintaining close and personal contacts with workers and evaluation of their work.

At this lowest management level technical knowledge and skill are required. It includes understanding and being proficient in using a specific activity; and usually consists of specialised knowledge and the ability to perform within that speciality.

To conclude, all the three skills and management functions (planning, organizing, leading and controlling) are important at each level, but their importance tends to vary across levels, i.e., the time spent by managers for each managerial function and skill differs. The top managers spend more time on planning and organising and more of conceptual and less of technical skill. To the contrary first level managers spend more time in leading and supervising and require more of technical rather than conceptual skill. The middle level managers spend relatively similar time in all functions and skills (Lee and David, 213).

The following two figures show the knowledge and skill required and the time spent by different management levels.

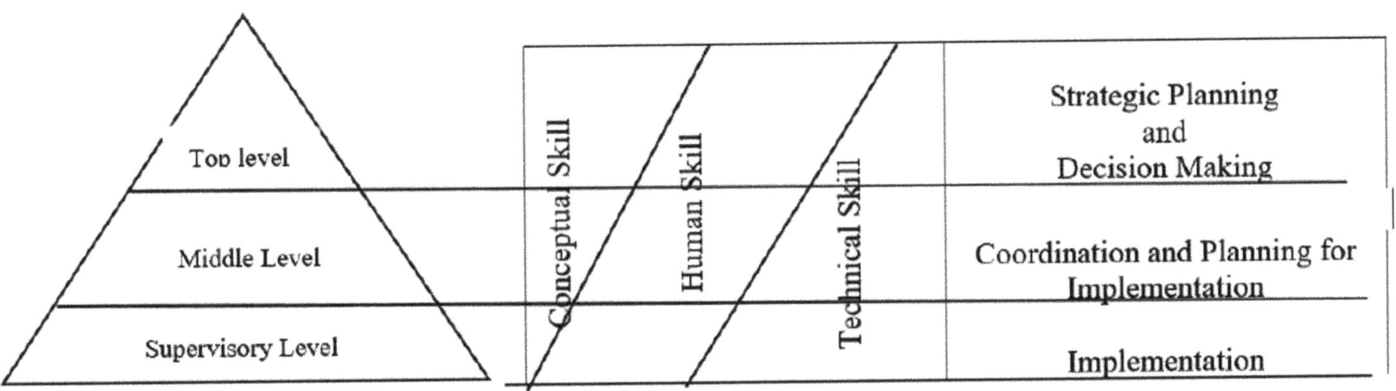

Figure 1.2 Managerial levels, required skills, and primary responsibilities.
Source: adopted from: Robbins, S.P. and Coulter, M.K. "Management". Pearson Education India.2009.

Knowledge and skills required for management vary with the organisation level.

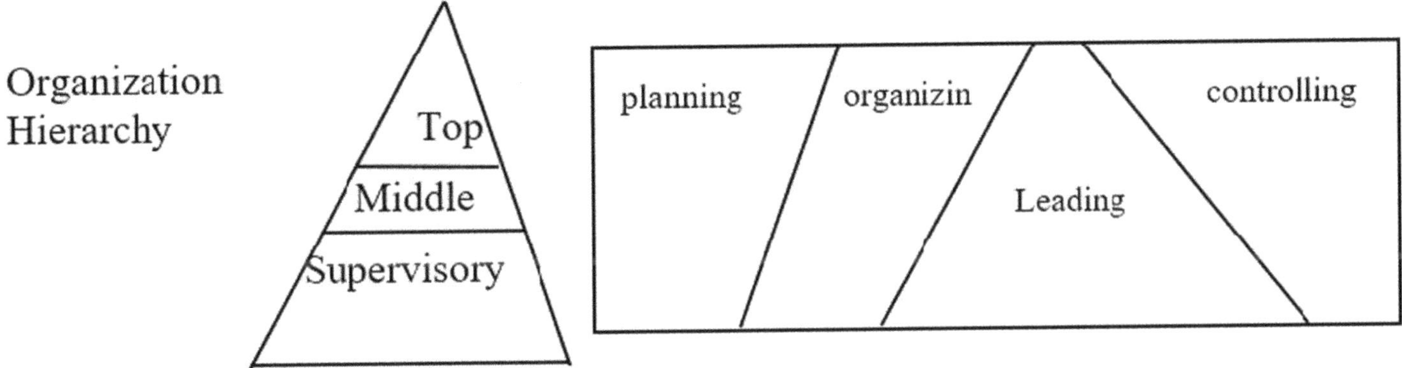

Figure 1.3 Time spent in carrying out managerial functions.
Source: adopted from: Robbins, S.P. and Coulter, M.K., 2009. Management. Pearson Education India.

1.7.3 Managerial Roles:

Managerial functions are general administrative duties that need to be carried out in all productive organizations. Managerial roles are specific categories of behaviour/managerial behaviour. Managerial functions involve "desired out comes". These outcomes are achieved through the performance of managerial roles (actual behaviour). In other words, Roles are the means and functions are the ends of the manager's job.

Henry Mintzberg identified ten different but interrelated organized sets of behaviour, or roles. These ten roles can be separated into three general groupings:

1. **Interpersonal roles:** three managerial roles are enacted when the manager engages in interpersonal relationship. They are:
    - **Figure head role:-** this role is played by managers who are required to perform duties of ceremonial and symbolic in nature such as signing documents, receiving visitors, etc. e.g. When the president of a university hands out diplomas at commencement.
    - **Leader role:-** managers play this role through hiring, training, motivating and disciplining employees to get the job done properly.
    - **Liaison role:-** managers play this role by contacting people outside the group, ^ by serving as a link in a horizontal (as well as vertical) chain of communication.
        - e.g. the sales manager who gains information from the personnel manager with in the same company- Internal liaison.
        - The sales manager who has contact with other sales executive by making trade association. – External liaison.
2. **Informational roles:** - All managers, to some degree, will receive and collect information from organizations and institutions outside his or her own. Managers play:
    - **Monitor/Nerve Centre Role:-** as a monitor /nerve centre, the manager tries to keep informed about what is happening in the organization or group. Managers serve as a focal point for non-routine in formation; they receive all types of information from news reports, trade publications, magazines, clients, etc.
    - **Disseminator role:-** the information a manager gathers as a monitor must be gleaned and transmitted to appropriate members of the organization. As a disseminator, a manager sends out side information into the organization and internal information from one subordinate to another. /Transmitting selected information to subordinates.
    - **Spokesperson role:** - it is the role of a manager in transmitting selected information to outsiders. It is played by a manager whenever he/she represents the organization or its position to other groups, including government agencies, customer, and trade organizations.
3. **Decisional Roles**: - It involves decision-making. The manager plays this role as:
    - **Entrepreneur**: managers as an entrepreneur initiate and oversee new projects that will improve their organization's performance. (Designing and initiating changes within the organization.
    - **Disturbance handler:** - taking corrective actions in none routine situations/the manager deals with situations our which he or she has little control. These may involve conflict between people or groups or unexpected events outside the company may affect the firm's operations.
    - **Resource allocates:-** managers play this role when they are in a position to decide exactly who should get what resources. (These resources include time, money, people-people, physical resources)
    - **Negotiator:-** participating in negotiating sessions with other parties (e.g. vendors and unions) to make sure the organizations interests are adequately represented. Managers perform this role, in which they discuss and bargain with other units to gain advantages for their own unit.

1.8 The Functions of Management

The five basic functions of management are:

1. Planning
2. Organising
3. Staffing
4. Leading, and
5. Controlling

1. Planning

Planning is generally accorded a position of primacy among the functions of management since logically it is the first function performed[4]. Planning is determining what is to be achieved, identifying appropriate action – plans. Planning centres on determining goals and the means to achieve them[2].

Planning involves selecting missions and objectives and the actions to achieve them. It requires decision making, that is, choosing future courses of action from among alternatives.

No real plan exists until a decision- a commitment of human or material resources or reputation-has been made. Planning bridges the gap from where we are to where we want to be in a desired future. It strongly implies not only the introduction of new things but also sensible and workable implementation[6].

Thus planning is a decision making process that determines what, how, why, when and by whom it is to be done.

2. Organising

Organising is establishing an intentional structure of roles for people to fill in an organisation. It is intentional in the sense of making sure that all the tasks necessary to accomplish goals are assigned and, it is hoped, assigned to people who can do them best. The purpose of an origination structure is to help in creating an environment for human-performance[6].

Organising turns plans in to action potential by defining tasks, assigning personnel, and supporting them with resources. In short organising is the process of determining the role by which an individual plays and the individual roles are inter-related and integrated to achieve, the common organisational goal. Organising thus involves:

a) Identification of activities to achieve the predetermined objective
b) Grouping these activities in to working units
c) Assignment of responsibility to each unit with corresponding authority
d) The creation of intentional organisational relationship so as to enhance co-ordination.

For example, a special task force on new product development is established: people are assigned, meeting facilities are made available and necessary technical support is established.

3. Staffing

Staffing involves filling, and keeping filled, the positions in the organisation structure. This is done by identifying work-force requirements, inventorying the people available, recruiting, selecting, placing, promoting, planning the career, compensating, and training or other wise developing both candidates and current job holders to accomplish their tasks effectively and efficiently.

Staffing is the process of providing needed human resources to the organisation, represents the life blood of any firm. Generally staffing is thought to include all the activities of recruitment, selection and placement. Some authors consider staffing as included in an organising function.

4. Leading

Leading is influencing people so that they will contribute to organisation and group goals: it has to do predominantly with the interpersonal aspect of managing. Since leadership implies follower ship and people tend to follow those who offer a means of satisfying their own needs, wishes and desires, it is understandable that leading involves motivation, leadership styles and approaches, and communication[6].

Leading is guiding the work efforts of other people in directions appropriate to action plans. Leading involves encouraging work efforts that support goal attainment. After plans have been made, the structure of the organisation has been determined, and the staff has been recruited and trained, the next step is to arrange for movement toward the organisation's defined objectives. This function can be called by various names; leading, directing, motivating, actuating and others. But whatever the name used to identify it, this function involves getting the members of the organisation to perform in a way that will help it achieve its established objectives. Whereas planning and organising deal with the more abstract aspects of the management process, the activity of leading is very concrete; it involves working directly with people.

5. Controlling

Controlling is measuring and correcting of activities of subordinates to ensure that events conform to plans. Although planning must precede controlling, plans are not self-achieving. The plan guides managers in the use of resources to accomplish specific goals. Then activities are checked to determine whether they conform to plans[6]. Establishing a sound plan, organising the component activities required, assigning responsibility and delegating authority, and actuating members do not ensure that the undertaking will be a success. Discrepancies, misunderstandings, unexpected hindrances may arise and must be communicated to the management, so that corrective actions may be taken timely. To conclude the function of controlling involves the following.

1. Establishing standards or expectation of performance pertains, for example, to the quality of products or services, amount of production, absenteeism, sales, etc
2. Evaluating or measuring current performance (actual) and comparing it to expected standards.
3. Detecting deviations from standard goals in order to make corrections before a sequence of activities is completed.
4. Taking corrective action when standards are not met or in anticipation that they may not be met.

1.9 The Environment of management

The management environment can be divided in to internal and external environment. The internal environment includes all the activities that are performed with in the organisation. As the name implies these factors are under the control of the management. Examples include personnel production, marketing, finance and other service departments depending on the nature and size of the organisation. However we are more concerned with the external environment on which the existence of the organisation depends. Organisations are open system and therefore have continuous interaction with their external environment[1].

Every organisation is a subsystem of its environment that provides it with resources input and utilises the organisations outputs. An organisation depends on its external environment; it is a part of larger systems such as the industry to which it belongs, the economic system and the society. The major types of external factors include economic, technological, social, political and legal, and ethical.

1. The Economic Environment

The economic environment has a great importance to both business and non-business organisations. Both of them are highly affected by this environment. Most of the inputs of any organisation are taken from the economic environment.

For example, government agency takes resources, usually from taxpayers, and provides services desired by the public. A church takes contributions from members and serves their religious and social needs. A university takes resource inputs from taxpayers, students, and contributors of various kinds and transforms these in to educational and research services. The significant factors of economic environment are:

Capital:

Almost every kind of organisation needs capital – machinery, buildings, inventories of goods, office equipment, tools of all kinds, and cash. Some of this may be produced by the organisation itself, for example, when a business builds its own machinery. Or cash resources may also be generated within an organization to buy capital items from outside[6]. Thus, the source of capital may be from within the organisation or from outside suppliers whose job is to produce capital items the firm requires for its operation. This means that all kinds of operations are dependent on the availability and prices of needed capital items. Eventually, the availability and price of capital may vary from one society to another. For example, railroad facilities (capital item) may be in short supply in Brazil but in plentiful supply in USA and Western Europe countries.

Labour:

Another important input from the economic environment is the availability, quality and price of labour, that is, the operation of the organisation is greatly affected by the availability, quality and price of labour. Hence, the management of the organisation should consider all these factors in making decision on labour inputs.

In some societies, untrained common labour may be plentiful, while highly trained labour may be in short supply. For example, engineers may be scarce at one time and plentiful at another.

Also, the price of labour is extremely important economic input to an enterprise. The relatively high wages in the United states and many European countries often create cost problems for producers in these countries. Many items can be produced at a lower cost in countries such as China, Mexico, Korea and Taiwan. It is not surprising that many products requiring high labour input are often made outside the United States.

Price Levels:

The input side of an enterprise is clearly affected by price level changes. And this input price changes have a direct effect on product price. For instance, inflation not only upsets businesses but also has highly disturbing influences on every kind of organisation through its effects on costs of labour, material and other items. Thus management should take in to account the price levels when deciding the quantity of inputs and the resulting outputs.

Government Fiscal and Tax Policy

Although these (fiscal and tax policy) are, strictly speaking, aspects of the political environment, their economic impact on all enterprises is tremendous. Government control of the availability of credit through fiscal policy has considerable impact not only on business but also on most non business operations. Similarly government tax policy affects every segment of our society. The way taxes are levied is also important, not only to business but to people generally. For example, if taxes on business profits are too high, the incentive to go in to business or stay in it tends to drop, and investors will look elsewhere to invest their capital. If taxes are levied on sales, prices will rise and people will tend to buy less. Therefore though these factors are out of the management, the firm should consider the various effects of the government fiscal and tax policies.

Customers

One of the most important factors for success of enterprise is customers. Without them, a business can't exist. But to capture customers, a business must try to find out what people want and will buy. Also it has to see their capacity to buy.

To be sure, the expectations and demands of various publics served by organised enterprises are influenced by non-economic as well as economic factors in the environment

The principal ones of none economic are the attitudes, desires, and expectations of people, many of which arise from cultural patterns in the social environment. The Economic factors still play a major role.

Another factor in the market is the appearance of substitute products. The needs of customers (buyers) change as the products change, new processes are developed and as different equipment and materials come on the market. In the long run, any enterprise (at least in free economies) has to serve the different and changing needs of customers. To do otherwise is a sure road to enterprise failure. Therefore, an organisation has to consider the non-economic and economic factors, the market appearance of substitute products in deciding to produce products.

2. The Technological Environment

Technological change, another component of the environment has become very important in most industries and most types of organisation in recent years, especially in the computer industry. The term *technology* refers to the sum total of knowledge we have of ways to do things. It includes inventions, techniques, and the vast store of organized knowledge about everything. But its main influence is on ways of doing things, on how we design, produce, distribute, and sell goods as well as services. Or technology is the combination of equipment, knowledge, and work methods that allows an organization to transform inputs in to out puts.

Impact of technology: the impact of technology is seen in new products, new machines, new tools, new materials, and new services. To say a few of the *benefits* from technology; greater productivity, higher living standards, more leisure time, and greater variety of products.

But the benefits of the technology must be weighed against the *problems* associated with technological developments, such as traffic jams, polluted air and water shortage of energy, etc. What is needed is a balanced approach that takes advantage of technology and at the same time minimises some of the undesirable side effects. Besides any organization should cope with the technological changes.

3. The Social Environment

The Social environment is made up of the attitudes, desires, expectations, degrees of intelligence and education, beliefs, and customs of people in given group or society. The social environment is relevant to all organisations. Changes in the social environment can most easily be seen in new laws and /or changes required by government bodies, these are clearly evident laws relating to the environment and to product safety.

Managers of various enterprises have been criticised for not being responsive to the social attitudes, beliefs, and values of particular individuals, groups or societies.

But attitudes and values are different for workers and employers, rich and poor people, college student and alumni, accountants and engineers, urban dwellers and the rural dwellers. Hence, this variety of values makes it difficult for managers to design an environment conducive to performance and satisfaction. It is even more difficult to respond to these forces when they are outside the enterprise.

Modern society is an interdependent system, and the internal activities of the enterprise have an impact on the external environment. This implies that the enterprise has social responsibility- seriously considering the impact of the company's action on society.

Due to the interweaving complexity of the environmental elements makes their study and comprehension exceptionally difficult. Even to forecast them, that a manager can anticipate and prepare for change is very difficult. Although it is difficult to forecast the social environment and prepare for changes, the management should try to consider and anticipate them as much as possible because social desires, expectations, and pressures give rise to laws and standards of; ethics, because laws are passed and react when a crises is at hand[6].

4 The Political and Legal Environment

The political and legal environment of managers is closely intertwined with the social environment.

The Political Environment

Political environment-the attitudes and actions of political and government leaders and legislators do change with the ebb and flow of social demands and beliefs. Government affects virtually every enterprise and every aspect of life[6]. Governments influence organizations through laws and regulation. In respect to business it promotes, constrains and discourage business. Sometimes governments promote businesses by subsidising, by giving tax advantages in certain situations, by supporting research and development, and even by protecting some businesses through special tariffs (eg, to facilitate or encourage import substitution programs). Government is also the biggest customer, purchasing goods and services.

The Legal Environment

As noted above, the other role of the government is to constrain and regulate business. Every manager is encircled by a web of laws, regulations and court decisions. Some are designed to protect workers, consumers, and communities. Others are designed to make contracts enforceable and to protect property rights. Many are designed to regulate the behaviour of managers and their subordinates in business and other enterprises.

Many of our laws and regulations are necessary, even though many become obsolete. But they do present a complex environment for all managers. Therefore, managers are expected to know the legal restrictions and requirements applicable to their action. Thus, it is understandable that managers in all kinds of organisations and in business and government especially, usually have a legal expert close at hand as they make their decisions.

5. The Ethical Environment

The ethical environment consists of sets of generally accepted and practised standards of personal conduct. The standards may or may not be codified by law, but for any group to which they are meant to apply, they sometimes have virtually the force of law. The ethical standards may differ from one society to another. Thus managers should take in to account the ethical standards of the society before law forces them. An organisation must understand what is good and bad of the society.

All persons, whether in business, government, a university, or any other organization is aware of ethics. Ethics is defined as, "The discipline dealing with what is good and bad and with moral duty and obligation" thus,

- Personal ethics has been referred to as "the rules by which an individual lives his or her personal life"
- Accounting ethics pertains to "the code that guides the professional conduct of accountants."
- Business ethics is concerned with truth and justice and has a variety of aspects such as expectations of society, fair competition, advertising, public relations social responsibilities, consumer autonomy and corporate behaviour in the home country as well as abroad. Business ethics is the moral codes governing business behaviour

Ethics is beyond legal responsibilities, thus it fills the gap between legal requirements and the actual decisions that managers must make. Beyond the strict term of legal obligation, management or organization should see what is bad and good and what is right or wrong. Actually, our conception of bad or good depends on the custom, religion belief, intuition and tradition of the society.

For instance, when a close relative, say a child of someone is died, there is no legal obligation that the employer has to allow him/her to burry his/her child in the working hours. However, the moral code of the society (ethics) obliges the employer or organisation to make the father or mother rest for some days and pay for. There are no legal guidelines for this and other similar conditions. The guidelines are the moral and ethical code of the society and the understanding of the businessperson. Therefore, managers have the responsibility to consider and adhere the ethical codes of the society by integrating the ethical concepts in their decision-making.

Ethical Environment

How do managers know when they are facing ethical issues in reaching organizational decisions? To answer this question, it is necessary to define ethics, while understanding that ethical issues may change as the values of society change.

Ethics is a process by which individuals, social groups, and societies evaluate their actions from the perspective of moral principles and values. This evaluation may be on the basis of traditional convictions of ideals sought, of goals desired, of moral laws to be obeyed, of an improved quality of relations among humans and with the environment. When we speak of 'ethics' and ethical reflections, we mean the activity of applying there various yardsticks to the actions of persons and groups[1].

Ethics of a society rest on a collection of shared beliefs. Thus, *ethics* often referred to as moral philosophy consists of a code of values for a particular group of people, a code that provides the guidelines for their interactions with one another.

For managers, ethical issues arise from attempts to reconcile the competing interests of buyers, sellers, clients, shareholders, and the managers themselves. Ethics is a code of conduct that deals with the rightness or wrongness of certain actions and the goodness or badness of the persons and the objectives of these actions.

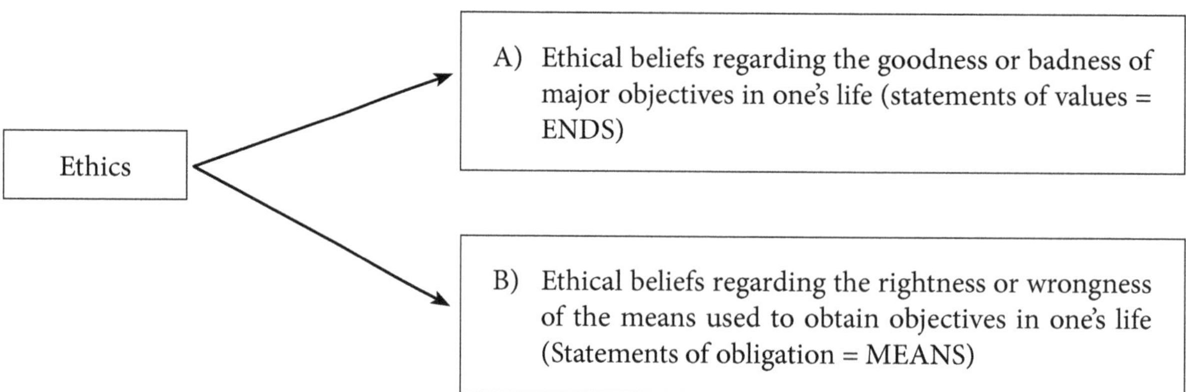

A) One's first exposure to ethical beliefs occurs early in life when parents make one aware of the distinction between good and bad. This distinction refers to major end values in life. Such distinction is reinforced by friends, teachers, and certain values are thus acquired.

B) This presupposes 'A'. Given that a person knows what is good and should be sought in life (prosperity, freedom and so on) the question becomes, what is the 'right' way to seek such an outcome? To mention some

A	**B**
Prosperity	Ambition and hard work
Stimulating, active life	Open-mindedness
Achievement	Competence
World peace	Cheerfulness
Harmony in nature and art	Cleanliness
Equality	Courageousness
Personal and family scrutiny	Forgiving nature
Freedom	Helpfulness
Happiness	Honesty
Inner peace	Imagination
Mature love	
National security	Independence and self-reliance
Pleasure and enjoyment	Intelligence

Religion and salvation	Rationality
Self-respect	Affection and love
Social respect	obedience and respect
Friendship	Responsibility
Wisdom	Self–discipline
	Courtesy

Review Questions

1. What is management?
2. Why do organizations need management?
3. Discuss the nature of management?
4. Is management science or art?
5. How can you justify that management is profession?
6. Why is management divided into levels?
7. What roles do managers play?
8. Discuss the functions of management.
9. Why management is universal?
10. Management is a set of interconnected roles and functions. how can you describe that?
11. Managers require a number of skills; discuss three of the required skills.
12. Explain the four levels of management in the firm.
13. How can Management control over the Macro environment?
14. How do you explain the pandemic COVID19 from macro environment perspective?

Short Case:

Axiom Company (hypothetical company) is doing business in the furniture sector since 2008; the company has three main branches Khartoum, Addis Ababa and Abuja, the main factory is located in Abuja, and the other two branches are assembling and selling what is made in Abuja, but in 2014 the company started to face some troubles with competition and sales as well the profitability it is not clear what reason caused the profitability and sales problem. Some executives blamed the marketing department, and some were blaming operations and design because of the lack of innovation in the company products. after that, the company consulted an experienced manager reported management issues.

From your point of view, what could be the management styles/ approach?

CHAPTER TWO

DEVELOPMENT OF MANAGEMENT THOUGHT

     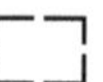 

LEARNING OBJECTIVES

1. develop an understanding of the evolution of the management, main schools of thought, development of the concept and contributors
2. understand the needs and motive for principles development.
3. Understand the contribution of Taylor, Henri Fayol and Elton Mayo to the development of management.
4. Explain the Contemporary Schools and Approached of Management

Overview

The pioneers' scholars of management initiated principles for managers, and those principles became as main guidelines for the late scholars and practitioners. When educated, workers and employees were few, and most of the tasks were manual; therefore, most of the jobs were performed in a classical way with a low level of innovation and change.

From the practices and observation of the early management scientist, the principles were developed and introduced as the first organized and theoretical nucleus for management science; this chapter cover pre-scientific, scientific school, Bureaucracy, Behavioural, Human Relations school.

2.1 The Evolution of Management thought

Despite the inexactness and relative crudity of management theory and science, the development of thought on management dates back to the days when people first attempted to accomplish goals by working together in groups.

Although modern operational management theory dates primarily from the early twentieth century, there was serious thinking and theorising about managing many years before.

The first known management ideas were recorded as long ago as 3000-4000 B.C. One example is provided in the building of the pyramids in Egypt. One pyramid built by Cheops in 2900 B.C required the use of 100,000 men for 20 years.

The pyramid covered thirteen acres and measured 481 feet in height. It was constructed with 2.3 million stone blocks each weighing an average of 2 1/2 tons. To produce such a building monumental achievement required planning, organizing guiding and directing, monitoring and decision-making.

The second example is provided in the Bible, in chapter 18 of Exodus. In this discussion Moses is advised by his father in-law, Jethro, to divide work and put specific individuals in change of specific activities. That is, here indicates "consulting" or giving an advice about the concepts of delegation, management by exception and span of control.

Ancient Greek literature points to the existence of administrative apparatus like councils, courts and boards of military personnel to manage the affairs of the state. The success of the Roman Empire depended on the ability of the rulers to organize their forces according to the scalar principle, neatly defining the area of authority and responsibility of each official.

Roman Catholic church was one of the most effective formal organizations in the history of western civilisation. The church had a set of well-defined objectives and effective and efficient organizational set up to achieve them.

Military organizations also contributed in their own simplistic way to the development of managerial practices such as line and staff authority.

Until about the middle of 18th century, the people of Western Europe used basically the same methods and implements of production that had been used for centuries. Management practice in business, government and the church remained quite stable through the centuries. It was carried on trial and error basis. Then within a few decades a series of inventions were discovered and the whole picture of industrial activity was enormously altered.

This new period, commonly referred to as Industrial Revolution was a land mark in human history. Essentially the industrial Revolution brought about a substitution of machine power for man power via the steam engine, and within a few short decades the entire picture of industrial activity was dramatically altered. Greater utilisation of machines and improved transportation and communication systems brought about centralisation of production activities, the establishment of new employer-employee relationships, and the separation of consumers from producers[3].

These factors brought the need of more thoughtful, resourceful and dynamic management. Problems of management become significant. In fact they opened new vistas. The importance of utilising adequate methods and principles in solving problems of management was realised. Management on traditional lines become useless. Rules of thumb could no longer exist. It had to be replaced by logical and rational principles, scientific approach and psychological handling.

Although the systematic management has a recent origin the practice of management is old as human beings have been living in-group since the very beginning. However the study of how managers achieve the results is predominantly a 20th century phenomenon. In early stages management study could not develop because of low esteem to business in society, indifferent approaches of economists, political scientists, sociologists, psychologists etc. towards business organization, treatment of management as an art and not as a science and the attitudes that successful managers are born but not made. This all obstacles didn't create a situation for the systematic study of management. So in the 20th century, the situation changed rapidly. Some of the factors that contributed to the need for a systematic management are:

a. The development of capitalism and the emergence of industries, mass production, the concentration of workmen and organization of trade unions, the growing competition for markets, technological invasions, the increase in capital investment, increasing obsolescence of instruments of production etc., forced organizations to be efficient or to find out ways for efficiency.

b. The complexities of organization. Society became more complex. The complexities of society were generated by:

   - The increasing size of organizations
   - High degree of division of labour and specialisation
   - Increase in government regulations and controls.

- Organised trade-union activities
- Pressure of various conflicting interest groups in society.

These complexities have increased the demand for efficient management and have resulted in the divorce of ownership and management. These forces have been vital for the development of systematic management principles and concepts. The principles have evolved through continuous experiments and observations.

Pre - Scientific Management Era

Though Frederic W. Taylor is known as the founder of scientific management, many persons before him make considerable contributions to the development of management thought.

1. James Watt and Bonlton:

They were responsible for the management of an Engineering factory in Britain in 1796, developed many management techniques. They were interested in market research, costing planned machine layout in terms of work-flow requirements, production planning, calculation of cost and profit, training and development of workers and managers, study and payment by results, welfare programme etc.

2. Robert Owen

He carried out most of his experiments in the area of personnel management when he was a manager of textile mills in Scotland between 1800-1828. Owen provided working conditions in the factory. He provided meals, housing, and marketing facilities to the employees in the factory.

3. Charles Babbage

Sometimes referred to as the patron saint of operation research. Charles Babbage began to search for method of improving worker productivity with the use of work measurement and cost determination. He was a professor of mathematics at Cambridge University (1828-39), was interested in division of labour and assigning on the basis of skills- with the division of labour by its level of skill reduces learning time since a given worker must learn only one operation rather than all operations, saves manufacturing time, too, because less time is lost changing from one operation to another, and high degree of skill can be acquired since each worker is learning only one task repeating it many times. Secondly, he provided a means for determining the feasibility of replacing manual operation with machinery, that is, developing of scientific principles governing the manager's use of facilities, materials and labour to get the best possible results. He also emphasised human relation aspects in the factory. His main contributions are in the areas of costing, engineering, wage and in certain systems.

Scientific Management Era

In 1980's an altogether new approach to management was suggested. It called for management on scientific lines. In effect this implied substitution of exact scientific investigation and knowledge in the place of the old individual judgement or opinion in all matters done in the establishment. This was the spirit of times.

2.2. The Schools (Theories) of Management Thought

Management problems are as old as human existence. But management as a science is the product of 20th century. Though it is late in evolution and growth, management thought and practice today has developed in to a dependable set of guidelines. However, since the persons who contributed to this process belonged to different disciplines, e.g, industrial engineering, political science, sociology, psychology, etc. there have naturally been different thought patterns as to management.

The Need for Management Theory

Theory is essentially a body of principles which are offered to explain certain phenomena and, by doing so, give a clear and systematic view of the subject. Or "theory, is principle or set of principles designed to explain the relationship between two or more observable facts." It is obvious that such principles tend to be interrelated because they are offered as explanations, truths of fundamental nature, basic to the understanding of the subject and having a predictive value.

It is important to realize that there is no single best theory of management. Each of the many theories of management has some worthwhile applications and some limitations. Management today is both a reflection of and a reaction to past management theories.

What does theory contribute to the practice of management? The theory of relativity, for example, helps physicists control the atom; through the laws of aerodynamics, engineers can predict the effects of a proposed change in airplane design. Similarly, the theories and principles of management make it easier for us to understand underlying processes and, on that basis, decide what we must do to function most effectively as managers. Without theories, all we have are intuition, hunches, and hope these all of which are of limited use in today's increasingly complex organisations.

The first objective of a general theory of management should be to help improve the practice of management. A general theory of management facilitates training. Management development and training depends on the conceptual understanding of the essence of management. It helps spell out a managers tasks. It makes management teachable. With the rapidly advancing management science, there is a great danger of managerial practitioners being out dated and obsolete.

There are a number of schools of management thought. Some of the schools of management thought that have developed in recent years are discussed as follows. The theories of management can be grouped as:

I. Classical Theories of Management
II. Neo-Classical (Behavioural) Theories of Management
III. Modern Theories of Management

2.2.1 Classical Theories of Management

There are three branches of the classical approach to management:

1. Bureaucratic organisation theory
2. Scientific management school
3. Process /functional/ management school

The classical schools of thought share the assumption that people are rational and economic in their orientation toward work. (That is every manager makes assumptions about the people with whom he or she works - be they subordinates, superiors, peers, customers or suppliers. And, people are most responsive to economic incentives; that is, they will rationally consider opportunities made available to them and do whatever is necessary to achieve the greatest economic gain. Each branch of classical management theory reflects this assumption)[2]

1. Bureaucracy (Max Weber 1864-1920)

The first pillar in the classical organization and management theory was systematically provided by Max Weber, a German sociologist. Weber offered bureaucratic model for management of any large and complex organization in any branch of human activity. He considered bureaucracy as the most efficient form for complex organizations.

Weber's Elements of Bureaucracy: these elements or characteristics are the vital parts of modern business, governmental, educational and other complex organizations. These are

1. Hierarchy of authority involving superior subordinate relationship and chain of command.
2. Clear cut division of work, based upon the competence and functional specialisation. An ordered hierarchy takes the advantage of specialization (i.e., division of labour by functional specialisation). [1]

3. A system of rules, regulations and procedures. (A system of rules, conveying the rights and duties of employees)[1] Behaviour is subject to systematic discipline and control.
4. A rule by law leads to impersonality of interpersonal or mutual relations. Interpersonal relations are based on positions and not on personalities (that is impersonal relations between people.)
5. A system of work-procedures dealing with work situations (i.e., standardising work procedures)
6. Selections and promotion of employees based on managerial and/or technical competence.
7. Authority and power rests in the office. Weber's concepts of bureaucracy recognize these only a legal power (authority) given to each office of position in the organization.

The power doesn't belong to an individual. It is part of the office.

The word bureaucracy has for us many connotations today, which are not envisaged by Weber, (popularly it is used to characterize the red-tape, inefficiencies of governmental administrator, long registration lines, and the like). Weber looks bureaucracy "organization with a legalized formal and hierarchical structure". He felt the bureaucracy should be rational and legal. It is rational that- the specific objectives are laid down rationally and the organization is rationally designed to achieve the objectives; and it is legal because authority stemmed from a clearly defined set of rules and procedures. Bureaucracy applies in formal organizations and seems to evolve as organizations become larger and more complex.

Advantages of Bureaucracy

Bureaucracy has many positive outcomes, but they occur only when the bureaucracy operates ideally. Some of the positive consequences are as follows:

1. Employee behaviour is consistent because of set policies, procedures and rules. Although rules and policies can be enforced too strictly, they are needed for efficiency. Consistent treatment of employees is required by law (non-discrimination)
2. Overlapping or conflicting job duties are eliminated because jobs are defined clearly. Also precise job definitions can assure the manager that all necessary tasks will be accomplished, and they may prevent wasted actions due to overlapping jobs.
3. Behaviour is predictable because there is a hierarchy of authority
4. Hiring and promotion are based on merit or expertise. It is effective to promote individuals on the basis of merit and expertise, allowing them to move up the hierarchy as they gain expertise and experience.
5. Employees develop expertise in their jobs because they specialize in those jobs. Specializing in their jobs helps individuals become "experts" on those jobs; thus they can perform more effectively.
6. There is continuity in the organization because it emphasises the position rather that the person, that is, when one person leaves a position, another person assumes that same position. For example, if the president leaves another person is simply promoted and the organization continues.

Disadvantages of Bureaucracy

The negative aspects of bureaucratic organization invite many criticisms about large organizations such as the federal government. Some of the changes made are:

1. There is too much red tape and too much paper work which wastes time that could be spent in more productive ways.
2. Employees don't care about the organization. Employee is unwilling to break a rule or exercise individual judgement. If a problem is not covered by a written rule or policy, many employees are afraid to make decision or take action to resolve the problem. This reliance on rules may lessen creativity, employee development and initiative.

3. Employees are treated impersonally (according to the rules). They are not treated as individuals but like machines.[1]It neglects the human aspects of organization members, assuming they are motivated only by economic concerns. Nowadays, as educational levels affluence, and work expectations have risen, this criticism has become more severe. The impersonal treatment can lead to employee indifference (absence of interest or feeling) toward the organization and job performance.
4. It doesn't suit to rapidly changing and uncertain environments. Formalized bureaucratic organization have difficulty in changing their established procedures.

In sum, the bureaucratic approach can have some important advantages, but it also has significant negative side effects.

2. Scientific Management School (F.W Taylor)

The series of ideas that became known as scientific management grew from the work of Frederick Winslow Taylor, who is known as " the father of scientific management". Scientific management is management carried out scientifically as opposed to traditional management in which managerial principles are subjectively derived. They depend on the whims, views and prejudices of the manager in charge. This school believes in the application of scientific method to resolve problem situations. Scientific management is a management approach, formulated by Frederick W. Taylor and others between 1890 and 1930, that sought to determine scientifically the best methods for performing any task, and for selecting, training and motivating workers.[5] According to them, a manager has to find the "one right way" of doing the job. They used time and motion study for developing the right way.

Aims (concepts) of Scientific management:

1. **Replacing rules of thumb with science**

   Each person's job should be broken down in to elements and a scientific way to perform each element should be determined. Under scientific management, each element (component) of a work and the motions required to perform it are scientifically analysed to determine the standard time, and standard methods of doing it with maximum efficiency. Similarly, the kinds of tools to be used and the working conditions are also arranged scientifically. There is no scope in all this for a hit or miss or rule of thumb approach.

2. **Harmony, not discord (obtaining harmony in group action, rather than discord)**

   Scientific management provides for a better pay to workers for producing more as also it shows the way to do it. As a result, workers perform their jobs sincerely and enthusiastically. Since management stands to gain as a result of increased productivity, it doesn't mind paying the workers more as batter pay is assumed to motivate workers to higher productivity. Thus, there is a complete harmony of interests between workers and management leading to mutually beneficial relationships.

3. **Co-operation, not individualism.**

   Scientific management lies on the co-operation between workers and management and as between workers. Management can look forward to larger profits only if workers perform their jobs with maximum efficiency and economy. If either the management or the workers seek to grab (take roughly or selfishly snatch) all the gains of increased productivity for themselves, they will both be losers because success of scientific management depends on co-operation rather than individualism on their part. Scientific management also promotes co-operation as between workers. The fear of reduced earnings forces workers to help and cooperate with one another for smooth working at all levels..

4. **Maximum output not restricted out put**

   Under scientific management, both management and workers are interested in attaining maximum output. Maximum output can be attained when management provides workers with standard materials, standard tools, standard working conditions and when workers perform their jobs most efficiently and economically.

5. **Development of each man to his greatest efficiency and prosperity.**

 Scientific management advocates that workers be selected and trained in accordance with the requirements of the jobs to be entrusted to them. Workers should be selected to the jobs who have the right abilities for the job. When a worker gets the work for which he is both physically and mentally well-equipped and when he is provided regular training to update his skills, naturally he becomes quite efficient. This efficiency enables the worker to earn higher wages and to get mental satisfaction.

Taylor published a book called "Principles of Scientific Management" in 1911 that established him as a father of scientific management. This was the time when the field of management theory was born.

Taylor advocated replacement of individual judgement by exact scientific investigation and knowledge. In his view, scientific knowledge together with a mental revolution on the part of both management and workers was essential to the existence of scientific management. Taylor and others who pleaded (argue in favour of) for scientific management suggested a number of definite and concrete steps to make scientific management a reality.

The following are the techniques or elements suggested for management of industrial establishments along scientific lines

1. Work -study

Work-study is a combination of several techniques, which can be applied to all kinds of efficiency problems. It is not, if it is concerned only with labour productivity problems. The main objective of work-study is to improve efficiency. Improvement in efficiency means using fewer resources in an activity and yet getting the same result or alternatively, using the same resources to get a better result.

The objective of work study can thus be defined as reduction in the number of men on every job, designing of a plan costing less than the old one, reduction in wastage of materials, scrap ratios, and so on. In this way it will lead to the determination of a standard task. In scientific management, therefore, an effort is made to find out in a scientific way as to what amount of work a worker should put in if the conditions of work were standardized.

The techniques for setting the standard task are:

i) *Method study*- to keep the costs incurred whenever any factor of production is used in an enterprise to the minimum.
ii) *Motion study*- to identify and eliminate unnecessary and wasteful motions by both operators (workers) and the machines operated by them (that is, increases efficiency).
iii) *Time study*- (work measurement) aimed at determining the time required to perform any job in the best possible way. It is concerned with labour productivity.
iv) *Fatigue study*- to find out how long a worker can perform the standard task without any adverse effects on his health and efficiency.

2. Scientific task planning

Task planning would mean answering the following questions:

a) What work is to be done?
b) Why is it to be done?
c) Where is it to be done?
d) How is it to be done? and
e) When is it to be done?

The objects of scientific task planning are:

i) to lay down the production target
ii) to ensure strict quality control
iii) to minimize cost

iv) to bring proper division of labour
v) to maximize sales, and
vi) to offer necessary cost information

Scientific task planning involves *routing, scheduling, despatching* and *follow up.*

Functional foremanship

Taylor regarded planning as the very basis of scientific management. He also knew that planning is a complicated job requiring specialized knowledge and experience. He thought workers should concentrate on doing the work assigned to them and they shouldn't be burdened with the task of also planning their own work.

Taylor recommended that there should be functional foremanship even at the shop level where workers have to produce goods. Accordingly, he divided the work of the single foreman into eight separable functions with a separate person in charge of each function. Thus, the executive functional bosses in the factory (implementation (action) of the plan) are to be:

a. *Gang boss*, to feed the worker with all the necessary material so that the worker will not be idle.

b. *Speed boss*, controls the workers' speed vis-à-vis the predetermined standard speed.

c. *Inspector*, to control the worker whether he is producing quality products and

d. *Repair boss*, workers may damage, so to make sure that the machines are most destine-full as against the above four executive functions.

The functional bosses (can be called as planning departments) are designated as:

i) *Instruction card clerk*, tells the worker what to do today (e.g., to produce beer)

ii) *Order and work clerk*, tells the work flow, the movement form one operation to another (e.g. take the bottled ones to the store)

iii) *Time and cost clerk*, controls the workers performance on specified time, and

iv) *The disciplinarian,* in the planning room controls unnecessary noise and other things that disturb the work process.

3. Scientific selection and training of workers

Scientific management emphasises the need for proper selection and training of workers. But how to select workers who are physically, technically and psychologically competent for the jobs to be handled by them is the problem involved in this connection. To this end,

a. Selection of workers should be made the responsibility of a specialist in this field. The practice of assigning this work to foremen may be risky because generally foremen don't possess adequate knowledge and experience to select the right man for the right job.

b. The procedure of selection should also be determined carefully. This calls for approaching the right sources for recruitment of workers. Then, standard procedures should be devised to test the qualities and capabilities of persons from among whom selection is to be made.

c. The worker should be given proper placement. Placement means familiarising the worker with the job to be handled by him. It means acquainting the worker with the aims, objectives, and policies of the enterprise and with his co-workers.

Scientific management also doesn't ignore the need for proper employee training. Either the enterprise provides systematic training to its workers or else the workers will train themselves. When they do it themselves, the enterprise will have to bear the losses resulting from unscientific and "trial" and "error" n methods employed by them in the process.

4. Standardisation

Standardisation means setting of standards or measuring sticks by which the extent and quality, value and performance or service may be guided or determined. Under scientific management, for everything there is a predetermined standard. There is a standard task for every department and worker which is set after a detailed analysis of the job and the capacity and capability of the various factors of production such as men and machines. The machines and tools to be used to perform the task are standardised. The methods of production are standardised. Not only this, the working conditions are also standardized through necessary innovations and improvements from time to time.

5. Mental revolution

This element states that the management and the workers should try to create such an atmosphere in the organisation that they must feel that both have a common goal. There is no clash of interests. Both would gain it, by their efforts, they make the enterprise prosper. For this, therefore, care should be taken to promote and maintain harmony and co-operation between the worker and the management. The workers should give up their hostility towards the management. They shouldn't entertain the idea that the management is out to exploit them. At the same time the management shouldn't think that all the workers are shirkers and require very strict handling. The managers must realize that, the management creates leadership responsibility because it is an activity.

Contributions of Scientific Management Theory

1. The methods of scientific management can be applied to a variety of organisational activities. The efficiency techniques of scientific management, such as time and motion studies have made us aware that the tools and physical movements involved in a task can be made more efficient and rational[5].
2. The stress it placed on scientific selection and development of workers has made us recognize the importance of both ability and training in increasing worker effectiveness.
3. The importance that scientific management gave to *work design* also encouraged managers to seek the "one best way" of getting a job done[5].
4. Scientific management not only developed a rational approach to solving organizational problems but also pointed the way to the professionalization of management.

Limitations of Scientific Management Theory

1. Proponents of scientific management considered human behaviour was indeed a component of a large productive machine. Taylor failed to understand the complexities of human behaviour. Thus Taylor and his followers over looked the social needs of workers as members of a group and never considered the tensions created when these needs were frustrated.
2. The proponents of scientific management also overlooked the human desire for job satisfaction.
3. Taylor's principle of management applies to the field of production, industry. It is shop or task management. That the focus was not on the enterprise as a whole, but on a single segment of it.

Process /Functional/ or Administrative Management School (Henry Fayol 1841–1925)

Another classical approach to management focuses on administration. There are several important names in this administrative-principles school of thought, including Mary Parker Follet, James D.Mooney, and Lyndall Urwick. Among them, Henry Fayol stands out as s successful manager as well as scholar and writer[2]. Perhaps he is the real father of modern management theory. Henry Fayol was a high executive in French industry. Fayol was a contemporary of Taylor (belonging to the same period), and it is important to note that, while Taylor was basically concerned with organizational *functions*, Fayol was interested in the total organization.

Unlike Taylor, Fayol's efforts dealt with "classical administration", the focus was on the enterprise as a whole, not on a single segment of it. Although his book, written in French, first appeared in 1916, his contributions were somewhat clouded until 1949, when the English translation become widely available.

This approach dealt less with the individual workers and their jobs and more with the operation of the total organization. Fayol developed a unified concept of management. Whereas scientific management was concerned primarily with tasks at the worker level, Fayol focused on managerial levels and the organization as a whole. Like scientific management, administrative management is oriented toward increasing production, but in a different way and at a higher level.

Classification of Business Activities

Henry Fayol expressed the opinion that although specific activities differ from enterprise to enterprise, generally they (activities) can be divided in to six main categories.

1. Technical activities (production, manufacturing, adaptation)
2. Commercial activities (buying, selling and exchange)
3. Financial activities (search for and optimum use of capital)
4. Security activities (protection of property and persons)
5. Accounting activities (stock taking, balance sheet, cost, statistics)
6. Managerial activities (planning, organizing, commanding, co-ordinating and controlling)

These six functions had to be performed to operate successfully any kind of business. Of these, the first five are according to Fayol, quite well known. Therefore, he concentrated on the analysis of the sixth, i.e., managerial activities[6]. Moreover, he pointed out that the last function, i.e. the ability to manage, was the most important for upper levels of manager.

Principles and Elements of Management

Henry Fayol's monograph can be divided in to three categories

1. Elements of management
2. Managerial qualities and training
3. Principles of management.

1. Elements of management

Elements of management refer to the functions which management performs. They are planning, organizing, commanding, co-ordinating and controlling. These will be explained in the forth-coming chapters.

Managerial qualities and training

Fayol prescribes a number of qualities, which a manager should possess, to be effective on his job. The qualities relate to the following:

i) **Physical**-This relates to the state of health. A good manager should have a good health. A healthy person with a good physique can attend to his managerial duties properly. He can communicate well, guide, direct and also motivate.

ii) **Mental** - More physical fitness is not enough. Mental ability includes ability to understand, appreciate, learn, judge and decide. It includes the quality or the capability to distinguish and decide what is proper.

iii) **Moral** - Moral qualities refer to the ethical values, beliefs and habits of the manager. He should be able to abide by the promise he executes. He should be loyal (true and faithful), true to his words, tactful, dignified, firm yet flexible and exhibit initiative and derive. He should be willing to shoulder responsibility and must not shirk.

iv) **General and technical education**- A good manager should have a solid educational background. Apart from a general education, he should have a thorough knowledge of the particular branch, which he is supposed to look after. Thus the production manager should have a sound knowledge of the particular branch of engineering. A sound technical education along with a good base of general education will make a good manager.

v) **Experience**- Perfection comes with practice. A manager becomes proficient in his field of activity by working at it for a number of years. Experience helps a person to discharge his functions efficiently and confidentially.

Fayol also laid a great emphasis on managerial training. For this purpose, he suggested that the enterprise should arrange training courses and programmes. Management schools should also be set up for this purpose.

While technical qualities are much in demand at lower levels of functioning, these become less and less important as the employee move up, status wise. At higher levels, managerial ability is most essential.

To this end, Fayol advocated the need for principles (theory) of management and for imparting training in them. The two places where managerial ability can be acquired are, according to him, the school and the workshop.

General Principles of Management

Fayol, based on his experience in the field, listed fourteen principles of management these are:

1. **Division of work**: Man acquires greater skill when he specializes in single operation. This avoids the wastage of time caused by changes from one work or process to another. This division leads to have maximum productivity and efficiency. Both technical and managerial activities can be performed in the best manner through division of labour and specialization. It is applicable to all kinds of work, managerial as well as technical. The more people specialize, the more efficiently they can perform their work.

2. **Authority and Responsibility**: Authority is the right to give orders, the right to command, and obtain obedience. And responsibility is its counterpart or corollary of authority arising from authority. Responsibility is the obligation to accomplish objectives or expected results or performance. Please note that authority and responsibility are the two sides of management coin. They exist to gather. They are complementary and mutually interdependent. Acceptance of authority implies acceptance of responsibility for the performance of assigned work. Authority and responsibility go hand in a hand. Responsibility flows from, and is the direct result of authority. An authority can't exist without responsibility. Responsibility is the constitutional and moral obligation of a person to see that the work allotted to him is done properly and also ensure that the desired result is achieved with the available resources and within the required time. No performance can be expected without authority. At the same time, authority without responsibility is meaningless.

3. **Discipline:** Discipline implies obedience and respect for the agreements between the firm and its employees. Clarity and fairness promote this respect. The objectives, rules and regulations, the policies and procedures must be honoured by each member of the organization. Discipline is the cornerstone of success not only for any group activity but even for individual activity. Applied to a group activity, discipline is the voluntary and instant obedience of the orders issued by the rightful authority. According to Fayol, "Discipline is an essence of obedience (respect for agreements which are directed at achieving obedience), application, energy behaviour and outward mark of respect observed in accordance with the standing agreement between the firm and its employees." Discipline demands that these agreements whether oral or written, whether expressed or implied must be obeyed in totality, without any dissent. This is absolutely essential for smooth running of any business. Discipline can be enforced only if the following conditions exist.

    1. Good superiors at all levels
    2. Agreement as clear and fair as possible
    3. Sanctions (Penalties) judiciously applied.

    For Fayol discipline will result from good leadership at all levels of the organization, fair agreements (such as for rewarding superior performance) and judiciously enforced penalties for infractions or for non-obedience or indiscipline.

4. **Unity of command:** each employee must receive instructions, orders about a particular operation from only *one* person[5.] There should be one and only one boss for each individual employee. If there are two or more superiors for an employee, conflicts in instructions and confusion of authority will result, it will endanger discipline and disturb order and stability.

5. **Unity of direction:** All units in the organization should be moving toward the same objectives through co-ordinated and focused effort, or, all members of an organization must work together to accomplish common or same objectives. Their efforts shall be directed towards one common super-goal.

   Fayol advocates, "one head and one plan" for a group of activities having the same objective. Without unity of direction, "unity of action, co-ordination of strength, and focusing of effort" can't be achieved. A group with two heads or two or more divergent plans can't succeed in doing anything.

6. **Subordination of individual interest to group interests.**

   This is self-explanatory. It is also called principle of co-operation. The interests of one employee or group of employees shouldn't prevail over that of the company or broader organization. The interests of the organization should take priority over the interests of any one individual employee. Each small work for all and all for each.

   Employees shouldn't take precedence over the interests of the organization as a whole. General or common interest must be supreme in any joint enterprise be it formal or informal. The general interest is not sacrificed at the altar of individual interest. When personal (individual) interest becomes supreme and general interest is sacrificed, the organization will collapse. However due to such factors as ignorance, ambition, selfishness, laziness, weakness and such like human passions, general interests may sometimes be ignored in favour of individual interests. Wherever such a conflict appears, action should immediately be taken to restore the supremacy of general interests. The management has so serve the general interest and not the individual interest.

7. **Remuneration of personnel:** The overall pay and compensation for employees should be fair to both employees and the organization. It has to be fair and afford the maximum satisfaction to both employee and employer[6.] No good performance can be expected unless the management personnel are properly and adequately paid. The payment should be sufficient to ensure a decent (satisfactory) standard of living. The wage plan should take into consideration factors such as the cost of living, availability of personnel, financial position of the business and economic conditions in general. The wage plan should also sufficiently compensate to the more efficient workers by giving bonus or some other form of compensation. Sound scheme remuneration includes adequate financial and non-financial incentives. However, it must be kept in mind that in an attempt to remunerate an enterprise must not overpay. i.e., the payment should be fair.

8. **Centralization;** Decreasing the role of subordinates in decision-making is centralization; increasing their role is decentralization[5]. Management should decide the extent of centralization in the working of the enterprise. Centralization is the situation where a single manager controls the entire work or most of it. For Fayol, the question of centralization of decentralization is a simple question of proportion, a matter of finding the optimum degree for a particular concern. Henry Fayol didn't favour any of the two (centralization or otherwise). An organization should have to balance subordinate involvement through decentralization with managers' retention of final authority through centralization. An organization will have to decide itself, the degree of centralization or decentralization it will have. The aim here is to attain the point of best overall output per worker. Extreme centralization and decentralization must be avoided. The problem is to find the best amount of centralization in each case.

9. **Scalar chain**: Scalar denotes steps Fayol defines scalar chain as the "chain of superiors " ranging from the ultimate authority to the lowest rank. It is a hierarchy or the line of authority in an organization often represented today by the neat boxes and lines of the organization chart-runs in order of rank from top management to the lowest level of the enterprise. Management should be set on the basis of a system of authorities. And the chain of superior-subordinate relationships from top to bottom is called scalar chain. It sets a line authority to be followed in the organization structure. Communication follows the chain. There should be no bypassing of it. If this (scalar chain) is to be followed it will maintain the principle of the unity of command. It is an error to depart needlessly from the

line of authority. As much as possible the hierarchy shouldn't be too long from top to bottom. But at times, adherence to the prescribed route or channel of communication may delay matters. Fayol maintains that if there is likely to be undue delay in following the line of authority, and quick results if it is ignored, then the subordinates concerned should be bold enough (don't feel something) to ignore the line of authority and use the " gang plank" (the contact between two or more immediately concerned officials).

10. **Order:** This principle relates to, people and materials should be in the right place at the right time Breaking order in to "Material" and " Social" order. Thus, "a place for everything and everything in its place" means material order, and "a place for every one and every in his place" means social order. Material order demands that the materials used in the enterprise should be properly stored. At the same time, all the materials should be available at the required time without difficulty.

    Social order calls for proper selection of the workers so that every employee is in his right place. This requires proper selection, training and placement of workers.

11. **Equity:** means a combination of fairness, kindliness and justice. Managers should be both friendly and fair to their subordinates. Employees can be made to put in their best only when they are given kind (friendly attitude), fair and just treatment. A superior must treat his subordinates equally. It is not only the chief executive out to apply equity in his dealings with subordinates, rather it is the duty of the chief executive himself to ensure that managers at all levels apply equity in their dealings with their own subordinates.

12. **Stability of tenure of personnel:** A high turnover rate is not good for the efficient functioning of an organization. Hence, the employees should be assured of their employment unless something unforeseen happens. It is only under this assurance that an employee will work well. Once appointed after a thorough examination and scrutiny, the services of an employee should be secured. There shouldn't be frequent termination and changes. The employer too will not gain anything from it. In a bigger organization the employees take time to adjust and to know people. So enough time must be given to the worker to acquire competence. Frequent change of personnel does no good. For example, a mediocre (neither very good nor very bad) manager who stays infinitely in the organization is preferable to an outstanding manager who comes and goes. Any such change (turnover) should be made only when it seems unfavourable as in the case of illness, retirement or death of an employee. Changes may also be made where an employee proves his ability to handle bigger and more important jobs, or if he proves himself to be unfit for the present job. Fayol points out its dangers and costs.

13. **Initiative**: Initiative is the power of thinking out a plan and ensuring its successful implementation. It stimulates human endeavour. This gives zeal and energy to the organization. Initiative is conceived of as the thinking out and execution of a plan. So workers should be encouraged to develop and carry out their plans for improvements. The employees or subordinates be given the freedom to conceive and carry out their plan, even though some mistakes may result[5]. Workers should be inspired to show initiative. A manager shouldn't be ashamed to acknowledge workers initiative and other good points. A manager who induces his subordinates to think and act on their own, is always better and more successful than the one who doesn't.

14. **Esprit de corps:** This is a French term, literally it means the spirit of loyalty, true, be faithful and devotion to the group or society to which one belongs. Management should promote a team spirit of unity and harmony among employees. Unity is strength and it comes from the harmony of the personnel.

    Esprit de corps means "spirit of cooperation", i.e., union is strength. But unity demands cooperation. If the workers of the organization work with a team spirit, in cooperation and harmony, the results are bound to be good. The management should strive to create harmony and understanding among the workers and impress upon them the need of united action. To this end the following are suggested:

    There should be proper coordination of work at all levels.
    ii) Subordinates should be encouraged to develop informal social relationship among themselves.
    iii) Efforts should be made to create enthusiasm and keen ness among subordinates so that they work to the maximum of their abilities.

iv) Employees with proven merit should be suitably rewarded and those not up to the standard should be given opportunity to improve their performance.
v) Subordinates should be made conscious of the fact that what they are doing is of value to the undertaking and to the community at large.
vi) It should be established by word and deed, that the management is deeply interested in the welfare and well-being of all subordinates.
Vii) Divide and rule policy should be avoided
viii) Oral communication should be preferred to written communication

Fayol made it clear that the above principles can be modified or changed by managers according to situations. They can also add to these principles or delete some, if they consider necessary.

2.2.2 Neo-Classical (Behavioural) Theories of Management

Neo means new or modern. Neo classical theory is a group of management ideas that developed throughout the period from the 1920_5 through the 1950s. Neo-classical theory is called human relation and behavioural science movement. It is built on the basis of classical theory. It modified, improved and extended the classical theory. Classical theory concentrated on job content and management of physical resources. They didn't emphasize the human side (factor). Neo-classical theory gave a greater emphasis to human factor or to man behind the machine and stressed the importance of individuals as well as group relationship in the plant or work place.

The predominant characteristic of these ideas is the emphasis on the social needs, drives and attitudes of individuals. The neoclassical writers felt that employees couldn't simply respond "to rules, chains of authority, and economic incentives. Such writers believed that employees brought their social need with them to the organization and that, consequently, effective management required a more human oriented approach. The behavioural science approach and human relations is the core of the neo-classical theory. They both pointed out the role of psychology and sociology in the understanding of individual as well as group behaviour in an organization. It advocated the importance of human values in business. The two schools of neo classical (behavioural) theory of management are:

1. Human Relations school (Elton Mayo 1880-1949)
2. Behavioural science school

1. Human Relations School (*Elton Mayo 1880–1949*)

George E. Mayo and his associates conducted Hawthorne studies in the Hawthorns plant of Western Electric Company in the USA between 1929 and 1932. Mayo was born and educated is Australia, Mayo joined the faculty of Harvard university in 1926. He was the pioneer of human relations movement.

Their study began as an attempt to investigate the relationship between the level of lighting in the work place and the productivity of workers - the type of question F. Taylor and his colleagues might well have addressed. The experiments followed by Hawthorne studies were:

i. Illumination experiment
ii. Relay Assembly Test Room Experiments
iii. Bank wiring Room Experiment
iv. Massive interviewing

i. Illumination Experiment: The initial experiment in the Hawthorne studies was illumination experiment. In this experiment workers were divided into two groups-,i.e., an experimental group and a control group. The experimental group was subjected to deliberate changes in lighting, but, the control group remained the light constant throughout the experiments.

As expected the output of the experimental group increased with each increase in light intensity. But the performance of the control group didn't remain constant as expected. Control group production increased at about the same rate as that of the experimental group. Later, the lighting in the work area of the experimental group was reduced and again, the output of the experimental group continued to increase, as did the output of the control group. Finally a decline in productivity of the experimental group did occur, but only when the intensity of light was roughly the equivalent of moon light. Clearly something other than illumination caused the changes in productivity. Something besides lighting was influencing the workers' performance. Surprisingly, this study showed that whether lights were turned up or down employee productivity increased. The researchers thus concluded that some factors other than light were responsible for the increased productivity.

ii. Relay Assembly Test Room Experiment Following the illumination experiment, some workers were placed in the relay assembly test room and various experiments under different work conditions were conducted. Such as a small group of workers were placed in a separate room (5 female assemblers, 1 layout designer, and one observer) and number of variables were altered: wages were increased; rest periods of varying lengths were introduced; the workday and work week were shortened. The researchers, who now acted as supervisors, also allowed the groups to choose their own rest period and to have a say in other suggested changes. Again the results were ambiguous (surprising). Performance tended to increase over time.

iii. Bank Wiring Room Experiment: A final experiment was conducted in the bank wiring room with a small group of employees (9-wiremen,3-solder men, 2-inspectors = 14 people). In this experiment researchers discovered that the production quota set by the company (using scientific management technique) was not the number of units actually produced by the workers. The researchers discovered that the workers had developed their own idea of the level of output that was fair. This informal standard of behaviour, called a *norm*, was enforced by the work group to the point that output was restricted. Any worker who produced more than that number was pressured by co-workers to comply with the norm.[1] To generalize, a) the workers deliberately restricted output b) other than the formal relationship, they created an informal relationship among them.

The experiments led researchers to two conclusions

(1) Strong informal groups exist.

(2) Non economic factors affect employees' behaviour at work.

iv. Massive Interviewing:

As a result of these experiments, about 20,000 interviews were conducted. Interviewers asked employees about the company, the work environment, the type of supervisors and their interpersonal relationships. From this information, the Hawthorne researchers realized that people were not leaving their feeling, attitudes and emotions at home. The employees were not at work simply for economic benefits. Other dimensions also affected their performance.

The Hawthorne Effect

The Hawthorne studies showed that social and psychological factors exert a powerful influence on productivity. The participants respond to social, psychological experience of participation rather than to the experimental variables being studied have become known as the Hawthorne Effect.

The improvement in productivity was due to such social factors as morale, satisfactory interrelationship between members of a work group and effective management - a kind of managing that would understand human behaviour, specially group behaviour, and serve it through such interpersonal skills as motivating, counselling, leading and communication.

To conclude:

1. Employees are essentially social beings, not merely rational economic beings. Individuals are motivated by social needs.

2. As social beings, employees are members of groups, therefore, managers should always relate to individuals with full awareness of the nature of groups and their influence on individual behaviour. People obtain their sense of identity through interpersonal relationships.
3. Managerial effectiveness often depends on a relationship of mutual trust between employees and their superiors.
4. Employees respond to provisions for their social needs and acceptance offered by management.
5. Because if industrial progress and routinization of work, work has become dissatisfying.
6. Employees are more responsive to the social forces of peer groups than to incentives and controls of management.
7. The business organization is not just a techno-economic system. Basically it is a social system.
8. The employee can also be motivated by many social and psychological wants and not solely by economic incentives because his behaviour is also influenced by feelings, emotions, and attitudes.
9. Democratic rather than authoritarian leadership is essential in order to honour psychosocial demands. Management must learn to develop co-operative attitude and not rely merely on command.
10. Management must take greater interest in employee development and workers' satisfaction, as there is a very close connection between morale and productivity. In other words productivity and satisfaction go hand in hand.
11. Informal group and Informal organization must be recognized. Group psychology plays an important role in any enterprise. We must rely more on group efforts.
12. Management must develop social skills in addition to technical skills.

The neo-classical theory tried to solve the man - machine equation by emphasizing that man is a living machine and he is far more important than the inanimate machine. Hence, key to higher productivity lies not in technological development alone but in reality it lies in employee morale. Where moral is high, output is also high. Man- to-man relationships, team spirit, group harmony should be given top preference by management.

2. Behavioural Science School

Initial human relations studies tended to concentrate on employee satisfaction and moral implying thereby direct connection between moral and productivity. Later on behavioural science approach through its objectives and scientific research of individuals-behaviour and motivation indicated the relationship between moral and productivity was over simplified.

Behavioural sciences qualify as science only because of their methods. These methods are essentially statistical in nature.

Behavioural science movement was a further refinement and it covered much wider scope in interpersonal roles and relationships. Earlier human relation experts were referred as now sociologists. Contended workers were considered productive workers just as contended cows could give more milk.

The behavioural science school of management thought started in 1940 and it gave special attention on understanding individuals and their interpersonal relations. Maslow developed a need hierarchy to explain human behaviour within an organization and motivation.

A Theory of Human Needs (Abraham Maslow)

A need is a psychological or physiological deficiency a person feels the compulsion to satisfy. From a managerial perspective, this is a significant concept because needs create tensions that affect a person's work attitudes and behaviours. Abraham Maslow was an eminent psychologist who identified five levels of human needs. Physiological, safety, social, esteem, and self-actualization.

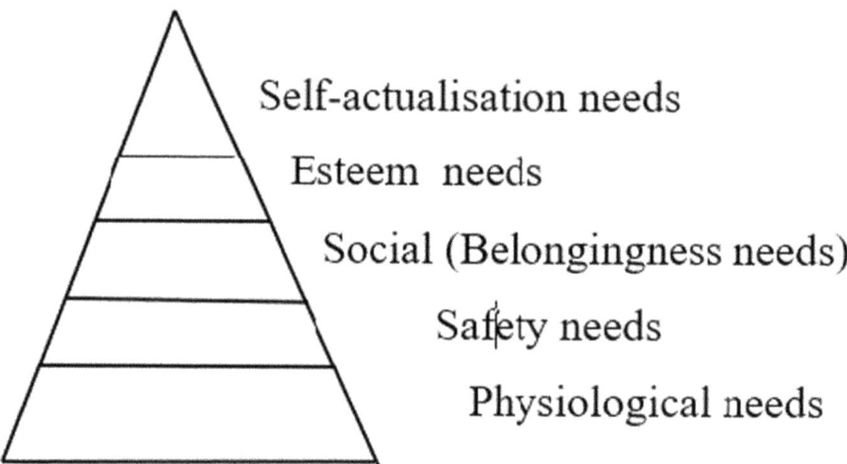

Figure 2.1 Maslow's Hierarchy of Needs.

Lester, David. "Measuring Maslow's hierarchy of needs." *Psychological reports* 113.1 (2013): 15-17.

1. *Physiological needs* - Most basic of all human needs: need for biological maintenance; include need for air, water, food and sex etc.
2. *Safety needs* - Need for security, protection and stability in the physical and interpersonal events of day to day life; includes the need for safety, order and freedom from fear or threat
3. *Social (Belongingness and love) needs* - Need for love, affection, sense of belongingness in one's relationship with other persons.
4. Esteem needs- Need for esteem of others; respect, prestige, recognition; need for self-esteem, personal sense of competence, mastery, achievement and respect from others.[2and5]
5. *Self-actualisation* - Highest need level; need to fulfil oneself; to grow and use abilities to fullest and most creative extent, to feel fulfilled and to realize one's potential.

Maslow's theory of human needs is based on two fundamental principles:

1. The *deficit principle* - A satisfied need is not a motivator of behaviour; people act to satisfy "deprived" needs that is, needs for which a satisfaction "deficit" exists.
2. The *progression principle* - The five needs exist in a hierarchy of precedence; a need at any level only becomes activated once the next lower-level need has been satisfied.

These two principles view people as seeking to satisfy sequentially the five levels of need in their work. A deprived need dominates individual attention and determines behaviour. Once this deficit is satisfied, the next higher-level need is activated and progression up the hierarchy occurs. When the level of self-actualisation is reached, the deficit and progression principles cease to operate. The more this need is satisfied, the stronger it grows.

This theory suggests that a manager's job is to:

1. Provide avenue for individual need satisfaction that also supports essential organization and work-unit goals, and
2. Remove any obstacles blocking need satisfaction and causing frustration, negative attitudes, or dysfunctional behaviour.

Maslow's theory has much in common with the Hawthorne studies: managers who satisfy human needs will achieve productivity.

Elements of Neo-Classical Theory

There are three elements of the neo-classical theory.

1. **The Individual**: The classical theory ignored the difference among individuals. The neo-classical theory emphasises that individual differences must be recognized. An individual has his own feelings, emotions, perceptions and attitudes. He has ever changing psychology. Each person is unique. Each is bringing to the job situation certain attitudes, beliefs as well as skills, technical, social and logical. Each person has certain hops, aspirations and expectations. Each individual has certain meaning of his job, his supervision, working conditions, his group, etc. The inner world of the worker (ignored by classical theory) is more important than the external relations at work determine the rise or fall in productivity. Of course, physical and economic conditions must be satisfactory. Ease of work (physical and mental ease) gives speed of work. Unidimensional economic model of motivation is firmly discounted. Instead, proponents of human relation advocate the adoption of multidimensional model of motivation, which is based upon economic, individual and social factors. Hence, the package deal of motivation includes financial and non-financial incentives in the right proportion.

2. **The Work-Group**: An individual in a group develops social wants, e.g. a desire to belong, to be accepted by, and stand well in his work group. Workers are not isolated, unrelated individuals; they are social beings and should be treated as such, by management. The existence of informal organization is natural. It can't be denied. On the other hand, management must recognize its importance and it must be integrated with formal organization. The informal communication (the grapevine) is often very speedy and often accurate. It can't be eliminated.

   The neo-classical theory described the vital effects of group psychology and behaviour on motivation and productivity. Each work group has its own leader, unwritten constitution and its own production standard imposed by social sanctions on the group members. Classical theory ignored the importance of informal organization. Human relation theory brought out its importance.

3. **Participative Management**: The emergence of participative management is inevitable when emphasis is given on the individual and work groups. Neo- Classical writers advocated worker participation in management. Allowing labour to participate in decision-making primarily to increase productivity was a new form of supervision. Taylorism was opposed to such participation. Taylor wanted only experts in job analysis and planning of job operations.

Classical theory was job oriented and it focused its attention on scientific job analysis. Neo classical theory focuses its attention on the worker and it is employee-oriented. Now we have a shift in managerial style from product-centre approach to employee and group cantered approach. Worker is the centre in a modern plant. Plant layout, machinery, tools etc must offer employee convenience and facilities. Neo-classical theory is built upon the success of classical theory. The pillars of classical approach - order, rationality, structure, etc have been modified by the neo-classical movement. Classical approach satisfied the basic economic needs of the organization and society. Now neo-classical approach is trying to satisfy personal security, and social needs of workers. Both approaches must be suitably integrated to emphasise the need not only for recognition of human values but also for recognition of productivity simultaneously. Modern management must have the twin primary objectives - productivity (classical approach) and satisfaction (neo-classical approach).

2.2.3 Modern Theories of Management

Modern management theories indicate further refinement, extension and synthesis of all the classical and neo-classical approaches to management. These trends started after 1960 and there are three main streams under the modern management theory.

1. Quantitative approach to management (operations research)
2. Systems approach to management
3. Contingency approach to management (situational).

Modern management theory highlights the complexity of modern organizations and integrates ideas from the other management theories. Likewise, since individuals are complex and people's motives, needs, aspirations and potentials vary, there can be few static or universal managerial principles. It is this distinction (few static or universal principles) that characterized modern managerial theories.

1. Quantitative Approach to Management (Operations Research Or Management Science)

Process management school centred around the functions of a manager. Human relations and behavioural sciences emphasised the human aspect of an organization and its management. However, quantitative approach to management could offer systematic analysis and the solutions to many complex problems faced by management in the real world. The quantitative school of management is also called operations research or management science. This school sees management as a logical entity, the actions of which can be expressed in terms of mathematical symbols, relationships, and measurable data. This school is primarily concerned with decision-making. New mathematical and statistical tools are now applied in the field of management, particularly in decision-making on complex problems. Examples of the quantitative techniques suggested by this school are linear programming, game theory, queuing (waiting line theory), simulation theory, and probability theory. These all together (quantitative decision making tools) are called operations research science.

Where,

- Linear programming - Calculating how best to allocate scarce resources among competing uses.
- Game theory:
- Queuing theory - Computing the number of service personnel or stations that will minimize customer waiting time and service cost.
- Simulation - Making a model of a problem and using a computer to solve the problem many times under various decision circumstances.

Production scheduling, replacement of capital equipment, inventory control, plant location, transportation problems, and many other complex managerial problems are being solved today with the help of operations research and computers.

Churchman has defined operations research as an application of scientific method to problems arising in the operations of a system, which may be represented by means of mathematical models and equations and solving of these problems by resolving the equations representing the system.

There are two main characteristics of the quantitative school:

(1) Optimising or minimizing input-output, and

(2) Using mathematical models

Optimising or minimizing means that which is most desirable for a selected factor is chosen from an entirety such as an entire organization department, or work group and any alternative would be less desirable. Optimising is usually associated with sales, gross margin, machine utilization, service or productivity.

In contrast, minimizing (to seek a minimum amount) is typically used for cost and time taken. Suppose our objective is to maximize production profits, to achieve this we consider the common portions of most enterprises to be (1) input, (2) process, and (3) output.

A mathematical model makes the optimising or minimizing work feasible. A mathematical model is a symbolic representation showing all pertinent factors quantitatively and reflecting the relative influence of each factor on the entire situation and the impact of a change in any one, or group, of the factors on the remaining factors and on the total. The mathematical model can be a single equation or a series of equations depending on the complexity and number of factors involved.

The development of models to represent system under study requires the skills of many branches of knowledge such as mathematics, statistics, economics, engineering, physical science, behavioural science and cost accounting as well as management expertise. Of course, these mathematical models must represent the real world for best results. Operations research teams constitute teamwork of diverse specialist and analysts are directly attached as staff members to top management in planning and decision-making. Management science represents the use of scientific method to facilitate management planning and decision - making. There is no doubt that the quantitative measurement school supplies a powerful tool for solving complex problems.[3] This approach is especially effective when applied to the measurable physical problems of management - such as inventory, material and production control - rather than to problems where measurement is difficult such as human behaviour. Note that risk in not eliminated by the use of this approach, but assistance is provided to enable the manager reduce risk increase probability. That is MS/OR managers play a crucial role in the planning and decision making of organization.

Operations research, computer, and management information system are the modern tools of management decision making problems. Quantitative management specialists are sometimes criticized for their lack of sensitivity to this additional human factor. A well-rounded and truly comprehensive view of problems, including both technical and human resource considerations is the ideal direction advocated by systems approach and contingency approach to management.

2. Systems Approach to Management

Systems approach means the application of systems concepts to the process of management and organization of any enterprise. Formally speaking, a *system* is a collection of interrelated parts that function together to achieve a common purpose. Or a *system* is some organized whole (e.g., a company) made up of parts connected in some fashion (eg, finance, accounting marketing and production departments) and directed to some purpose (eg, to make products or profit) [3]. The system approach to management attempts to view the organization as a unified, purposeful system composed of interrelated parts. Rather than dealing separately with the various segments of an organization, the systems approach gives managers a way of looking at an organization as a whole and as part of the larger, external environment. In so doing, systems theory tells us that the activity of any segment of an organization in varying degrees affects the activity of every other segment.

Some key concepts: as managers, we should be familiar with the systems vocabulary, so that we can keep pace with current developments.

- ***Subsystems***: the parts that make up the whole of a system are called subsystems. And each system in turn may be a sub system of a still larger whole. Thus a department is a subsystem of a plant, which may be a subsystem of a company, which is a subsystem of the conglomerate or industry, which is a subsystem of the national economy as a whole, which is a subsystem of the world systems.
- ***Synergy:*** the situation in which the whole is greater than its parts. In organization terms, the fact that departments that interact cooperatively can be more productive than if they operate in isolation. For example, it is more efficient for each department in a small firm to deal with one financing department in a small firm to deal with one financing department than for each department to have a separate financing department of its own.
- ***Open and closed systems:*** A system is considered an open system if it interacts with its environment; it is considered a closed system if it doesn't. All organizations interact with their environment but the extent to which they do so varies. An automobile plant, for example, is a far more open system than a monastery or a prison.
- ***System boundary:*** the boundary that separates each system from its external environment. It is rigid in a closed system, flexible in an open system.
- ***Flow:*** Components such as information, materials, and energy (including human energy) that enter and leave a system. These enter the system from the environment as inputs (for example, raw materials), undergo transformation process with in the system (operations that alter them) and exit the system as output (goods and services).
- ***Feedback:*** feedback is the key to system controls. As operations of the system proceed, information is fed back to the appropriate people or perhaps, to a computer, so that the work can be assessed and, if necessary, corrected. Through feedback, managers learn how well the organization's or subsystem's products or services are being received.

  From manager's perspective two major parts of systems theory are:

  1. Organization is an open system
  2. Interdependency of the parts components.

Generally the definition of *system* has three significant parts:

1. Every system is goal oriented and it must have a purpose or objective to be obtained. The objective provides the basis for evaluating functions performed within the system.
2. In designing the system we must establish the necessary arrangement of components. This is nothing but organizing function of management.
3. Inputs of information material and energy are allocated for processing as per plan so that the outputs can achieve the objective of the system, vis-à-vis, productivity and satisfaction. Figure 2.2 shows the design of a basic system

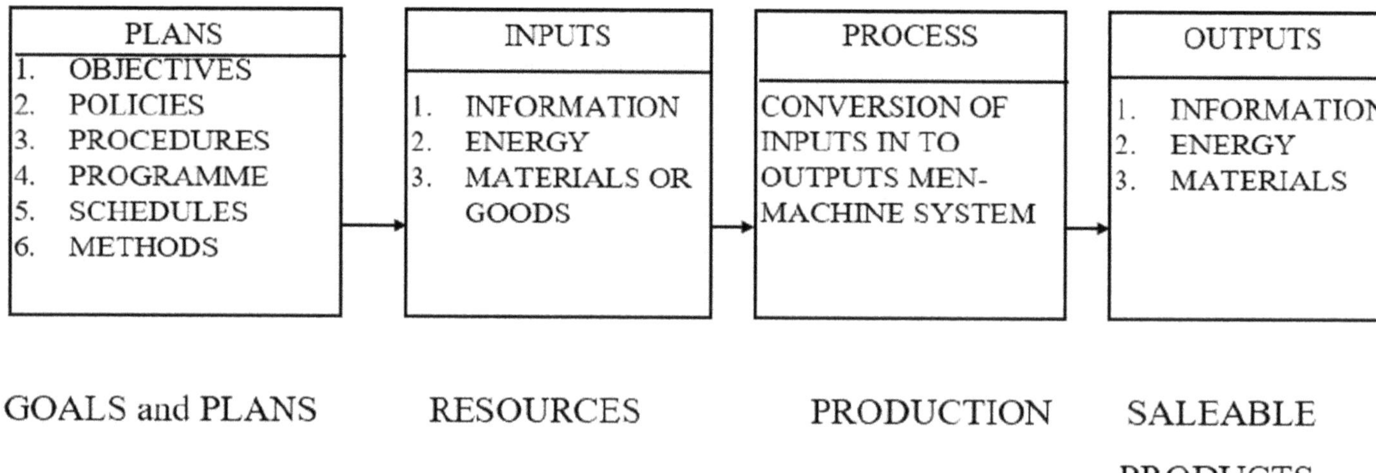

Figure 2.2 The design of a basic system.
Source: Daft, R.L. and Marcic, D. Understanding management. Cengage Learning. 2016.

Note: (1) Generally there are three basic inputs that enter the processor of the system, viz, information (technology), energy (motive power) and materials to be transformed in to goods. (2) If the output is service, materials are not included in the inputs (3) If we have a manufacturing company outputs are goods or materials. (4) If we have a consulting firm, output is information or advice. (5) If we have a power generating company, output is energy.

When systems approach is applied to organization, we have the following features of an organization as an open adaptive system:

1. It is a subsystem of its broader environment
2. It is goal oriented-people with a purpose
3. It is a technical subsystem -using knowledge, techniques, equipment and facilities
4. It is a structural subsystem- people working together on interrelated activities.
5. It is a psychosocial system-people in social relationships
6. It is coordinated by a managerial subsystem creating planning, organizing, motivating, communicating and controlling the overall efforts directed towards set goals.

Open Systems and the Environment

The environment is a critical element in the open systems perspective on organization. Because it is a source of resources and feedback, it has a significant impact on organizations. As the environment changes over time, for example, it is the manager's job to stay informed and help the organization respond in a productive way.

Feedback is also central to an open system. It reflects the environment's evaluation of an organization or subsystem. Through feedback, managers learn how well the organization's or subsystems' products or services are being received. Based on feedback constructive action can be taken by managers to maintain or improve organizational productivity.

When properly used, feedback helps ensure the survival and long-term prosperity of the enterprise. Figure 2.2 show the Organization as an interacting and open system

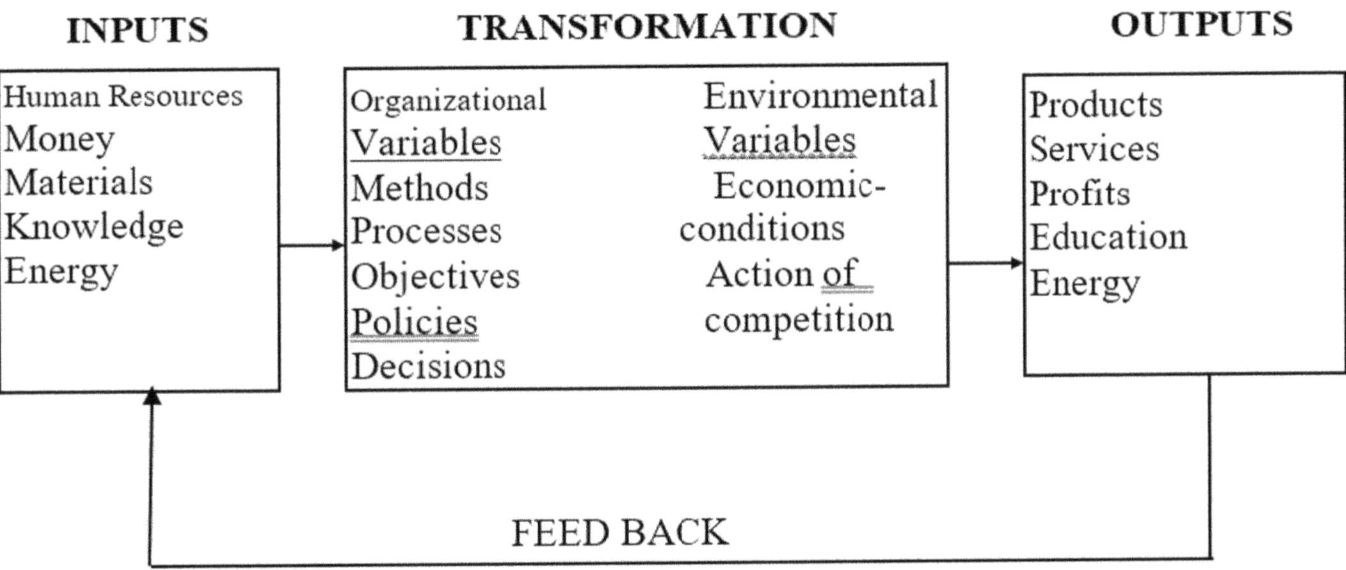

Figure 2.3 Organization as an interacting and open system'
Source: adopted from: Daft, R.L. and Marcic, D. Understanding management. Cengage Learning. 2016.

Contingency theories have done an especially good job of extending the implications of the organization environment relationship for managers.

3. Contingency Approach to Management (Situational)

Contingency management theory evolved out of the systems approach to managing organizations. [3] Systems approach emphasizes that all subsystems of an organization along with the supra system of environment are interconnected and interrelated. Contingency approach analyses and understands these interrelationships so that managerial actions can be adjusted to demands of specific situations or circumstances. The essence of the contingency perspective is to help managers analyse and understand situational differences and choose responses that best facilitate productivity in each circumstance. Thus contingency approach enables us to evolve practical *answers* to the problems demanding solutions. Organization design and managerial actions most appropriate to specific situations will have to be adjusted in order to achieve best possible results under the given situation.

Hence, we can't have universal principles of organization and management appropriate to all situations and in all environments. In other words, there is no *one best way* (as advocated by Taylorism) to organize and manage. Decentralization as well as centralization can work under given set of situations. Even bureaucracy can work under certain circumstances and it has not totally outlived its utility. Similarly, democratic or participative managerial style may not be fit in a certain situation, and we may have to adopt tight control under certain circumstances. Leadership style to be adopted always depends on the situation and not merely on leadership qualities and characteristics of the followers. Motivation through financial incentives can work wonders if the environment is favourable. We can't say that non-financial incentives can work in any situation of environment.

The basic ideas of four important contingency viewpoints are:

- Organization structure must match environmental demands
- Organization structure must match technological demands
- Structures of organizational subsystems must match the unique demands of their respective environments
- Leadership behaviours must be appropriate to the situational demands of various work groups.

The contingency approaches advocate that managers carefully analyse the unique characteristics of situations and respond accordingly in their decision-making and problem-solving efforts. Depending on such things as environmental demands, technological factors, and work group characteristics the manager's actions will vary from one situation to the next. What is a good managerial response for one type of situation may be a poor one for another and vice versa. If the condition is A, then action X may be considered most effective. However, if the condition is B, then action Y should be used, which is contingency approach is a realistic view in management and organisation. There is no 'one best way' of management or organization. Situation decides the pattern of organization and management most appropriate in practice.

Review questions

1. Outline the main evolution stage and theory in the history of the management.
2. What problems did the school of thought principles solve?
3. A cement factory is characterized by frequent loss and deterioration of productivity; and its CEO wants to find a solution for the problem the company is facing. What will be your focus if you are
   a. Proponent of Taylor
   b. Proponent of behavioural management theory
3. Contingency view believes in that there is no one best way to manage. So, does it violate management science? If not, why?
4. Discuss the general principles of H. Fayol. Can we apply all principles of Fayol?
5. What lessons do we take from Hawthorne experiment?
6. Differentiate between Objectives based on MBO School perspective, Long and short-term objectives, Qualitative and Quantitative Objectives.
7. What were the weakness and problems of the management schools of thought?

Short Case:

1. If the company does not give a clear and correct guideline for the staff/employees in the unit/department, which principle is violated? What will be the impact of it?
2. as part of your learning requirements please visit a manufacturing company. Write down your observation about the supervisor and their subordinate, beside the means and methods of communication. Prepare your report and present it in front of your class.

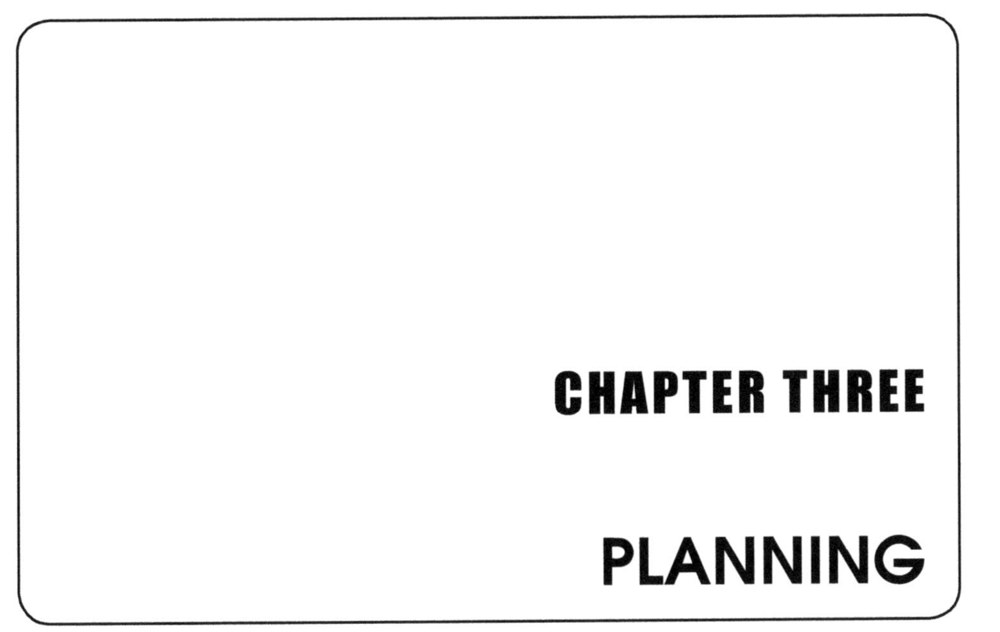

CHAPTER THREE

PLANNING

     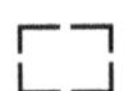 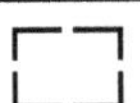

LEARNING OBJECTIVES

After studying this chapter, you will be able to:

1. justify the importance of planning.
2. Explain what managers do in the planning process.
3. identify the approaches of planning.
4. Discuss contemporary issues in planning.

Overview

This chapter will discuss the planning concept, process (steps), components, approaches and the role each planning stage plays in developing a successful plan. However, planning is surrounded by many factors constraining and affecting the plan performance; these factors have been considered in this chapter. Furthermore, planning mainly relies on forecasting the future; therefore, this chapter covers the forecasting process and types.

3.1 Meaning, Nature and Importance of planning

Planning is the primary function of Management. Every human activity is undertaken with a view to achieve something that must be preceded by planning. Since man is gifted with the power of reasoning, he rarely does anything without weighing the consequences of his action. Students plan their studies teachers plan their teaching work, the head of the family plans his expenditure etc.

For any organization to survive and grow, some degree of planning is necessary. In the field of business Management, the need for planning is all the greater. This is because of ever – growing competition, frequent fluctuation in demand, discovery of new products, the new ways in which these can be used, and a world-wide scarcity of resources. As such, it is necessary for those in business to plan to make fullest possible use of their available resources.

The process of management Involves looking ahead. Good mangers are able to assess the future and make provision for it PLANNING, the first of the four basic managerial functions, is how this responsibility is carried out. It is formally defined as a process of setting objectives and determining what should be done to accomplish them. Planning is an applied problem – solving and decision making effort (Robbins, and Coulter, 2012)

3.1.1 Meaning of Planning

Planning – means taking the hard decisions before events force them upon you, and anticipating the future needs of the market before the demand asserts itself.

To achieve effectiveness at any level of responsibility, a manger must be a good planner.

Planning has three action characteristics that present special challenges to the manager. Planning is:

1. Forward thinking: - through planning managers. decide what to do and how before it must actually be done.
2. Decision-making: - planning involves making decisions that identify desired future states of affairs and define the actions required to achieve them.
3. Goal oriented:- planning targets efforts on activities needed to accomplish objectives and arrive at a desired end result. According to Henry Fayol, "plan of action is at one and the same time
    - the result envisaged
    - line of action to be followed
    - the stages to go through and methods to use.

The term planning has been defined by various thinkers and from the various definitions given above that planning involves two things:-

1. Determining the aims and objectives of planning, and
2. Selecting, on the basis of past experience, present facts and circumstances and future possibilities the best course of action to realize the planning objectives.

Planning involves selecting missions and objectives and the actions to achieve them; it requires decision-making; that is, choosing future courses of action from among alternatives. Planning is determining in advance what is to be accomplished. Planning bridges the gap from where we are to where we want to be in a desired future (Karmakar., 2011).

3.1.2 The Nature (Characteristics) of Planning

We can highlight the essential nature of planning by examining its major aspects:

1. The contribution of planning to purpose and objectives

Every plan and all its supporting plans is to facilitate the accomplishment of the enterprise's objectives and purpose. This principle derives from the nature of organized enterprise, which exists for the accomplishment of group purpose through deliberate cooperation. This was emphasized by E. Gotez, when he said, "Plans alone can't make an enterprise successful, action is required; the enterprise must operate. Plans can however, focus on purpose. They can forecast which actions will tend toward the ultimate objectives, which tend a way, which will likely offset one another and which are merely irrelevant."

Managerial planning seeks to achieve a consistent, coordinated structure of operations focused on desired ends. Without plans, actions become merely random activity, producing nothing but chaos.

2. Primacy of plans

Since managerial operations in organizing, staffing, leading and controlling are designed to support the accomplishment of enterprise objectives, planning logically precedes the execution of all other managerial functions. Although in practice all the functions mesh (interlink) as a system of action, planning is unique in that it involves establishing the objectives necessary for all group effort. Besides a manger must plan in order to know what kind of organization relationships and personal qualifications are needed, along which course subordinates are to be directed and led, and what kind of control is to be applied. And, of course, all the other managerial functions must be planned, if they are to be effective.

PLANNING and CONTROL are inseparable the Siamese twins of management. An attempt to control without plans is meaningless, since there is no way for people to tell whether they are going where they want to go (the result of task of control) unless they first know where they want to go (part of the task of planning). Plans thus furnish the standards of control.

3. The pervasiveness of planning

Planning is the function of all mangers although the character and breadth of planning will vary with each manager's authority and with the nature of polices and plans outlined by superiors. If mangers are not allowed a certain degree of discretion and planning responsibility, they are not truly mangers.

One manger because of his/her authority or position in the organization may do more-or more important-planning than another, or the planning of one may be more basic and applicable to a larger portion of the enterprise than that of another. However, all mangers from presidents to first level supervisors all they plan. Even the head of a road gang or a factory crew plans in a limited area under fairy strict rules and procedures. While top executives plan the general direction of the firm, mangers at all levels must prepare their plans so that they contribute to the overall aims of the organization.

4. The efficiency of plans

Efficiency of a plan is measured by its contribution to our purpose and objectives, off set by the costs and other factors required to formulate and operate it, i.e., planning has to go with the goal and objective of the firm. A plan may enhance the attainment of objectives but at unnecessary high cost. Plans are efficient if they achieve their purpose at a reasonable cost, when cost is measured not only in terms of time or money or production but also in the degree of individual or group satisfaction i.e. plan can even make it impossible to achieve objectives if they make enough people in an organization dissatisfied or unhappy.

That is, the quality of planning depends on the quality of the intellectual activity and the precise goals and objectives. If these two aspects are carefully considered, there is no doubt that planning will lead to overall efficiency in the organization. Without clear objectives, mangers have no sense of direction. Failure to plan and direct an organization toward goals inevitably produces inefficiency.

5. It concerns future activity.

The essence of planning is looking ahead and is concerned with deciding in the present what is to be done in the future.

6. It has dynamic aspects

A manager. plans on the basis of some assumptions, which may not come true in the future. Therefore, he has to go on revising, modifying and adjusting plans in the light of the circumstances prevailing. Thus, planning is not only the primary function of management but it is also a continuous function of management. Planning is flexible as it is based on future conditions, which are always dynamic (Karmakar, 2011).

3.1.3 Importance of planning

As was emphasized on the nature of planning, all the managerial actions depend on planning, because planning provides a guideline to all managerial functions. Moreover, when all the functions are performed to give a certain result, this is compared with the planned result to ensure that organizational objectives are being achieved.

Koontz (1988) stresses the significance of planning in four important points.

1. **To offset uncertainty:** Future is always full of uncertainties and changes which makes planning necessity because planning foresees the future and makes provisions for it there by giving an added strength to the organization for continuous growth and steady prosperity. Just as the navigator can't set a course once and forget about it, so an organization? Manger can't establish a goal and let the matter rest. The future is seldom very certain, and further in the future the results of a decision must be considered. An executive may feel quite certain that within the next month orders, costs, productive capacity, output, cash availability and other factors of the business environment will be at given level. A fire, an unforeseen strike, or an order cancellation by a major customer could change all this, but in the short-run this is unlikely, However as this mangers plans further in advance, his/her certainty about the internal and external business environment diminishes and the rightness of any decision becomes less sure.
2. **To focus attention on objectives**: Because all planning effort is directed towards achieving enterprise objectives, the very act of planning focuses attention on these objectives. Well, mangers being typically interested in immediate problems, are forced through planning to consider the future and even consider the periodic need to revise and extend plans in the interest of achieving their objectives well, Managers being typically interested in immediate problems are forced through planning to consider the future and even consider the periodic need to revise and extend plans in the interest of achieving their objectives.
3. **To gain economical operation**: Planning minimizes costs because of the emphasis on efficient operation and consistency. Planning provides for a greater utilization of the available facilities of the enterprise. i.e. for any given period of time the best use is made of what is available. Planning substitutes joint directed effort for uncoordinated piecemeal activity, even flow of work for uneven flow, and deliberate decision for snap judgements.
4. **To facility control**: The twin of planning is controlling, which is performed to make sure the planning is bringing about the results sought. By means of planning, deadlines are determined for the start and completion of each activity and standards of performance are set. These serve as bases for controlling. i.e. mangers can't check on their subordinates' accomplishments without having planned goals which serve as standard, i.e. any attempt to control without plan is meaningless. Thus controlling is exercised in the context of planning.

3.1.4 Limitations of Planning

As against the potential benefits, planning has some limitations, though most of the limits are related with the uncertainties of the future.

Planning is based on reliable data- which is difficult to procure (get) further, forecasting is integral to planning which is based on the present data. Absence of accurate data will upset the plan that is supposed to remove uncertainty.

Planning is also an expensive and time-consuming activity.

A good amount has to be and spent on setting up the planning machinery, and collection of necessary data. Furthermore, planning involves a good deal of investment with respect to time. A lot of time has to be devoted to plan before actual operations start. Sometimes planning may lead to internal inflexibilities and procedural rigidities which may work against the best interest of the organization. Several factors beyond the control of an enterprise also put strain on the success of planning.

Koontz and Weirich (1988) identified the following major limitations by classifying into two categories, that is internal and external inflexibilities

1. **Internal Inflexibility**

Major internal inflexibility that may limit planning are:

a – human psychology

b – policies and procedures and

c – capital investment

a) **Psychological inflexibility:-** managers and employees may develop patterns of thought and behaviour that are hard to change. Particularly in old, established businesses, people develop patterns of thought that are resistant to change.
Mangers are often frustrated in instituting a new plan simply by the unwillingness or inability of people to accept the condition of change. This is a difficult planning limitation to overcome. To do so requires patient selling of ideas, careful dissemination of information, aggressive leadership, and intentional development of a tradition of change among the members of the org?
Policy and procedure inflexibility: Once policies and procedures are established these become ingrained in the enterprise, and changing them becomes difficult. This problem is common in most organization as they get order.
One of the most convincing evidences of bureaucracy, whether in business or government is the existence of complicated procedures designed to avoid mistakes. But usually progressive planning requires an environment of change, with some reasonable degree of freedom and willingness to assume the risks of mistakes; this is prevented in an enterprise bound by the straitjacket of policy and procedural inflexibility, i.e., progressive planning is very difficult to apply in such type of organization which are bound by policy and procedural inflexibility.
Capital Investment: in most cases, once capital is invested in a fixed asset, the ability to switch courses of future action becomes limited, and the investment itself becomes a planning premise. Similar inflexibilities also exist where investment is sunk in items other than what is normally what is regarded as fixed assets. An investment in training of a particular kind or in building up a certain customer reaction to a product through advertising, packaging, or otherwise-may become sunk. Unless the company can reasonably liquidate its investment or change its course of action or unless it can afford to write off the investment, these irretrievable costs may block the way of change. Although it may be a good axiom (suggestion) to disregard sunk costs in planning, their existence does influence planning.

2. **Externally Imposed Inflexibilities:**

Manger has little or no control over externally imposed inflexibilities. Some of the major external inflexibilities are:

a. Political climate
b. Labour unions (organization)
c. Technological change
d. Sociological and cultural
e. Educational variables

a) **Political climate:** Every enterprise to a greater or lesser degree is faced with inflexibilities of the political climate existing at a given time. If the local, state, or notional government actively regulates business or if the notional government adopts a high tariff or otherwise restricts trade, this must be taken into account in planning. Tax, antitrust, and fair trade policies also cause inflexibilities.

A change in government policy, such as import or export policy nationalization of some industries or trade will upset planned calculations. The political philosophy of the government in power can affect the planned programme in a major way, i.e., the basic attitude of government has significant effect in the business plan. Furthermore the procurement policies and programs of government agencies may cause rigidities in planning.

b) **Labour-Unions:** The existence of strong unions, particularly those organized on a national basis, tends to restrict freedom in planning. The numerous wages and working condition provisions of union contracts and the influence of union policies on employee productivity and attitudes must be taken into account. In addition to being important environmental influences, they often give rise to definite inflexibilities. An unforeseen strike, or lock fire out may cause considerable damage to production targets. In fact, the success of planned programs too will depend on the cooperation of the trade unions. It is therefore, advisable that trade union-leaders be taken into confidence regarding the planning targets.

c) **Technological Change**: the rate and nature of technological change also present external limitations upon planning. Technology changes rapidly, and one new development replaces another. But at any given time, the status of technical progress is relatively inflexible. (Technology includes inventions, techniques, vast store of organized knowledge. But its main influence is on ways of doing things, on how we design-produce, distribute and sell goods or services.)

d) **Sociological and cultural:** the important sociological cultural factors, which are relevant to the enterprise include:

- Inter-organizational and individual cooperation or conflict example are the means for advancement open to a person who is capable, regardless of any discrimination?
- view towards authority

  E.g. is participation of subordinates accepted and encouraged?
- View of achievement and work

  E.g. does the society value economic achievement through hard work as a desirable personal trait, or is achievement in the arts or preparation for life after death regarded as paramount?

  Creativity = the ability and power to develop new ideas.

  Innovation = the use of this ideas (new ideas).
- View towards change and risk taking.

  E.g. are nations, enterprise, and individuals willing to take reasonable risks?
- View of change E.g. do the people in a society maintain their basic faith in traditions old way of doing things or do they embrace change which promises to improve productivity? E.g. if a company wants to plan scientifically, you have to care, is the society interested in preserving traditional cultures and patterns or in following a given ideology, regardless of the logic involved or the empirical evidence and new discoveries available, or does the society understand the basic relationship between such economic factors as demand, price, wages, absenteeism, and turnover? etc.

e) **Educational Variables**: Among the major educational constraints noted are literacy level and attitude towards education, types of education and availability of specialized vocational and technical training, higher education's management training programmes, etc, and the extent to which education matches requirements for skills and abilities of the enterprise demand.

The limitation of planning may be overcome by applying more scientific measures and by introducing better system of motivation. In fact, there is no controversy between planning or no planning, it may be in the context of planning techniques planning is a must for every organization because unplanned operations produce chaos and disorders universally without any exception. Therefore, if we are aware of the limits, we can avoid many of the frustrations and insufficiencies of planning.

3.2 Elements of planning

Mangers deal with many different types of plans. Planning consists of several individual plans or component parts which are bound together in a consistent structured operations. It is easy to see that a major program, such as one to build and equip a new factory, is a plan. But what is sometimes overlooked is that a number of other courses of future action are also plans. Keeping in mind that a plan encompasses any course of future action, we can see that plans are varied. They are classified here as:

Figure 3.1 the hierarchy of plans.
Source: Robbins SP, Coulter M. Principles of management. Translated by Seyyed Mohammad Arabi and Mohammed Ali Hamid Rafiee and Behrouz Asrari Ershad, Fourth Edition, Tehran: Office of Cultural Studies. 2007.

1. **Purposes or Missions**

   Every kind of organized group operation has, or at least should have, if it is to be meaningful, a purpose or mission. In every social system, enterprises have a basic function or task, which is assigned to them by society. Mission is the organization's basic long-range objective. It provides a guidance and direction for the organization and defines the industry in which the organization intends to operate

   - the purpose of business generally is the production and distribution of economic goods and services,
   - the purpose of a state highway department is the design, building and operations of a system of state highways.
   - the purpose of the courts is the interpretation of laws and their application.
   - the purpose of a university is teaching and research, and soon.
   - Mission or purpose are that which they define for all concerned the organization's chosen role in society and the ways it intends to full fill this role, i.e. it offers a common sense of direction to all concerned of the reason of the company's existence.

2. **Objectives or goals**

   Objectives, or goals, are the ends toward which activity is aimed. Objectives are a desired future result. i.e. Objectives are the targets toward which mangers move in order to fulfil an organizations mission. All organizations have some mission that includes their reasons for existence. To be effective in this mission, the organization must have targets, the OBJECTIVES that managers. hope to achieve. To meet its mission, the hospital must set specific targets and state desired results. For example the hospital may wish to have an 80% average occupancy rate (that is, 400 of its 500 beds occupied on the average day so that it receives enough income to pay for its building debt, equipment, employees, and other expenses.

   Objectives do not only represent the end point of planning, but also the end toward which organizing, staffing, leading and controlling are aimed. While enterprise objectives are the basic plan of the firm, a department may also have its own objectives. Its goals naturally contribute to the attainment of enterprise objectives, but the two sets of goals may be entirely different. For example, the objective of a business might be to make a certain profit by producing a given line of home entertainment equipment, while the goal of the manufacturing department might be to produce the required number of television sets of a given design and quality at a given cost. These objectives are consistent, but they differ in that the manufacturing department alone cannot assure accomplishing the company's objective.

3. **Strategies**

The word "strategy" comes from the Greek strategia, which means the art or science of being a general. The Greeks knew the importance of generalist in winning and losing battles. Effective generals needed to define the purpose of leading an army, winning, holding territory, protecting a city from invasion, wiping out the enemy, and so forth. Each kind of objective required a different deployment (use) of resources-different programmes. Likewise, an army's strategy could be defined as the actual pattern of actions that it look in response to the enemy. Dating back to the Greeks, the concept of strategy thus was both PLANNING component and decision-making or action components.

Generally, Strategy is a military term, which means projecting and planning a military movement, and handling troops on the battlefield.

In the context of business management it concerns, "the choice of means by which the enterprise's forces (resources) may be employed most effectively in order to accomplish its intended goal. A strategy is the determination of the basic long-term objectives of an enterprise and the adoption of courses of action and allocation of resources necessary to achieve these goals. The heart strategic planning process is determining the actions necessary to accomplish the organizational objectives. A strategy is a plan for using and allocating the organization's resources to accomplish the organizations long-ran objective.

A corporate strategy, sometime referred to as grand strategy, is the overall, predominant strategy of an organization. The corporate strategy determines the direction for the total organization, it could be growth strategy, diversification strategies etc.

Thus a company has to decide what kind of business is it going to be in (engaged). It is a railroad or a transportation company? It is a container or a paper box manufacturer? The firm also has to decide on its growth goal and its desired profitability. The purpose of strategies, then, is to determine what type of action to use. Strategies do not attempt to outline exactly how the enterprise is to accomplish its objectives, since this is the task of countless major and minor programs. But they furnish framework for guiding, thinking and action.

Strategies also indicate the pattern of organization's response to its environment overtime. Strategy links the human and other resources of an organization on one hand, with the challenger and risks posed by the outside world, on the other. Therefore, strategy creates a unified direction for the organization in terms of its many objectives, and it guides the deployment of the resources used to move the organization toward those objectives.

4. **Policies**

A policy can be defined as a pre-determined, general course or guide established to provide direction for ensuring action, based upon a thorough analysis of enterprise objectives. A policy is a general guideline for decision-making. It sets up boundaries that-supply general limits and direction in which managerial action will take place. It sets up boundaries around decisions, including those that can be made and eliminating those that cannot.

Policies delimit (define) an area within which a decision is to be made and ensure that the decision will be consistent with, and contribute to overall objective. A policy defines the area in which decisions are to be made, but it doesn't give the decision. By keeping within these predetermined boundaries, but with freedom to decide within the stated areas, the manger's work is performed in keeping with the overall planning of the enterprise.

Policies tend to pre-decide (i.e. they decide issues) issues before they become problems, make it unnecessary to analyse the same situation every time it comes up, and unify other plans, thus permitting mangers to delegate authority and still maintain control over what their subordinates do.

There are many types of policies. Examples include policies, to hire only university-trained engineers to promote from within, not to do business in South Africa, to set competitive prices or to insist on fixed prices, etc.

Since policies are guides to decision making, they must allow for some discretion. Otherwise they would be rules. Policies leave little room for interpretation. Policies can be regarded as a means of encouraging discretion and initiative, but within limits. The amount of discretion or freedom possible will naturally depend upon the policy, which in turn reflects position and authority in the organization.

5. **Rules**

Rule is a must-restricting device. A rule is a very specific and detailed guide to action, which is set up to direct and restrict action in a fairly narrow manner. They are explicit statement of the plans, that tell what should be done and not to be done. Any rules are the simplest type of plan. Rules are frequently confused with policies and procedures. In fact, rules and policies provide guidelines for action. However, there is a difference between the two policies provide guide lines for decision making by marking off area of discretion but, rules don't allow any discretion in their application.

On the other hand, rules are unlike procedures in that they guide action without specifying a time sequence. In fact a procedure might be looked upon as a sequence of rules. A rule, however, may or may not be part of a procedure. Rules and procedures, by their very nature, are designed to repress thinking (not to think); we should use them only when we do not want people in an organization to use their discretion.

The essence of a rule is that it reflects a managerial decision that some certain action must-or must not-be taken. They do not allow any deviation from stated course of action (Example, "No smoking"). Unlike polices, rules eliminate giving of choice or allowance of discretion, to the employee. That means, what they expect from the employee is simply acceptance. They are ends by themselves.

6. **Procedures**

Procedures are plans that establish a required method of handling future activities. A procedure is a series of steps or functions established for the accomplishment of some specific project or endeavour. Procedures are truly guides to action, rather than to thinking and the detail the exact manner in which a certain activity must be accomplished. Their essence is chronological sequence of required action. Procedures provide a detailed set of instructions for performing sequences of actions that accurse often or regularly.

Polices are broad guidelines, whereas procedures are the methods used to carry out polices. Procedures are more specific in their action implications than organizational policies. E.g. a policy may state, " all new employees should be welcomed in the organization"; the procedure for carrying out this policy might specify a one-day orientation for all new employees. E.g. a policy of " refunds made, with a smile, on all merchandise returned within seven days of purchase";. The procedure for all clerk who handle such merchandise might then be (1) smile at customer (2) check receipt for purchase, date; (3) check condition of merchandise----and soon. Such detailed instructions guide the employee who perform these tasks and help insure a consistent approach to a specific situation.

Procedures are found in every part of an organization. Their pervasiveness in the organization is readily apparent. However they become more exacting and more numerous at the lower levels, largely because of the necessity for more careful control, the economic advantages of spelling out actions in detail, the reduced need for discretion, and the fact that many routine jobs can be performed most efficiently when management prescribes the best way to carry them out. A procedure should be somewhat stable yet flexible enough to allow emergencies and unique situations to occur.

7. **Programs:**

Programs are complex of goals, policies, procedures, rules, task assignments, steps to be taken, resources to be employed and other elements necessary to carry out a given course of action: they are ordinarily supported by necessary capital and operating budgets. Programs may be as major as that of an airline to acquire a $ 400 million fleet of jets, or they may be as minor as a program formulated by a single supervisor to make an improvement of the workers in a department production financial department, etc.

That is a program is a comprehensive plan that includes future use of different resources in an integrated pattern and establishes a sequence of required actions and time schedules for each in order to achieve stated objectives. The makeup of a program can include objectives, policies, procedures, methods, standards, and budgets, but it doesn't necessarily have to include all these categories of plants. Programs outline the actions to be taken, by whom, when, and where.

A program shows or it covers:

- the major steps required to reach an objective
- the organization unit or member responsible for each step, and
- the order and timing of each step.

8. **Budgets**

A budget is a statement of expected results expressed in numerical terms. It may be referred to as a "numberized" program. A budget is a statement of expected results, or resources set aside for specific activities, expressed in numerical or quantitative terms. Budgets are plans that commit resources to activities, projects, or programs. It may be expressed either in financial terms or in terms of labour-hours, units of products, machine hours, or any other numerically measurable term. It may deal with operations, as the expense budget does; it may reflect capital outlays, as the capital expenditures budget does; or it may show flow of cash, as the cash budget does. Making a budget is clearly planning. Budget is the fundamental planning instrument in many companies.

Budgets like all plans, is forward looking. A budget forces a company to make in advance-whether for a week or 5 years-a numerical compilation of expected cash flow, expenses and revenues, capital outlays, or labour or machine-hour utilization. Nothing can be done about the past, and what you are doing in budgeting is planning for things that are to happen. The best budget makers profit from experience. The budget is necessary for control but it can't serve as a sensible standard of control unless it refracts plans.

3.3 Types of Plans

There are many different types of plans with which you will become involved as a manager. These plans may be differentiated or classified in terms of the:

* Time frame (dimension)- it is common to classify or differentiate plans according to the time horizons they represent as-short-range plans, which cover one year or less, medium-range plans, which extend or cover up to a period of five years, and long-range plans which extend beyond five years and often ten and twenty years. Naturally the planning objectives in a manager's action agenda will be more specific in the short run and less clear-cut over the longer term. However, the choice of planning period is influenced by the subject and the purpose as well as the nature of the organization in question,
* Scope or hierarchical arrangement and function intended to perform-Master plans or strategic plans, which involve the overall organization plans and reflect longer term needs and directions of the organization, and Functional plans or operational plans by contrast, are more limited in scope and address those activities and resources required to implement Master plans. They represent each major unit and subunit, such as marketing plan, production Plan, financial plan, personnel plan, marketing research plan, etc. Because of this activating or energizing nature, operational plans are sometimes referred to as tactical plans.
* Use – plans can also be classified according to the frequency or repetitiveness of use – repeated use or standing plans – are plans that are continuing or recurring by nature, require continual adjustment to the ongoing situation. These types of plans are designed to be used again and again. They exist in the form of organizational policies, procedures, and rules. The advantage of such plans is that they provide a stable guide for a particular situation whenever it occurs and help to coordinate the diverse parts of the organization. At the same time they also conserve time used for planning and decision making because similar situations are handled in a predetermined, consistent manner.

Single-use plans:- are used only once. Such plans are designed to meet the needs of a unique or single situation such as for a special project or task. These plans are for a specified period of time or for the duration of the task for which they are designed. Budgets projects and programmes are good examples of typical single-use plans. They are designed to fit a specific project or time period and are discontinued when the project is completed or the time has expired. Example, a rapidly expanding firm, planning to set up a new warehouse, will need a specific single-use plan for the project even though it has established a number of warehouses in the past. It will not be able to use an existing warehouse plan, because the projected warehouse presents unique requirements of location, construction costs, labour availability, zoning restriction and so forth.

Example for standing plans, bank managers can more easily approve or reject loan requests if criteria are established in advance to evaluate credit ratings, collateral assets, and related applicant information. The same decision can be given for recurring issues of similar in nature about the request of loan. Plans may be classified by the degree of flexibility adapted to suit with the uncertainty of the environment with which they deal into.

Variable Plans:- Which state figures in terms of ranges to allow for the uncertainty of the environment. For instance, the time estimated to complete a phase a project might be stated as " three months plus or minus one week." The advantage of the variable plan is that one easily estimates the effect on the organization of deferent levels of operation.

Alternative plans:- Plans which are similar to variable plans in recognizing the environment uncertainties, but in this case the planner sets up two or more entirely separate plans. The plan that is finally chosen is the one that most closely accounts for the circumstances that arise. This kind of planning requires a careful definition of important environmental factors at the outset, and it is also costly since at least one plan will never be used.

Supplementary plans: - a third type of flexibility can be obtained through supplementary plans. Although the basic plan may set a firm ceiling on expenditures in a given area, the plan allows for the manger (the responsible unit) to request further resources should they the later be needed. Supplementary plans reduce the constraining effect of the original plan by providing a prearranged appeal channel.

Plans are also classified on the basis of regions or geographic feasibility. For instance, an organization, which operates on diverse regions, may formulate different plans for each region or territory of operation that would help the overall achievement of organizational objectives.

3.4 Principles of Planning

A principle is a general rule or truth that may be expected to apply under similar conditions anywhere to reach or get out comes. As G.R. Terry put, "a principle is defined as fundamental statement or truth providing a guide to thought or action." In order to build effective plan there are certain principles to be considered. Some of the principles are:

1. Plan for the right length of time.

There should be some logic in selecting the right time range for company planning. In general, since planning and the forecasting that underlies it are costly, a company should probably not plan for a longer period than is economically justifiable; yet it is risky to plan for a shorter period. The answer as to the planning period seems to lie in the "commitment principle". Logical planning encompasses a period of time in the future necessary to for see, as well as possible, the fulfilment of commitments involved in decisions made today or logical planning encompasses a future period of time necessary to fulfil, through a series of actions, the commitments involved in decisions made today.

There is no uniform or arbitrary length of time for which a company should plan. The commitment principle indicates, there may be different time spans for any plan and planning decision, depending on the nature of the commitment involved.

2. Planning should be coordinated

The effect of one plan should be taken into account in the light of its effect on another planned aspect of the concern. Coordination of short-range plans with long plan is vital. No short-run plan should be made unless it contributes to the achievement of the relevant long-range plans. Many of the wastes of planning arise from decisions on immediate situations that fail to consider their effect on more remote objectives. Sometimes short-range decisions not only fail to contribute to a long-range plan but actually impede (hinder) or require changes in the long-range plan.

Responsible managers (individuals or units) should continually scrutinize (make a detailed examination) immediate decisions to ascertain whether they contribute to long-range programs, and subordinate mangers should be regularly briefed on company long-range plans so that they will make consistent short-range decisions.

3. Building flexibility into plans

The ideal of planning is to be flexible – the ability to change directions when forced to do so by unexpected events, without undue cost. The flexibility principle states that "the more that flexibility can be built into plans, the less the danger of losses incurred by unexpected events; but the cost of flexibility should be weighed against the risks involved in future commitments made."

The flexibility principle applies to the building into plans of a practical ability to change direction, the ability to change a plan without undue cost or friction, to detour (round about away when the existing one is changed), to keep toward a goal despite changes in environment or even failure of plans has great value.

E.g. Lever Brothers did actually spend some $ 5 million in extra construction cost in building a soap and detergent factory so that it could, if the company later decided to do so, be changed into a chemical manufacturing plant.

E.g. if the coming future of Elala (Mekelle) seems to be business area, then a person now have contemplating to a place in that site for residence, he had better add extra cost and build a house that can be changed from residential house to business house when the need arises at later times.

4. Reviewing plans regularly (The principle of navigational change)

This principle states "the more planning decisions commit for the future, the more important it is that a manger. Periodically check on events and expectations and redraw plans as necessary to maintain a course toward a desired goal. Unlike the flexibility principle, which applies to the adaptability built into plans themselves, this principle applies to flexibility in the planning process. Built-in flexibility doesn't automatically revise plans; the manger, like the navigator, must continually check the course and redraw plans to meet a desired goal.

5. Principle of contribution to objectives.

The purpose and function of every plan and all derivative plans should be to facilitate the accomplishment of enterprise objective. Every plan has to support to the major plan.

6. Planning involves an open system approach.

As we have discussed it in the previous chapter, practitioners must necessarily take into account interactions with their total environment in every aspect of managing. Managing is not, nor could it be, a closed-system approach to enterprise operation. This is nowhere apparent than in the theory and practice of planning.

Objectives must obviously be set in the light of the economic, technological, social, political, and ethical elements of an enterprise environment. Planning premise represent a clear recognition that plans can't be constructed (made), nor decisions made, in the vacuum of an internal system. The interfaces and interactions plans with every element of the conditions and influences surrounding an enterprise are indeed many and complex.

7. Principle of facts and planning

To design an effective plan, it is necessary to obtain all the available pertinent (relevant) facts, face the facts and include the action that the facts dictate. Knowledge of the activities to be planned and their effect on their activities both internal and external to the enterprise is necessary for intelligent planning.

8. Plans should always incorporate standard to facilitate control

Planning and control are especially inseparable. The Siamese twins of management unplanned action can't be controlled and for control involves keeping activities on course by correcting deviations from plans, plans should, as much as possible, be clear and quantifiable or verifiable expectations. There is no control without plans and plans without control means no achievement.

9. Principle of communication

The making of plans in itself is not enough, they should be conveyed to all concerned with them. They should be communicated to all the bodies concerned. The more the plans (strategies, policies, rules, etc) are clearly understood, the more consistent and effective will be the framework of enterprise plans.

10. Principle of feasibility and planning

Plans shouldn't be a mere wish, but something that are actionable, attainable or realizable. In other words, planning involves, a conscious determination of expected targets and projecting a course of action to meet the established target. Therefore, in order to make plans practicable and not too ambitious, nor too timorous, they should be set out in relation to available human and non-human resources as well as the prevailing conditions.

3.5 The process of planning

The formal approach to the planning process may be depicted as follows. These steps can serve as a general model which can be applied with some modification, to the planning process of any organization. whether it be large or small, profit making or not-for profit. These steps are:

1. Identifying and defining the real problem

Although it precedes actual planning and is therefore not strictly a part of the planning process, an awareness of opportunities in the external environment as well as within the organization is the real starting point for planning. Being aware of opportunity in light of –the market, competition, what customers want, our strengths, our weaknesses etc, has to be primarily seen before formulating a plan. We should take a preliminary look at possible future opportunities and see them clearly and completely, know where we stand in the light our of strengths and weaknesses, understand what problems we wish to solve and why, and know what we expect to gain. Our setting of realistic objectives depends on this awareness. Planning requires realistic diagnosis of the opportunity situation.

2. Establishing clear-rut objectives

The second important step in planning process is establishing objectives for the entire enterprise and then for each subordinate work unit, for the long term as well as for the short range. Without a clear definition of goals, organizations spread their resources too broadly. Identifying priorities and being specific about aims enable organizations to focus their resources effectively.

Objectives specify the expected results and indicate the end points of what is to be done, where the primary emphasis is to be placed, and what is to be accomplished by the network of strategies, policies, procedures, rules, budgets and programs.

3. Establishing the planning premises, and constraints.

In order to plan, you have to make certain assumptions about the future. Thus premises are PLANNING ASSUMPTIONS in other words, they are the expected environment of plans in operation. These premises and constraints point out the background assumed to exist to validate the plan. They are ASSUMPTIONS about the environment in which the plan is to be carried out.

Knowledge of the organization goals and existing condition provide a frame work for defining which aspects of the environment will have the greatest influence on the organization ability to achieve its objectives. The purpose of environmental analysis is to identify the ways in which changes in organization economic, technological, social/cultural, and political/ legal environments can indirectly influence the organization. Direct influence is exerted on the n as these factors act on the organization market, industry suppliers, competitors, or key resources and skills, Here, real consideration should be made to the assumptions regarding the future made, inclusiveness of premises and coverage, and assumptions that should be watched in order to detect changes. The forecasts about the future or premises are the bases upon which planning and decision is to be made; i.e. forecasting is important in premising;

- What kind of markets will there be? What volume of sales? what products? What prices
- How long will last the world peace or war
- Competition from imports will level off or decline slightly or high. etc.

Because the future environment of plans is so complex, it wouldn't be profitable or realistic to make assumptions about every detail of the future environment of a plan. Stating clearly the major premise on which planning is based is a critical aspect of effective planning. Therefore, premises are, as a practical matter, limited to assumptions that are critical, or strategic to a plan, i.e., those that most influence its operation.

4. Identifying alternative course of action

The fourth step in planning is to search for and examine alternative courses of action, especially those not immediately apparent. There is seldom a plan for which reasonable alternatives don't exist, and quite often an alternative that is not obvious proves to be the best.

The more common problem is not finding alternatives but reducing the number of alternatives so that the most promising may be analysed. Thus, the planner must usually make a preliminary examination to discover the most fruitful possibilities. i.e. there are various possibilities to achieve the work to be done (the goal) but of these various possibilities of the alternatives, the most optimum has to be screened out.

Once the objective (goal) is known it is possible to formulate one or more potential solutions. Creativity is extremely important in this stage. Information is gathered, data analyzed, and the pros and cons of possible alternative courses of action established. Additional information is gathered where appropriate. This effort to identify, clarify and evaluate alternative solution is very critical. The end result can only be as good as the quality of the alternative solutions generated in this step.

5. Evaluating alternative courses.

Once alternative courses are generated and sought (examined) their strong and weak points, their pros and cons, then we must next evaluate them by weighing them in the light of premises and goals. One course may appear to be the most profitable but require a large cash out lay with a slow payback; another may look less profitable but involve less risk; still anther may better suit the company's long-range objectives. Therefore, make an adjustment for the forecast plan if any; see if the cost, speed, and quality requirement are satisfied and if mechanization expedite the work for the achievement of desired objectives in terms of each possible alternative course of action.

6. Selecting a course

This is the point of choice. This is the point at which the plan is adopted- the real point of decision-making. The decision is now reached regarding which plan to adopt. The plan's expediency, adaptability and cost are important. The considerations contributing to the proper and selection or the important points that has to be considered to properly select a course of action include:

(1) Flexibility of the plan, to be capable of adapting to the changing situation or condition.
(2) It has to get acceptance by the operating personnel.
(3) The capacity of the firm and need for new equipment, space, personnel, training and supervising will be needed.

Occasionally, an analysis and evaluation of alternative courses will disclose that two or more are advisable and the manager may decide to follow several courses rather than the one best course (Single course). To conclude, this is the step where the most suitable (or at least the most satisfactory alternative is taken. Or it is the step in which decisions about future actions are made.

7. Formulating derivative plans

At the point where a decision is made, planning is seldom complete, and there is a need to develop derivation plans required to support the basic plan. Such plans like, arrangement of detailed sequence and timing for the proposed plan should be made to assist and also facilitate the operation of the basic plan.

8. Numberizing plans by budgeting

After decisions are made and plans are set, the final step to give them meaning is to numberize them by converting them to budgets. This helps - to establish verifiable targets of achievement, to facilitate control. Here the planner should be able to arrange for sufficient reports and records over a reasonable period to make him enable to inform to proper management members and to measure results as well as to make remedial actions for significant deviations.

3.6 Skills Required in Planning

1. <u>Forecasting</u>

   In order to set realistic and achievable goals, mangers must try to understand what the future holds for them. In developing premises forecasting play a determinant role. Identifying aids and barriers to an established goal depends on an understanding future event. Figure 3.2 illustrate forecasting and planning process

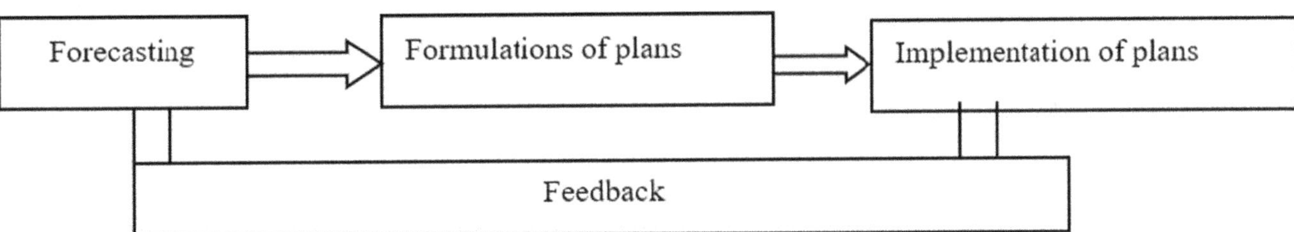

Figure 3.2 Forecasting and planning.
Source: Robbins SP, Coulter M. Principles of management. Translated by Seyyed Mohammad Arabi and Mohammed Ali Hamid
Rafiee and Behrouz Asrari Ershad, Fourth Edition, Tehran: Office of Cultural Studies. 2007

Forecasting is a systematic attempt to investigate and predict outcomes and future trends, that can serve as the basis for planning, by inferences from known facts.

Forecasting is an attempt to predict outcomes that will happen in the future. All good plans involve forecasts, but forecasting, in itself, is not planning. Planning is a more comprehensive activity that involve deciding what to do about the implications of forecasts once they are made. A forecast is a vision or perspective on the future that mangers can use as a planning premise. Forecasts thereby involve assumptions about what will happen in the future. When properly performed, they are a major resource to the manger in the planning process. Unfortunately this task is not as easy as it may seem. Could you for example, have foreseen the technological advances that enabled the manufacture of the cheap reliable pocket calculators readily available today? Could you have predicted the advent of the digital watch and the micro- or personal computer?. If the future could be forecast with accuracy, planning would be relatively simple. Thus plans are synthesis of various forecasts.

By relating the past and the present information or data, management should be able to anticipate the future environment. In developing premises, (the kind of markets, volume of sales, prices, products, technological developments, costs, tax rates and policies, policies with respect to dividends, the social and political environment long term trends etc.) of the future should be predicted with the help of forecasting.

Effective planning is made with the help of forecasting because planning itself is a future oriented course of action.

Accordingly, we have to assess the dynamism of both the internal and external environment. Therefore when mangers assess or evaluate the alternatives, they try to forecast how events both within and outside the organization will affect each alternative and what the outcome of each will be.

The significant areas of forecasting may be grouped into two.

A. Forecasting for Economic and Sales Information.

Our discussion of forecasting techniques will concentrate on these areas because of the importance of predicting future economic and sales trends. They predict the economic wellbeing of the region, nation, and / or world.

This technique can be performed either by qualitative or quantitative forecasting or both.

Qualitative forecasting: is appropriate when hard data are scarce or difficult to use. It involves the use of subjective judgments and rating schemes to transform qualitative information into quantitative estimates. Qualitative forecasting techniques use expert opinions to predict the future. In some cases a single person of special expertise or reputation may be consulted. (For example, it is common for ex-secretaries of state of the United States to advise large corporations on international affairs and the risks associated with doing business abroad. Because their job is straight forward to analyse political and economic events and forecast the risks associated with various operating strategies.)

Qualitative forecasting can't be expressed simply be numerical terms. Also past information doesn't have importance here. For instance, when a new product or technology is introduced, past experience is not a reliable guide for estimating what the near-term effects will be. It uses experts opinion, subjective judgment.

Examples include: jury of executive opinion, sales-force composite, survey of expert opinion, political stability, attitude of a city or state toward taxes, or the receptivity of style factors by potential customers etc.

Quantitative forecasting : extrapolates form the past or is used when there is sufficient "hard" or statistical data to specify relationships between key variable. These can be put into numbers, whether in USD, dollars, labour hours, square feet of space, machine hours, or units of product.

It is simply extrapolating future trends with the help of past and current data. But qualitative forecasting doesn't demand numerical or statistical data in the same way that quantitative forecasting does. Quantitative forecasting techniques use statistical analyses and mathematics to predict future events.

Inputs to qualitative forecasts are mainly the results of intuitive thinking, judgment, and accumulated knowledge. Specialists from a variety of fields are sometimes called upon to provide such input. Qualitative forecasting may be used alone or in combination with quantitative methods. Most (although not all) studies comparing the two forecasting techniques, however, find that quantitative methods are generally more accurate than qualitative ones.

Quantitative forecasting assumes that changes are gradual. It disregards political considerations, action of competitors, technological changes. It mere depends on the past and current trends. For instance, sales records are constant with regard to national income, industrial growth and population. Their rate of growth in the past will be assumed to be the same in the future.

Quantitative forecasting can be used if information exists about the past, if this information exists about the past, if this information can be specified numerically, and if it can be assumed that the pattern of the past will continue.

B. Forecasting Technological change

It is predicting what new technologies will be developed in the future and how current technologies will change. The rapid pace of technological change has led many firms, hospitals, government agencies and other institutions to recognize the importance of predicting future technological developments. As a manager, we may often have to ascertain what technological development are likely to occur in order to prepare our institution (organization) for change. Qualitative and quantitative forecasting techniques imply that the future often will be similar to the past, but as opposed to these techniques technological change anticipates that the future often will be quite different from what has gone before. Thus, it calls for deep investigation and continuous effort.

To conclude our forecast should be ***accurate, up to date, applicable*** and ***less costly*** as much as possible. These are the four important considerations in forecasting.

2. Decision Making

After studying this lesson, you will be able to:

- Develop understanding for decision making process.
- discuss the types of decisions and decision-making conditions
- Discuss contemporary issues in managerial decision making.

Decision making is defined as the selection, based on some criteria, of one best alternative from two or more possible alternatives; or it is process of choosing a specific procedure or course of action from among several possible alternatives. It is the means by which managers plan, organize, lead or direct and control. Thus, decision making is an integral of managers' job, even more an integral part of human life, because one has to take decisions in one's day-to-day life. In business or non-business organizations managers have always to decide. They have to determine what is to be done, who is to do it, when, where and how to do it, which is the core of their task.

Effective decision-making requires a rational selection of a course of action. But what is rationality? When is a person thinking or deciding rationally?

People acting or deciding rationally are; first they must be attempting to reach some goal that cannot be attained without positive action. Second they must have a clear understanding of alternative courses by which a goal could be reached under existing circumstances and limitations. Third, they must have the information and the ability to analyse and evaluate alternatives in the light of the goal sought. And finally, they must have a desire to come to the best solution by selecting the alternative that best satisfies goal achievement. Thus, rationality implies making decisions based on facts, experience, experimentation or research and analysis with distinct procedures.

The Decision Making Process

The steps in decision-making process include the following figure 3.3:

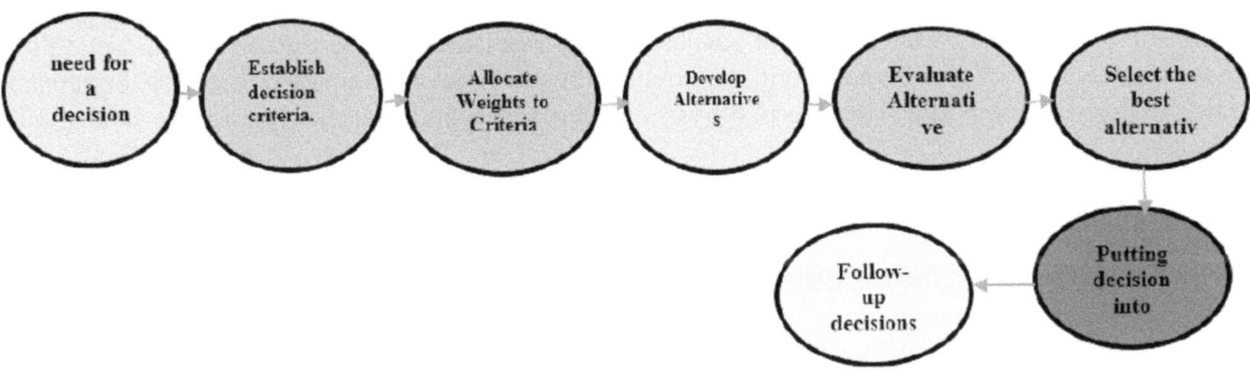

Figure 3.3 Decision making process.
Source: Daft RL, Daft RL. Principles of management. South-Western, Cengage Learning India Pvt. Limited; 2009.

1. Ascertain the need for a decision

The decision making process begins by determining that a problem exists; that is, that there is an unsatisfactory condition. This is frequently expressed as a disparity between what is and what should be. Before attempting to solve a problem, a manager must first become aware that a problem exists and that it is important enough for managerial action. (some individuals or managers may refuse to recognize that a problem exists because they are afraid to face the problem or because they do not know how to fully identify a problem) i.e. we have to find and identify the type of problem occurring. Like, what was the desired and what is actually happening? What is the reason for the disparity of the desired and actual?

2. Establish decision criteria

Once the need for a decision has been determined, there comes the need to establish decision criteria that requires identifying those characteristics that are important in decision-making. Which of two or more alternative decisions is best? That depends on the *CRITERIA*, the standards of judgment, used in evaluation. According to the decision theorists, these decision criteria need to be explicit; ideally, they are written out in order of their priority, and all this is done before the alternative strategies (solutions) are developed. If the criteria are decided upon afterward, or if the criteria are never made explicit, the alternatives them selves may influence the criteria used for their own evaluation.

A second aspect of establishing decision criteria concerns decision processes and calls for decisions about who will make the final decision, when the final decision will be made, and how much time and money, if any, will be allocated for finding a solution. Managers who neglect this phase of problem solving may spend excessive time or money on decisions that offer only a small return on investment while avoiding others that involve the survival of the firm. They may spend $ 50,000 to solve a $ 10,000 problem.

3. Allocate Weights to Criteria

The list of criteria must now be prioritised. Since some are obviously more important than others, you need to weight each criterion to reflect its importance in the decision.

4. Develop Alternatives

This involves developing a list of the alternatives that may be viable in dealing with the stated problem. Here once the problem is identified, it is possible to formulate one or more potential solutions. Creativity is extremely important in this stage of problem solving. Poor decision-makers often settle for the most available solution. They ask, "Will it solve the Problem?" rather than, "Is it the best solution obtainable within the limits of search we have set for ourselves?" The former question results in an accept- reject decision, while the latter demands a more complex comparison of alternatives. But some managers are driven to the accept – reject approach because of their inability to handle the information overload.

Since this step is the generation or developing of alternatives, it avoids the evaluation of choices, it draws on the decision maker's ability to comprehend a wide number of possible alternatives. However, it should be done in mind that it may not be possible to consider all the alternatives. In this context, the principle of limiting factors should be applied which suggests that common, but important elements in the various alternatives should be taken as the base for analyzing these alternatives.

5. Evaluate Alternative

Once the alternatives have been enumerated, the manager (decision maker) must critically evaluation each one. The strengths and weaknesses, benefits and costs, advantages and disadvantages of each alternative must be identified as they are compared against the established criteria and weights.

As we compare alternative plans for achieving an objective we are likely to think exclusively of QUANTITATIVE FACTORS (These are factors that can be measured in numerical terms, such as time or the various types of fixed and operating costs). No one would question the importance of this analysis (importance of quantitative factors), but the success of the venture would be endangered if intangible or qualitative, factors were ignored. QUALITATIVE FACTORS, (INTANGIBLE FACTORS) are those that are difficult to measure numerically, such as the quality of labour relations, the risk of technological change, or the international political climate. To summarize these illustration, in evaluating alternatives the importance of both quantitative and qualitative factors should be considered. They should not be ignored.

At this stage, a manager also has to think about the consequences of each alternative. For instance, a manager who is deciding whether to fire a supervisor should consider the impact of this action on other supervisors and employees. Whatever their basis for deciding, the more systematic the evaluation is, the more likely the forecasted result will be accurate and complete.

6. Select the best alternative

Study (evaluation) gives the information about the way different alternatives are contributing in the solution of a problem. This is the point of choice. Given the alternatives, along with pros and cons of each, a manager can choose a preferred course of action. A manager says in effect, "to deal with this problem, I believed that this solution is the best one,". The best among these should be selected. However, while selecting, factors such as risk, economy of efforts, timing and limiting factors should be considered adequately.

7. Putting decision into action

After an alternative (best alternative) has been selected it is put into action. Managers must implement once the decision is made. This is the point of action initiation and direction setting. This requires the communication of decision to subordinates, getting acceptance of the decision, and getting their support and cooperation for converting the decision into effective action. The decision should be effective (operational) at proper time and in proper way to make the action needed effective to achieve desired objectives.

8. Follow-up decisions

In spite of the use of various scientific and mathematical methods, a decision may not be absolutely correct, because a decision is based on some forecasts which they are not absolutely correct. Sometimes the relevant information may not be available for decision-making. As a safeguard against this incorrect decision, managers are required to institute a system of follow up to the decision so as to modify them at the earliest appropriate time. The manager should compare the actual results of action with the predicted results. If there is any deviation, this should analysed and factors should be located. If these factors lie in wrong decision, this can be modified. A successful manager (decision-maker) is one who modifies his decision according to the subsequent march of the events.

Following up is checking to see whether an action is accomplishing its intended results. It is important for two reasons:

1. Follow-up allows managers to become AWARE of newly developing problems associated with the solution.
2. Follow-up allows managers to evaluate their own decision-making skill.

If problems associated with a decision are detected soon enough, the solution can be modified before a major new problem develops. Thus, the follow-up stage thus serves as a mechanism for becoming aware of problems. Focusing only on results, without considering the entire decision making process ‘can be misleading

We have to monitor the action going on together with the decision made; i.e. are things working according to plan?. What is happening in the internal and external environment as a result of a decision? are subordinates performing according to expectations; what is the competition doing in response?. Decision-making is a continual process for managers and a continual challenge.

Types of Decisions: Several authors believe that there are two types of decisions: programmed & non-programmed decisions.

Programmed decisions: are the kinds that managers face time and again. These decisions are "programmable" because of a specific procedure can be worked out to resolve them based on experience in similar situations.

- Once a standard procedure has been established, it can be used to treat all like situations.
- They usually involve an organization's every day operational and administrative activities
- They are primarily found at the middle and lower levels of management.
- Data used in making a programmed decision usually are complete and well defined.
- Participants know the details and agree on how to resolve the problem.

Non-programmed Decisions: are used to solve nonrecurring problems.

- No well-established procedure exists for handling them, primarily because managers do not have experience to draw upon.
- In contrast to programmed decisions, available data are usually incomplete.

Non programmable decisions are commonly found at the middle and top levels of management and often is related to an organization's policy-making activities such as whether to add a product to the existing product line, to reorganize the company, or to acquire another firm, are examples

Decision making situations

1. Decisions under certainty:- decisions made in which the external conditions are identified and very predictable / whenever there is complete data & information/
2. Decisions under risk:- those decisions in which probabilities can be assigned to the expected outcomes of each alternative
3. Decisions under uncertainty:- it is a case where neither there is complete data not probabilities can be assigned to the surrounding conditions. Some conditions that are uncontrollable by management include competition, government regulations, technological advances, the overall economy, and the social and cultural tendencies of society.

3.7 Management by Objectives/MBO/

Learning Objectives

1. Develop an understanding of Management by Objectives
2. Describe several types of plans, including management by objectives.
3. Discuss the benefits of MBO and disadvantages of MBO

Overview

This section discusses management by objectives MBO, which involves nature, defining goals and developing plans with which to achieve them. the goals in the firms begin with strategic goals followed by tactical and operational goals. The section covers the process of MBO, how objectives will be developed, initiates, achieved, and measured the Managers roles in determining and assign the objective and responsibility besides the alignment goals and communicate them throughout the company structure.

Introduction

Objectives are the ends toward which enterprise activities are aimed (directed). Objectives should as much as possible be verifiable, i.e. at the end of the period one should be able to determine whether the objective has been achieved. The goal of every manager is to create a surplus, and clear and verifiable objectives facilitate measurement of the effectiveness and efficiency of managerial actions.

The Nature of Objectives

Objectives state end results and over all objectives need to be supported by sub-objectives. Thus, objectives form a hierarchy as well as a network. Moreover, organizations and managers have multiple goals, which are sometimes incompatible and may lead to conflicts within the organization, within the group, and even within individuals. A manager may have to choose between short term and long term performance and personal interests may have to be subordinated to organizational objectives.

A Hierarchy of Objectives: objectives form a hierarchy, ranging from the broad aim to specific individual objectives. The zenith (tip point) of the hierarchy is the purpose, which has two dimensions:

First – there is the purpose of society, such as requiring the organization to contribute to the welfare of the people by providing goods and services at a reasonable cost.

Second – there is the purpose of the business, which might be to furnish convenient, low-cost transportation for the average person.

The stated mission might be to produce, market and service automobiles. These aims, in turn, translated into general objectives and strategies, such as designing, producing and marketing reliable, low-cost, fuel-efficient automobiles. At the next level of the hierarchy, we find more specific objectives such as those in the KEY RESULT AREAS. (Peter F. Drucker Suggests the following key result areas; market standing, innovation, productivity, physical and financial resources, profitability, manager performance and development, worker performance and attitude, and public responsibility). These are the areas in which performance is essential for the success of the enterprise. The objectives have to be further translated into division, department, and unit objectives down to the lowest level of the organization (Daft., 2010).

<u>A Network of Objectives</u>: Both objectives and planning programs form a network of desired results and events. If goals are not interconnected, and if they do not support one another, people very often pursue paths that may seem good for their own department but may be detrimental to the company as a whole. Managers must make sure that the components of the network "fit" one another. Fitting is a matter not only of having the various programs carried out but also of timing their completion, since undertaking one program often depends upon first completing another.

It is easy for one department of a company to set goals that may seem entirely appropriate for it, only to be operating at cross-purposes with another department. The manufacturing department may find its goals best served by long production runs, but this might interfere with the marketing departments desire to have all products in the line readily available, or the finance department's goal of maintaining investment in inventory at a certain low level.

So it is bad enough when goals don't support and interlock with one another. It may be catastrophic when they interfere with one another. What is needed is a matrix of mutually supportive goals. So managers shouldn't see objectives from their own perspective – based on their self-interest – without understanding the total network of aims.

Definition of Management By Objectives

MBO emphasizes results or the achievement of objectives, instead of activities, and also places importance on human behaviour through the fulfilment of needs from work efforts. Management is purposeful: it is performed to attain accomplishment. But in many instances, accomplishment falls short of its intended mark because the objective is not clearly known to all who are affected by it, the scope within which a member is permitted to make decisions is too narrow, or the major problem areas are not given preferred attention. To correct these shortcomings, participation in formulating an objective can be done by the doers and users of that objective. This leads to a current practice in management sometimes referred to as management by objectives, management by mission, or results management, because results are the core of attention. MBO is a process of joint objective setting between a supervisor and subordinate.

MBO is defined as, "a comprehensive managerial system that integrates many key managerial activities in a systematic manner, and is consciously directed toward the effective and efficient achievement of organizational and individual objectives". It is a system in which each employee participates in determining personal (individual) objectives as well as the means by which he or she hopes to achieve these objectives. Developed within the overall boundaries set forth by superior, the objectives and plans for attaining them are discussed by the initiator and the superior, altered if necessary, and finally adopted if agreed upon. The specific expected results guide the direction of the operations and are also the standards of performance against which the subordinate is appraised. Result management tends to make each employee a manager of his or her own particular work. The individual plays a great role in her/his own work decisions and purposes. It diminishes the authoritarian practice of deciding and telling subordinates exactly what to do. MBO is a way of managing. It applies to managers in any kind and size of organization at all levels and in all functional areas.

The Systems Approach to MBO

Management by objectives has undergone many changes: it has been used in performance appraisal, as an instrument for motivating individuals, and more recently, in strategic planning. But there are still other managerial subsystems that can be integrated into the MBO process; they include design of organizational structures, portfolio management, management development, career development, compensation programs, and budgeting. These various managerial activities need to be integrated into a system.

One of the early research studies that investigated MBO as a comprehensive system of managing indicates that most key managerial activities can and should be integrated with the MBO process. The degree of integration, however, differs for individual activities. It was found, for example, that the highest degree of integration of MBO with managerial functions was in controlling, planning, and directing. But several key managerial activities in staffing and organizing also were well integrated into the MBO process. These findings suggest, that MBO, to be effective, has to be viewed as a comprehensive system. In short, it must be considered a way of managing, and not an addition to the managerial job.

The Process of MBO

Ideally, the process starts at the top of an organization and has the active support of the chief executive, who gives direction to the organization. It is not essential that objective setting start at the top, however. It can start at division level, at marketing -manager level or even lower.

As in all planning, one of critical needs in MBO is the development and dissemination of consistent planning premises. No manager can be expected to set goals or establish plans and budgets without guidelines.

1. Preliminary setting of objectives at the top (Top level goal Setting)

Given appropriate planning premises, the first step in setting objectives is for the top manager to determine what he or she perceives to be the purpose or mission and the more important goals of the enterprise for a given period ahead. Effective MBO programs usually start with the top managers who determine the organization's strategy and set preliminary goals. These goals can be set for a much shorter period or a much longer period depending on the circumstances. E.g. of quarter objectives set preliminary may be, "a 5 percent increase in sales next quarter", or for annual "no increase in overhead costs this year". This procedure gives both managers and subordinates a clearer idea of what top management hops to accomplish and shows them how their own work directly relates to achievement of the organization's goals.

The goals set by the superior are preliminary, based on an analysis and judgment as to what can and should be accomplished by the organization within a certain period. This requires taking into account the company's strengths and weaknesses in the light of available opportunities and threats. These goals must be regarded as tentative and subject to modification while the entire chain of verifiable objectives is worked out by subordinates. It is usually not advisable to force objectives on subordinates since force can scarcely give rise to a sense of commitment. Most managers also find that the process of working out goals with subordinates reveals both problems to be dealt with and opportunities they were not previously aware of or realized.

When setting objectives, the manager also establishes measures of goal accomplishment. If verifiable objectives are developed, these measures, whether in sales dollars, profits, percentages, cost levels, or program execution, will normally be built into the objectives.

2. Clarification of organizational roles

The relationship between expected results and the responsibility for attaining them is often overlooked. Ideally, each goal and sub-goal should be someone person's clear responsibility. By analysing an organization's structure, however, we often find that the responsibility is vague and that clarification or reorganization is needed. Sometimes it is impossible to structure an organization so that a given objective is someone's personal responsibility. In setting goals for launching a new product, for example, the manager of research, marketing, and production must carefully coordinate their activities. Their separate functions can be centralized by putting a product manager in charge. But, if this is not desirable, at least the specific parts of each coordinating manager's contribution to the program goal can and should be clearly identified.

3. Setting subordinates objectives

After making sure that subordinate managers have been informed of pertinent general objectives, strategies, and planning premises, the superior can then proceed to work with subordinates in setting their objectives. The superior asks what goals the subordinates believe they can accomplish, in what time period, and with what resources. They will then discuss some preliminary thoughts about what goals seem feasible for the company or department. The superior's role at this point is extremely important. Questions that she/he should ask include:

- What can you contribute?
- How can we improve your operation to help me improve mine?
- What stands in the way; what obstructions (block up) keep you from a higher level of performance?
- What changes can we make?
- How can I help?

It is amazing how many things can be identified that might obstruct performance and how many constructive ideas can be dredged up from the experience and knowledge of subordinates.

Superiors must also be patient counsellors, helping their subordinates develop consistent and supportive objectives and being careful not to set goals that are impossible to achieve. And one of the things that can weaken a program of managing by objectives is to allow managers set unrealistic objectives.

At the same time, when subordinates set goals, it doesn't mean that people can do whatever they want to do. Superiors must listen to, and work with, their subordinates, but in the end they must take responsibility in approving subordinates goals. Here, the superior's judgment and final approval must be based upon what is reasonably attainable, what is fully supportive of upper level objectives, what is consistent with the goals of other managers in other functions and what is consistent with the long-run objectives and interests of the department and the company.

Well-stated objectives must be objectives should be specific, time defined, understandable, verifiable, and challenging.

4. Conducting periodic and annual appraisal reviews

This targets the important consideration of results. Periodic reviews are essential so that excessive variations from the expected are recognized before they get too bad or continue for too long. A yearly diagnosis is totally inadequate. Reviews should be made when the manager believes they are appropriate. A company operating under a project concept should conduct appraisal reviews at the completion of each project. Annual reviews provide a good starting point for planning the next year.

Benefits and Weakness of MBO

Although goal-oriented management (MBO) is now one of the most widely practiced managerial approaches, its effectiveness is sometimes questioned. Often faulty implementation is blamed, but another reason is that MBO may be applied as a mechanistic technique focusing on selected aspects of the managerial process without integrating them into a system. Also, effectiveness is not easy to define and an increase or a decrease in performance may be due to factors other than MBO. It may take 2-5 years to implement an MBO program, and during that time many factors other than the program may influence the operation of the firm.

MBO is one of the most talked about and debated management concepts of the last some years. It is the subject of books and a target of research criticism. This criticism is useful because it helps identify things to be avoided and things to do in order to take maximum advantage of MBO as a management technique.

Benefits of MBO

1. Motivational aspect

The employees start with a self-appraisal of performances, abilities, and potential. From this, employees begin to know personal strengths and weakness to gain self-confidence, to receive feedback on accomplishments, to know why the actions being taken are performed, and to be a self-directed, and self-improved member. By participating in establishing their own goals, employees are encouraged to think about their work, to capitalize on experiences, and to believe in the objectives.

Result management (MBO) helps satisfy the human need for achievement. Result management supplies a special framework for participation. Decisions and actions that affect the person's job are determined jointly by the superiors and subordinates. This combination makes for high motivation.

In addition, result management tends to shift control from people to operations. The evaluation is not a radar of the person's traits and characteristic behaviour, but is centred on what is achieved. The subordinate here exercises self-control.

Further, the superior-subordinate relationship is improved. The subordinate has greater freedom and plays a more supportive role; communication about the organization becomes open. Opportunities to increase knowledge and skill are opened up and performance can be more effective and satisfying.

2. Better managing

MBO forces managers to think about planning for results, rather than merely planning activities or work. To ensure that objectives are realistic, it also requires managers to think of the way they will accomplish results, the organization and personnel they will need to do so, and the resources and assistance they will require. Also, there is no better incentive for control and no better way to know the standards for control than a set of clear goals.

3. Clarified organization

Another major benefit of managing by objectives is that it forces managers to clarify organizational roles and structures. To the extent possible, positions should be built around the key-results expected of people occupying them.

Managers shouldn't have to forget that to get results, they must delegate authority according to the results they expect. "If decentralized management is needed to make an organization work well and MBO is in need to make decentralization work."

4. Personal commitment

MBO encourages people to commit themselves to their goals. Once it is clearly stated the objective, no longer are people just doing work, following instructions, and waiting for guidance and decisions; they are now individuals with clearly defined purposes. They have had a part in actual setting of their objectives; they have had an opportunity to put their ideas into planning programs; they understand their area of discretion-their authority-and they've been able to get help from their superiors to ensure that they can accomplish their goals. These are the elements that make for a feeling of commitment. People become enthusiastic when they control their own fate.

5. Development of effective control

In the same way that management by objectives sparks more effective planning, it also aids in developing effective controls. Control involves measuring results and taking action to correct deviations from plans in order to ensure that goals are reached. And in MBO, a clear set of verifiable goals is the best guide to management control.

Weaknesses in MBO

With all its advantages, a system of MBO has a number of weaknesses. Most are due to shortcomings in applying the MBO concepts.

1. Failure to teach the philosophy of MBO:

As simple as MBO may seem, managers who would put it into practice must understand and appreciate a good deal about it. They in turn must explain to subordinates what it is, how it works, why it is being done, what part it will play in appraising performance, and above all, how participants can benefit. The philosophy is built on concepts of self-control and self-direction aimed at making managers professionals.

2. Failure to give guidelines to goal setters:

Management by objectives, like any other kind of planning, can't work if those who are expected to set goals are not given needed guidelines. Managers must know what the corporate goals are and how their own activity fits in with them. If corporate goals are vague, unreal, or inconsistent, it is virtually impossible for managers to tune in with them. Managers also need planning premises and a knowledge of major company policies. People must have some assumptions as to the future, some understanding of policies affecting their areas of operation and an awareness of the objectives and programs with which their goals interlock in order to plan effectively. Failure to fill these needs can result in a fatal vacuum in planning.

3. Difficulty of setting goals:

Truly verifiable goals are difficult to set, particularly if they are to have the right degree of stretch or pull, quarter in or quarter out, year in and year out. Goal setting may not be much more difficult than any other kind of effective planning, although it will probably take more study and work to establish verifiable objectives that are formidable but attainable than to develop many plans, which tend only to lay out work to be done. Participants in MBO programs report at times that the excessive concern with economic results puts pressure on individuals that may encourage questionable behaviour. To reduce the probability of selecting unethical means for achieving results, top management must agree to reasonable objectives, clearly state behavioural expectations, and give a high priority to ethical behaviour, rewarding it as well as punishing unethical activities.

4. Emphasis on short-run goals:

In most management by objectives programs, managers set goals for the short-run term, seldom for more than a year, and often for a quarter or less. There is clearly a danger of emphasizing the short-run, perhaps at the expense of the longer range. This means, of course, that superiors must always assure themselves that current objectives, like any other short-run plan, are designed to serve longer-range goals.

5. Danger of inflexibility:

Managers often hesitate to changes objectives. Although goals may case to be meaningful if they are changed too often and do not represent a well-though-out and well-planned result, it is nonetheless foolish to expect a manager to strive for a goal that has been made obsolete by revised corporate objectives, changed premises, or modified policies.

6. Other Dangers:

In addition to the above ones, there are some other dangers and difficulties in management by objectives. In their desire to make goals verifiable, people may over use quantitative goals and attempt to use numbers in areas where they are not applicable, or they may downgrade important goals that are difficult to state in terms of end results (Forge the favourable company image may be the key strength of an enterprise, yet it is difficult to state this in quantitative terms). There may also be a danger of forgetting that there is more to managing than goal setting.

But even with the difficulties and dangers of managing by objectives in certain situations, this system emphasizes in practice the setting of goals, long known to be an essential part of planning and managing.

Review Questions

1. What is planning?
2. What are the characteristics of planning?
3. Why do companies plan?
4. What are the limitations planning?
5. Discuss the elements in planning?
6. How do you differentiate missions, objectives and strategies?
7. Differentiate single use plans from standing plans.
8. What are the varieties in planning based on their degree of flexibility?
9. When do we apply qualitative forecasting?
10. Why decision making is the core part of manager's job?
11. How can you differentiate between programmed and non-programmed decision?
12. Based on your experience, work, school mention two wrong decisions you have made or observed before.
13. Describes the approach and model of decision making?
14. What can explain luck and skill in decision making?
15. What is decision making? What is the difference between programmed decision and non-programmed decision?
16. What is MBO? What benefits organizations get from MBO? What shortcomings does MBO have?

Short Case:

You are the chief executive officer CEO of Sahra company Ltd. You seek to establish the rationality of decision-making at the various levels of management in the company, as all executive managers were selected according to professionalism, experience, competence and talents. Their actions and decisions were rational and objective, and therefore you, as CEO, would expect them to continue the same approach, but business conditions and the business environment sometimes make some wrong decisions or accidental mistakes; despite all this, the issue of rationality and responsibility of the decision cannot be overridden.

Questions:

1. Determine the decision-making process you would prefer to follow.
2. outline the main characteristics of rational decision-making.
3. What are the main difference between a successful and an unsuccessful decision?

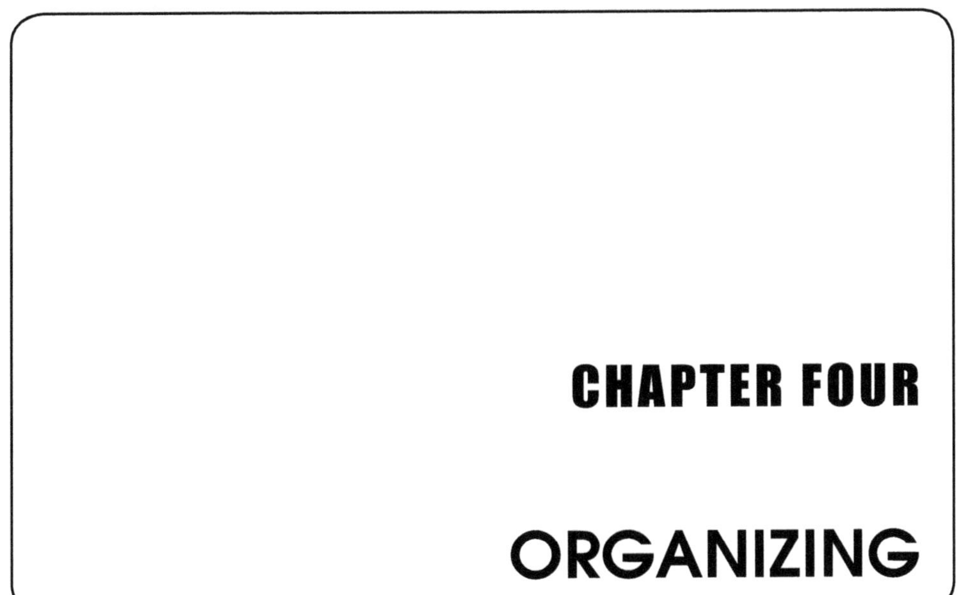

CHAPTER FOUR

ORGANIZING

     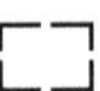 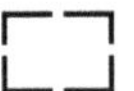

LEARNING OBJECTIVE

After studying the unit students will be able to:

1. understand the meaning and fundamental practices of organizing, such as work specialization, chain of command, etc..
2. 2.discuss the principles of organization
3. 3.develop an understanding of Process of organizing formally and informally
4. 4.Identify the organization structure types
5. Describe functional and divisional approaches to structure.
6. Explain the need for coordination across departments

Overview

This chapter the discuss the concept of organizing and fundamental features of organizing, such as work specialization, chain of command, span of management, and the process of organizing, formal organization, informal organization. Organizing is a function For smoothing the functioning of organization well established principles of organizing need to be followed.

This chapter also discussed organization structures implanted by business firms. Each type of structure has its own advantages and disadvantages, Organizational Relationships and Behaviour.

4.1 Meaning of Organizing

Organizing is the second management function. Once plans are created, the manager's task is to "organize" the human and physical resources properly to carry them out.

The word "organizing " originates from the word "organism" which means a structure with its parts so integrated that their relation to each other is governed by their relation to the whole. It is also called a system with parts that work together or a system with parts dependent up on each other. Different scholars (authors) have defined organizing in different ways. Organizing is establishing an intentional structure of roles for people to fill in the organization. Organizing is a function identifying classifying grouping and assigning various activities and prescribing authority relationships to create an organism or a structure capable to accomplish predetermined objectives (Koontz., Weihrich, and Cannice., 2020).

4.2 Basic Concepts of Organizing

The following factors may be considered to highlight the basic characteristics of the organizing function of management.

1. Division of labour

Division of labour is essential to maximizing the output of workers and machines. Division of work means dividing large tasks into smaller activities (packages) or functions of work. Division of labour is the basis of all organizing functions.

Why is division of work necessary?

Division of labour becomes necessary because the work is too much for any single individual. This work specialization allows an employee to master the task in a shortest time with a minimum of effort. For example, for a business organization the work, may be divided according to the function into production, marketing, finance, personnel etc. It is tire some for a single employee to work in the theses different functions.

2. Unity of function (coordination)

The organization has to establish correct and adequate relationships between one department or sub-department and another, between an employee and his work, one employee and another to attain the major goal. In an organization different persons are assigned with different functions. But the objective or aim of all is ONE. This can be achieved if and only if they make adequate relationship among them. Failure to establish such relationships may result in the divisions (department or persons) to follow different paths which make the achievement of the goal difficult.

3. Communication

Every organizing function should be able to create an organization, which has its own channels and methods of communication. Management to be successful effective communication is vital. Since management is concerned working with others, therefore, unless there is proper understanding between people it can't be effective. The channels of communication may be upward, downward, or horizontal.

4. Authority and Responsibility

Authority and responsibility are the two sides of management coin. Authority is the right to give orders and instructions or the right to command and obtain obedience, and responsibility is the obligation to accomplish the needed result. There has to be parity of authority and responsibility.

The flow of authority and responsibility to every individual should be clearly defined. And it is necessary to provide for a proper balance between authority and responsibility. For example, if the responsibility assigned to a manager is not matched with the authority delegated to him, he'll not be able to control the performance of his subordinates. His subordinates may disregard, even disobey, for the simple reason that he lacks authority to secure performance from them. On the other hand, if a manager is given more authority than responsibility, he may become dictatorial and irresponsible. Hence, there has to be parity between the two.

5. Unity of command

Each employee should receive orders and commands from only one superior. Each person should be accountable to a single superior. For example, when an office worker is made accountable to several superiors, each of whom may've varying standards for judging the finished job, confusion results, moral and organizational discipline may eventually be destroyed.

6. Unity of direction

This principle is expressed as " one head one plan." Unification and coordination of activities at various levels can't be achieved in the absence of unity of direction.

7. Span of control or (span of management or supervision)

Determining the optimum number of subordinates to be supervised by each manager, i.e., the number of subordinates reporting directly to given manager. Determination of the optimum number depends on many factors. Generally, a manager can supervise fewer subordinates at the upper levels and their number can be conveniently increased at lower levels because the tasks allocated to subordinates at the lower level are specific and precise. But at top the tasks may involve the consideration of many factors into account in decision making. The appropriate span of management (control) can't be calculated from any single formula or rule of thumb. However, there are guidelines that indicate whether a span should be relatively broad or narrow.

The guidelines include:

a. *factors relating to the situation:* It could be relatively broad to the extent that the work is

   - fairly routine
   - fairly stable
   - work of subordinates is similar

b. *factors relating subordinates:* The span can be relatively broad to the extent

   - subordinates are well trained for the work

c. *factors relating to the manager:* The span can be relatively broad to the extent

   Manager is well trained and highly capable. A manager with demonstrated competence can, for example, perform more jobs than an inexperienced person. Hence, mangers with similar competence can have different spans of control depending on the nature of the jobs they manage.

   - the fewer non managerial responsibilities assigned to the manger, the wider the span of control can be. The span of control can therefore, be different for managers at the same level.

d. *The closer the physical proximity of the jobs, the wider the span of control can be.*

The span of management may affect the efficient utilization of managers and the effective performance of their subordinates. There is a relationship between span of management throughout the organization and organizational structure. For example, narrow spans of management result in "tall" organizational structure with many supervisory levels between top and lowest levels. Whiles, wide spans, for the same number of employees, mean fewer management levels between top and lowest levels. Average human brain can effectively direct three to six subordinates. The essence or ideal span of control is one that facilitates effective control, supervision, easy and smooth communication between managers and their subordinates.

8. Management by Exception (Exception principle)

Top management is not burdened with making decisions in respect of all organizational problems, complex or routine. The top management should concern itself with only those matters that are either so important and wide ranging that they can't be left to be decided at lower level management or so complex that they can't be fully understood by subordinates. Problems involving unusual matters should be referred to the high level (programmed decisions of repetitive nature and routine can be handled by standard procedures).

Management by exception dictates that only highly significant and extraordinary activities should be performed by higher level managers in order to conserve their time and energy for the most complex and important activities of their organization. The other routine type problems can be handled competently by lower level managers. This principle states that only significant deviations from policies and procedures should be brought to the attention of managers.

This principle underlines the importance of widespread delegation of authority so that even those at the lowest levels can be free to make decisions within the established limits.

Maximum efficiency can be achieved only when top management concentrates its time and energy on broader and wide ranging issues rather than on routine and procedural matters.

9. Scalar principle (scalar denotes steps)

Scalar chain in an organization is the chain of superiors ranging from the ultimate authority to the lowest ranks. Organizations should have a chain of authority and communication that runs from the top to the bottom and should be followed by managers and subordinates. This principle suggests that there must be a clear line of authority running step by step from the highest to the lowest level of the organization This clear line of authority makes it easier for organization members to understand

- to whom they can delegate authority
- who can delegate to them
- to whom they are accountable.

It has to be clearly drawn leaving no doubt in any body's mind as to who is his superior. Communication should be sent up or down through the proper channel. This ensures unity of command.

10. Flexibility (continuity)

Is building flexibility into every structure devices and techniques for anticipating and reacting to change because every organization moves towards its goal in a changing environment. When the company or department is first established, from then, it is the process of reorganizing that takes place. Major changes keep on taking place in the relationships of an enterprise or its departments due to factors as:- increase in costs, internal conflicts, pressure from competing products or services.

In order to meet best or handle any change in circumstances, re-organizing can be possible only where the organization structure is flexible enough to adopt it self to meet the needs of changing circumstances. Hence, the organization structure has to be flexible enough to be adaptable to changing circumstance, it shouldn't be ridged or inelastic.

4.3 The process of organizing

To organize means to arrange different elements into a whole of inter dependant parts, i.e., putting persons and things in their proper places and in relation to each other, with each person or thing having proper and well-defined functions to perform. Thus, organizing is concerned with arranging a complex of tasks in to manageable units and defining the formal relationships among the people who are assigned the various tasks.

The important steps in organizing process are as follows:

1. Determination of the basic activities that must be performed to achieve organizational objectives. The required activities are derived from the objectives of the organization, i.e., identifying the work (activities) needed to execute plans and policies (objective) of the organization. This is the basic step of organization process.
2. Breakdown the required work into component activities The basic functions (work to be done) must be divided into reasonably homogeneous or similar activities. Functional differentiation of the activities is the next requirement of the organizing process.
3. Group the activities into practical units based on similarity, importance or who will do the work. After the functional differentiation, the next logical step is to combine the work of the enterprise in a logical and efficient manner into units or group of activities capable to be directed in a unified manner to fulfil the desired purpose.
4. Provide the physical means or all necessary facilities such as equipment and tools for each activity or group of activity to be performed. For example desks, chairs, telephones, shelves, etc.
5. Assign qualified or potentially trainable personnel. This step involves -placement of the right man for the right job (the staffing function -supplying the right people in the right positions at the right time)
6. Inform each member what accomplishments are expected and what formal interrelationships exist. This step involves the delegation of authority and assignment responsibility throughout the organizational hierarchy to avoid confusion as – who is to do what, who is accountable for whom.

4.4 Important Elements of Organizing

The organizing process has three key elements. These are:

1. Departmentation
2. Delegation and
3. Decentralization

4.4.1 Departmentation

Departmentation is one fundamental part of the organizing process. In the context of management, departmentation means dividing and grouping the activities and employees of an enterprise into various departments or into organizational units. The division of the total work of an enterprise into individual functions and sub functions. Then either on the basis of similarity of work or efficiency, these various functions and sub functions are grouped together into work units. The work units so formed may be called departments, divisions, units, or any other names.

Through departmentation we-obtain organizational units of manageable size that can utilize managerial ability based on specialization to secure maximum results, which helps in increasing the efficiency of organization. The following chart indicates the organizational chart of food and paints manufacturing organization.

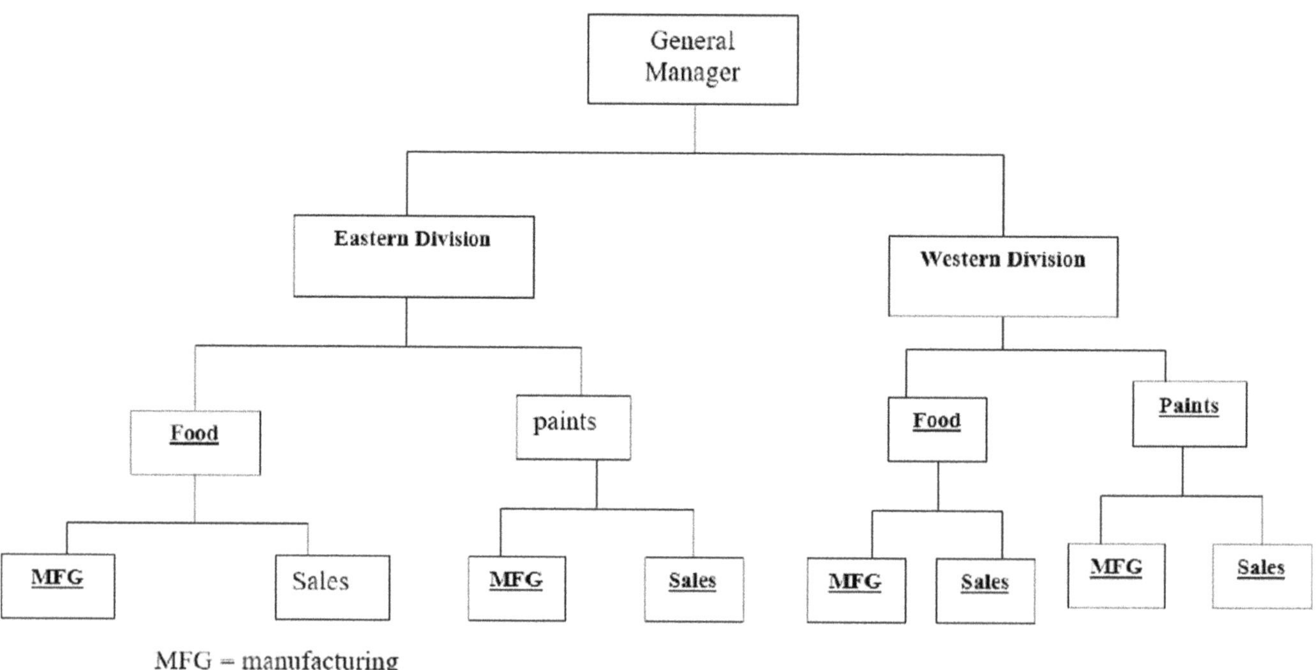

Figure 4.1 Manufacturing organization chart.
Source: Daft RL, Daft RL. Principles of management. South-Western, Cengage Learning India Pvt. Limited; 2009.

Bases of Departmentation

The activities necessary to achieve the organizational objectives are basic considerations in organizing.

The bases more commonly used for departmentation are

1. Departmentation by function
2. Departmentation by product
3. Departmentation by territory or geographic area
4. Departmentation by customer
5. Departmentation by process
6. Departmentation by task force or project
7. Departmentation by matrix

1. Departmentation by function

Is the process of grouping an organization's activities into logical units on the basis of the essential functions that must be performed to attain the enterprise's goal. This basis of departmentation is the primary, most common or very popular method of grouping tasks. Under this method tasks involving similar activities are grouped together, i.e the separate functions (units) are based on specialization or homogeneity of activities.

For example, the manufacturing company depicted below shows this method of departmentation. Figure 4.2 Departmentation by function

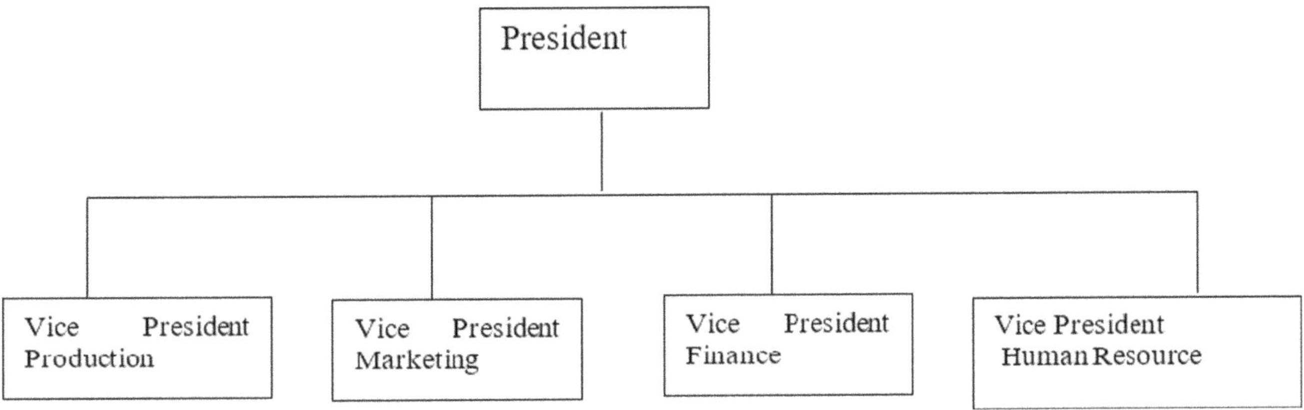

Figure 4.2 Departmentation by function.
Source: Robbins SP, Coulter M. Principles of management. Translated by Seyyed Mohammad Arabi and Mohammed Ali Hamid Rafiee and Behrouz Asrari Ershad, Fourth Edition, Tehran: Office of Cultural Studies. 2007.

This type of classification is a very familiar form of division work (it groups together in a common organizational unit people performing similar or closely related activities).

In this structure, all production problems are the responsibility of the production vice president, marketing problems are the province of the marketing president and soon. Such grouping on the basis of similar activities may increase specialization and employees technical expertise.

However, this method can include failures to communicate across department lines and lack of responsiveness to interdepartmental issues as each department refers problems up its hierarchy for resolution. Besides it becomes more difficult to get quick decisions or action on a problem because functional managers have to report to superiors and may be made to wait for a long time.

Advantages: -

- It is logical, scientific and time-tested method because it groups like or similar activities together which facilitates specialization. (efficiency is fostered through specialization.)
- It makes supervision easier, since each manager is an expert in only a narrow range of skills.
- Tight control of all functional units is assured, because the top managers are responsible for the end results.
- It simplifies training.

Disadvantage:

- People in a functional department may lose sight of the overall operations of the business; it in turn invites employees to de-emphasize the overall company objective.
- Workers may develop highly specialized skills, but not general managerial abilities. Consequently, functional departmentation is not an ideal training ground for top-level managers.
- Although there is strong relationship between within a function, co-ordination between functions is reduced.
- Sometimes conflict develops among departments as each unit competes for resources.
- The geographic area served; or the type of product or product line produced may require a different type of departmentation.
- Responsibility for profit is at the top.

Despite its disadvantages, it is widely used by various managers.

1. Departmentation by product

Under this method, activities are grouped according to product lines. For each major product manufactured by the enterprise, there is a separate department looks after. Each department is responsible for a product or related family of a product. This method stresses the utilization of specialized knowledge, and encourages a sensible degree of specialization. It is used in many types of productive enterprises such as drug, food, clothing machines automobiles etc.

For example the following are some examples of organization taking the advantage of product departmentation.

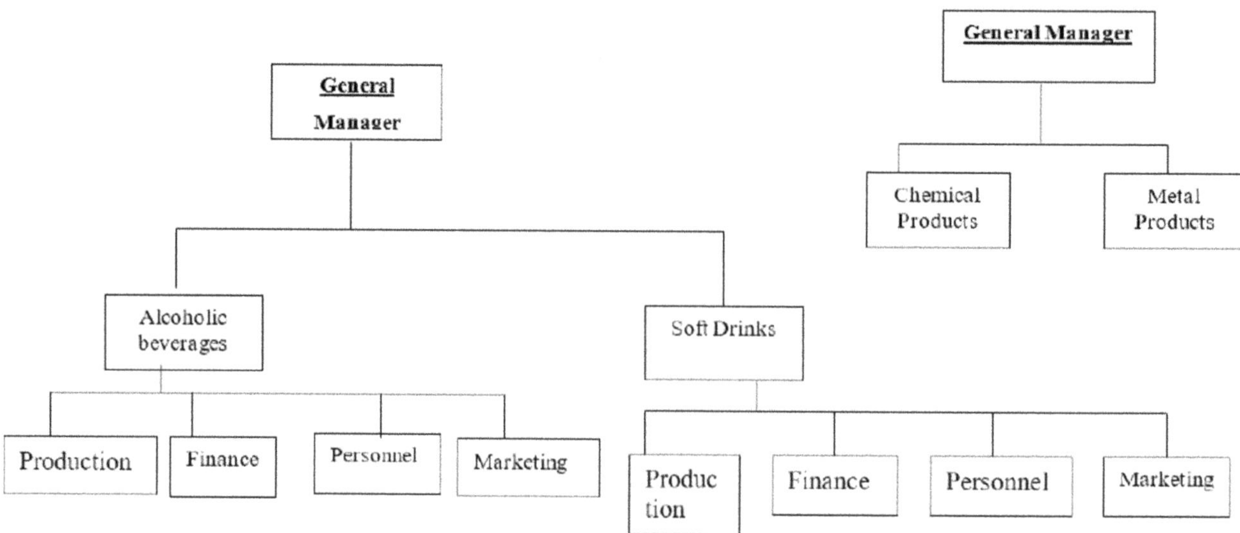

Figure 4.3 Departmentation by product,

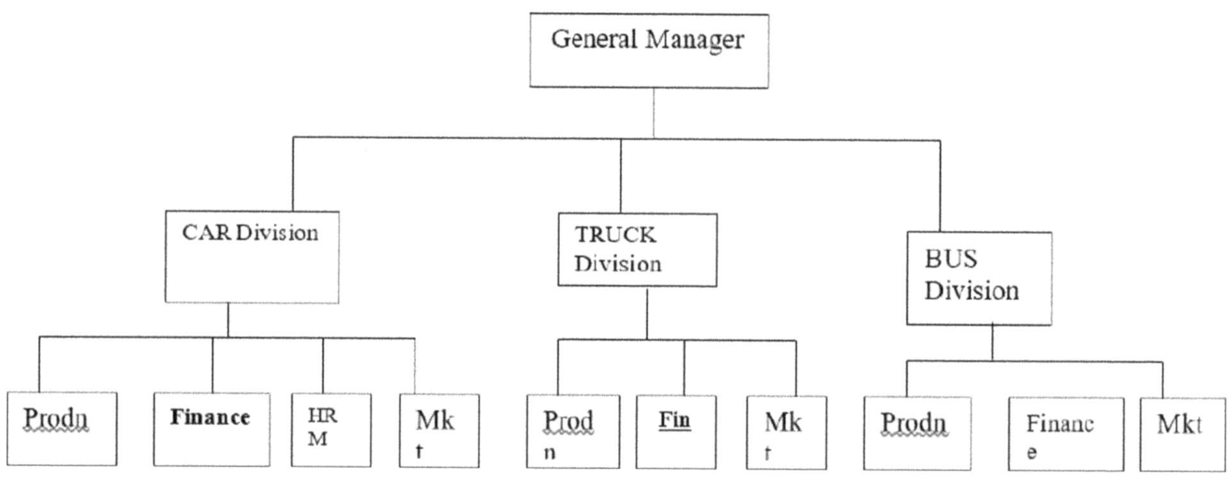

Figure 4.4 Departmentation by product.
source: adopted from Robbins SP, Coulter M. Principles of management. Translated by Seyyed Mohammad Arabi and Mohammed Ali Hamid
Rafiee and Behrouz Asrari Ershad, Fourth Edition, Tehran: Office of Cultural Studies. 2007

Each division is a separate profit centre by itself and in each division we have basic functional departments as manufacturing, personnel, finance, and marketing.

Advantage:

- It enables the enterprise to focus attention effort on product lines, making it easier for to management to see the efficiency and effectiveness of production determining which product is profitable or not.
- It improves co-ordination between functions relating to a particular product.
- Furnishes measurable training ground for general managers.
- Facilitates use of specialized capital, facilities, skills and knowledge.

Disadvantages:

- Requires more persons with general manager abilities.
- There is an ever-present danger of duplication of activities.
- It presents increased problem of top management control.

2. Departmentation by Territory/ Geographical Area/ Location

Geographic departmentation is a process of grouping activities based on the geographic location and assigning them to a given manager. This method is highly suitable for enterprise whose activities are widely spread. The factors that are important in deciding to use geographic departmentation are:

- *Economic factors:* such as low cost of operation, for example, mining and oil producing companies
- *Climatic factors*: attractive local conditions and the southern region wouldn't stock the same amount or type of winter clothing as the northern region.
- *Legal and political considerations*
- *Convenience to customers*: customer preference of the same product may vary from place to place.

For example, The Ethiopian Insurance Corporation, the Ministry of Education the Ethiopian Postal Service and the Commercial Bank of Ethiopia have different branches in different regions of the country, that they can use this method of departmentation. figure 4.5 illustrate Departmentation by Territory/ Geographical Area/ Location

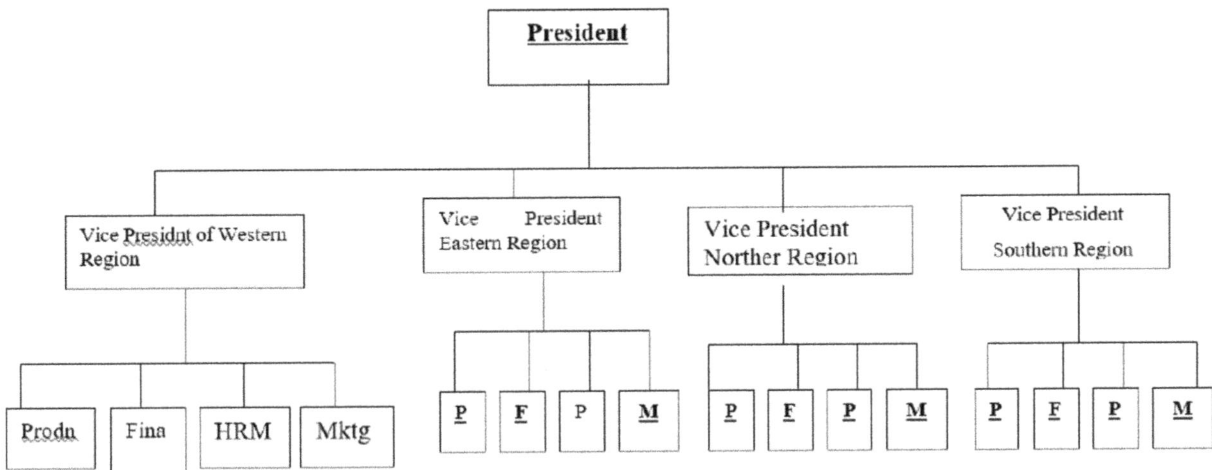

Figure 4.5 Departmentation by Territory/Geographical Area/Location,
Source: Robbins SP, Coulter M. Principles of management. Translated by Seyyed Mohammad Arabi and Mohammed Ali Hamid Rafiee and Behrouz Asrari Ershad, Fourth Edition, Tehran: Office of Cultural Studies. 2007.

Advantages:

- Results in great saving in time and money. The enterprise can benefit from lower freight, lower rents and lower labour costs. Thus, it takes advantages of economics of local operations (places emphasis on local markets and operations)
- Places responsibility at lower level (There will be quick decision.)
- Places measurable training ground for general managers.
- Better face to face communication with local interests.

Disadvantages:

- Requires more persons with general manager abilities /it is costly to implement.
- Duplication of effort
- Increase problem of top management control (This is because of having flat span of management.)

4. Departmentation By Customer

It is the grouping of enterprise activities based on customers' interests. Companies that must provide special services to different groups set up departments by types of customers, using customer departmentation. For example, a manufacturer may have both an industrial products division for its industrial customers and consumer products division for other consumers. An airlines company may make departments its selling departments for travelling agencies, government passengers, tourists and other customers. Normally, setting up departments by customers is not a primary form of departmentation. It is used instead within some other framework. This method takes into account the various needs of customers. It is used when the emphasis is upon being better able to serve buyers of the enterprise's products or services, departmentation by customer is suggested.

Electric company organization chart

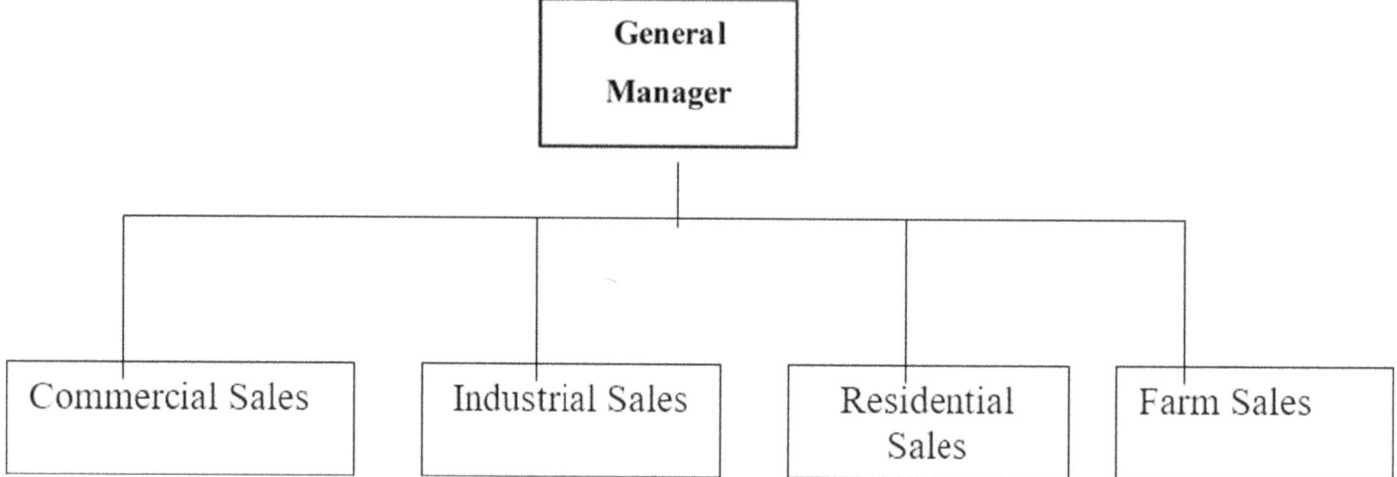

Figure 4.6 Company organization chart.
Source: Ahmady, Gholam Ali, Maryam Mehrpour, and Aghdas Nikooravesh. "Organizational structure." Procedia-Social and Behavioral Sciences 230 (2016): 455–462.

Advantages:

- Encourages concentration on customer needs
- Giving customers feeling that they have an understanding supplier
- Develops expertise in customer area.

Disadvantage:

- May be difficult to coordinate operations between competing customer demands.
- Requires managers and staff expert in customer's problems
- It may result in under utilization of resources in some departments.
- Customer groups may not always be clearly defined.
- There may be duplication of activities.

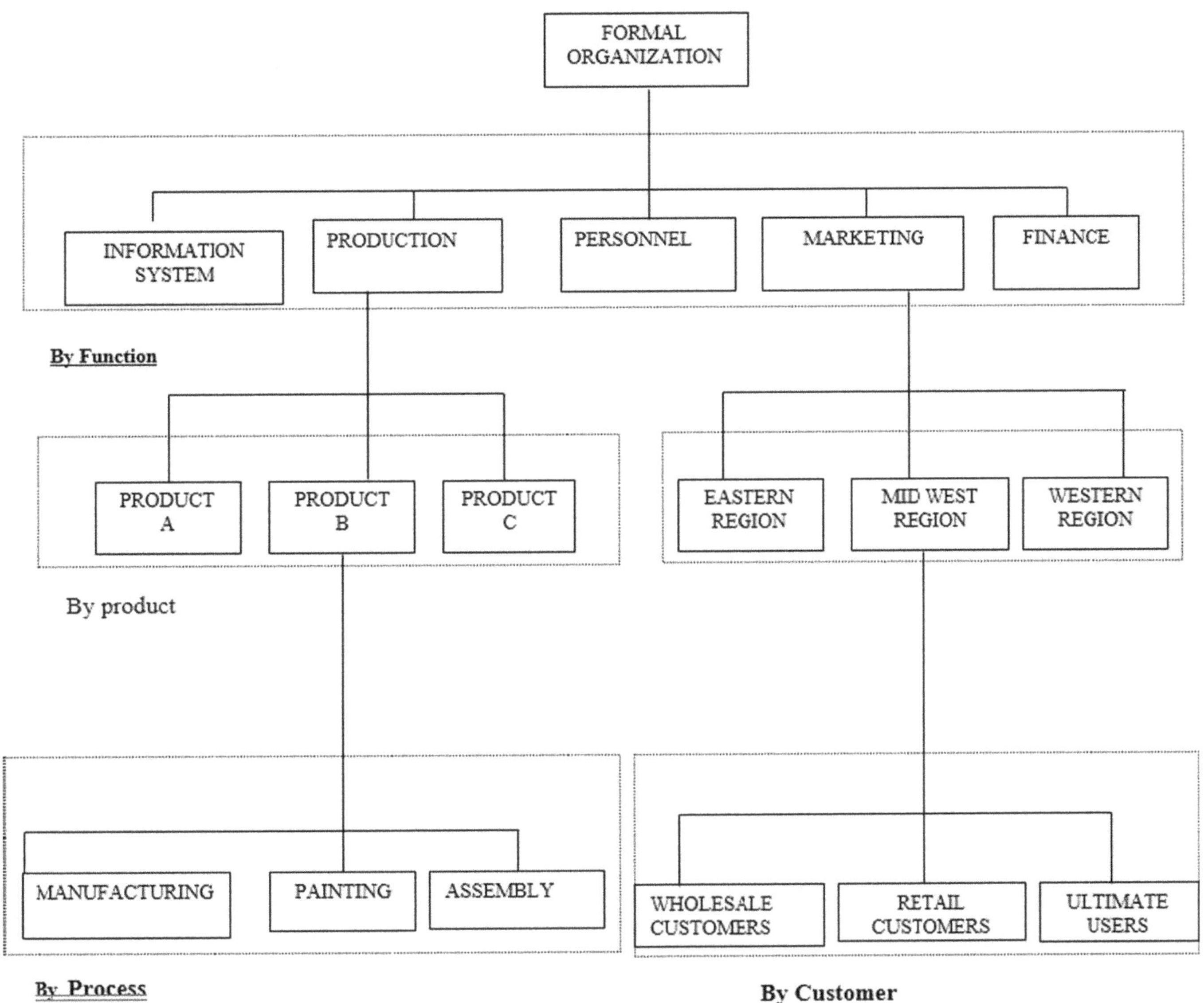

Figure 4.7 Organization Chart Showing the Break Down of Business Systems Into Subsystems.

5. Departmentation by Process (Equipment Departmentation)

It is the grouping of enterprise activities according to the products' manufacturing process. This method of departmentation is logical and used when the machines or equipment used require special skill for operating and are of large capacity which eliminate organizational diving or have technical facilities which strongly suggest a concentrated location. For example, a textile factory may be classified in to Spinning, Weaving, processing, etc. Economic and technological considerations are the foremost reasons for adopting process departmentation. It is mostly found in production departments.

It is used when the machine or equipment require special skill for operating and are of large capacity. Here, economic and technological considerations are the foremost reasons for adoption of this method and is commonly practiced in production areas frequently at the operative levels.

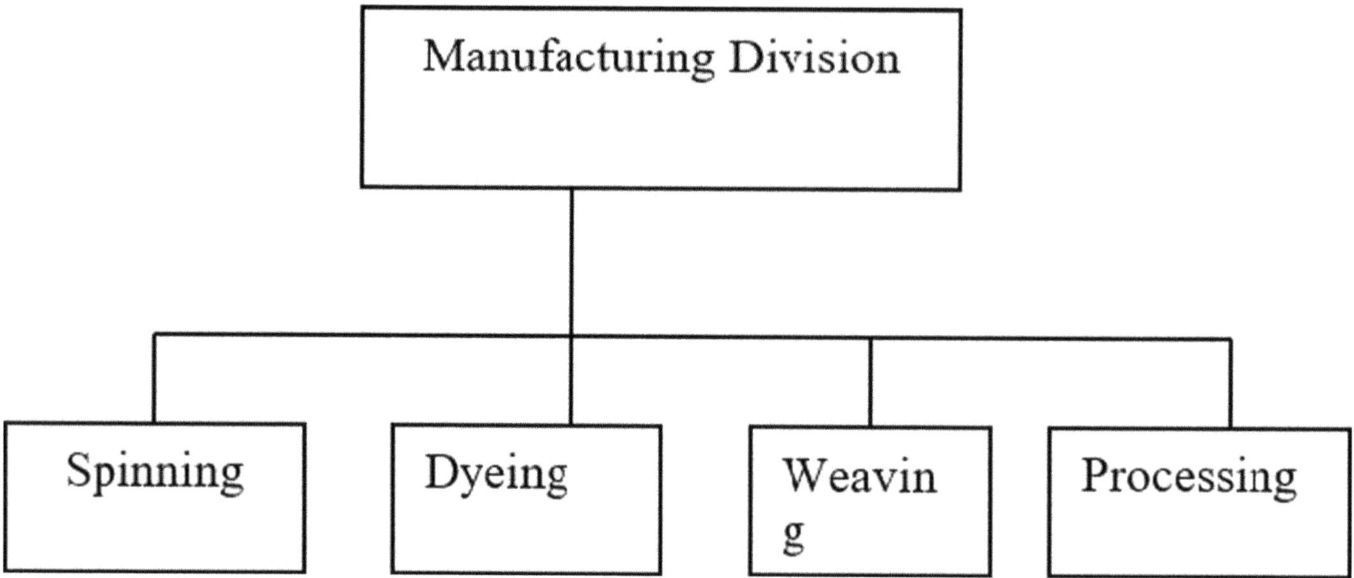

Figure 4.8 For example, textile department.
Source: Ahmady, Gholam Ali, Maryam Mehrpour, and Aghdas Nikooravesh. "Organizational structure." Procedia-Social and Behavioral Sciences 230 (2016): 455-462.

Advantage:

- Achieves economic advantage
- Uses specialized knowledge
- Simplifies training
- Sues specialized technology

Disadvantage:

- Coordination of departments is difficult
- Responsibility for profit is at the top
- It is unsuitable for developing general managers

6. Departmentation by Task Force or by Project

This method is used to carry out a specific mission or purpose, to carry out a specific project. The basis of departmentation is a project or block of work, which extends from the beginning to the completion of a wanted and definite work. For example, big companies, in which its major work is contracting construction activities may use this method for its departmentation tasks as road constructions project department, building constructions project department, dam constructions project department, etc.

7. Matrix Departmentation

It is an organizational arrangement that developed because of the need for quick completion of highly technical projects that required significant contributions by two or more functional groups. It begins with functional stricture and then another structure organized by product or by client /customer or by project is overlaid upon the original structure. The result is that employees are assigned to a basic functional department and, at the same time, they are assigned to work on a particular product/project or for a particular customer/client. The essence of matrix organization normally is the combining of functional and product departmentation in the same organization structure. Figure 4.9 shows the matrix departmentation

Advantage

- Since there are a number of managers, there are more channels of information
- It is oriented toward end results. (The project objectives are clear.)
- Professional identification is maintained.
- Resources are used efficiently because workers are assigned to different projects as needed and groups or projects can share equipment.

Disadvantage

- Conflict in organization authority exists (it lends it self to power struggle.
- Possibility of disunity of command exists
- It also /results in higher over head costs because more managerial positions are created.
- Requires manager effective in human relations.

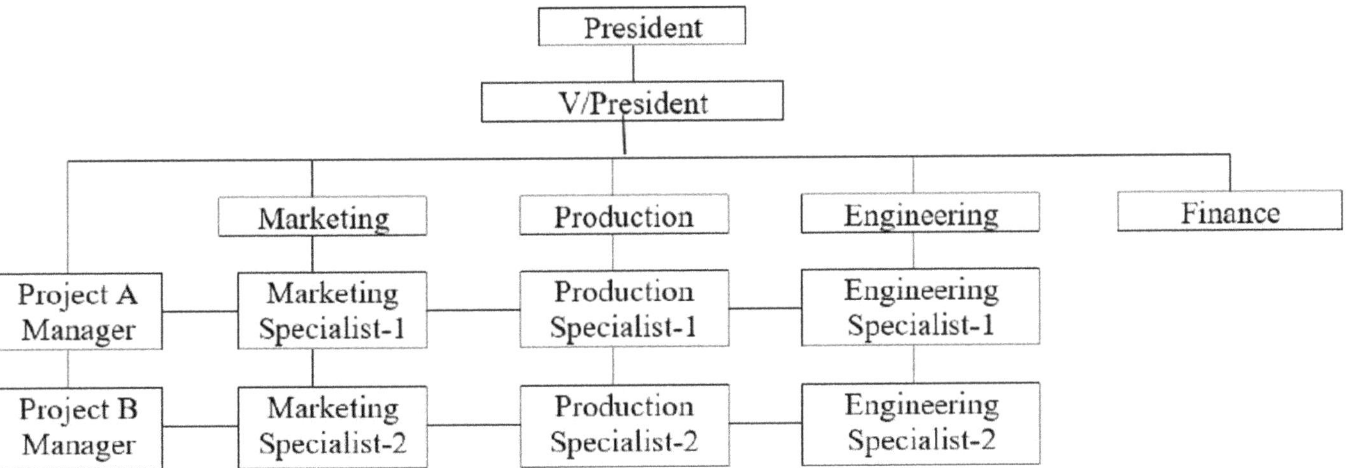

Figure 4.9 Matrix Departmentation.
Source: Ahmady, Gholam Ali, Maryam Mehrpour, and Aghdas Nikooravesh. "Organizational structure." Procedia-Social and Behavioral Sciences 230 (2016): 455-462.

To generalize a manager may use any means of departmentation individually or by combining of two or more methods, but the method adopted should facilitate specialization, coordination, control, minimization of cost and suitability to the existing personnel and given condition.

4.4.2 Delegation

Delegation is the process of distributing and entrusting work to other persons to accomplish them. Delegation occurs when the workload of an individual manager becomes so great that he has to get help from others to get his work done. Since it is impossible for any single person in an enterprise to execute all the tasks necessary for the accomplishment of group activities, similarly it is impossible for a single person to exercise all the authority for decision making so the need to delegate becomes evident.

In a very small set-up there may be no need of delegation but in bigger organizations it is difficult to function without it. Hence the need of delegation is felt in big organizations. No one, however, is capable of performing all the jobs alone in a modern business organization. One must divide and share the work and responsibilities with others. All managers decide how much work they should do themselves and what should be assigned to others. The process of delegation involves:

a. Delegation of authority
b. Assignment of responsibility and
c. Accountability for performance of duties and exercise of authority

Assignment of tasks without delegation of adequate authority is meaningless. Delegation of authority without specifying the tasks to be performed will mean leaping in the dark. And assignment of tasks and delegation of authority without accountability, will be a blind bargain.

a. Authority

Managerial authority is the official and legal right vested to act, command, of direct the action of others in the attainment of organizational goals. In every organization there is an ultimate authority and since it is not possible for the ultimate alone to perform all duties or to exercise all authority, it delegates authority to persons at all levels.

It is impossible for the ultimate authority to exercise all authority, therefore, it has to delegate to the lower levels, i.e., the superior delegates authority to subordinates. The delegated authority is generally in the form of power to make decisions, issue instructions, hire and fire employees and supervise and control work performance at different points.

Authority once delegated can be enhanced, reduced or withdrawn depending upon the requirement. For example,. The purchaser of a department may've an authority to purchase supplies up to a USD 5000 limit. S/He can't buy beyond USD 5000. To buy beyond USD 5000 S/he has to get additional approval from his boss. Because it is out of her/his authority to buy. Due to the competency of the purchaser it may be enhanced to USD 10000 or reduced to USD 2500 or total withdrawal from purchasing supplies.

A manager can't delegate authority which s/he herself/himself doesn't possess. Moreover, s/he doesn't delegate the entire authority to her/his subordinates because if she/he surrenders or delegates all the authority s/he can't work, thus, some authority has to be left for the manager to work.

b. Responsibility

Responsibility is synonymous with duty in many senses. Both of them are used interchangeably. In the context of management, responsibility is the obligation of a subordinate to accomplish the task assigned to him. Managerial responsibility is contractual responsibility because it is the result of the contract of service. And it is moral responsibility to be discharged honestly and efficiently. Responsibility may be in respect of

- ***performance*** – when one is assigned a duty to finish a certain task – if the person completes the task – it will be assumed as the responsibility is over, however, if the person did not complete the task he/she will be questioned for not completing the task. This type of responsibility can be also called as *discontinuous* responsibility. For example,. An accountant engaged to finalize the company's accounts for a single year. Responsibility can be in respect of – ***non-performance*** – being a continuous obligation that does not get finished at a particular specified period of time. For example, the relationship between general manager and the production manager signifies this type of relationship. This type of responsibility can be also called as *continuous* responsibility. Responsibility can be assigned only when there is superior subordinate relationship between the persons concerned. Responsibility can't be delegated, it is absolute. It doesn't flow down wards. No superior can escape responsibility for the activities of subordinates, for it is the superior who has delegated authority and assigned duties.

c. Accountability

Accountability means an obligation or answerability for the performance of an assigned task. The process of delegation doesn't end with mere assignment of duty or responsibility and delegation of appropriate authority for the performance of that duty or responsibility. It comes subordinate is called upon to give answer. Unlike authority, accountability always flows from the bottom up. Accountability is the point at which authority and responsibility meet.

The requirement for a subordinate is to answer to the superior for result accomplished in the performance of any assigned duties. If the subordinate fails to perform the duty, he is liable to punishment. For example, if the purchase manager is assigned the task of purchasing raw materials for the factory and is also given the authority to make payments for the raw materials, he is liable to punishment if he doesn't ensure adequate availability of raw materials when required or if he doesn't make payments to suppliers in time. Accountability can be enforced through demanding regular reports from the subordinates concerned and through on-the-spot inspection of the subordinates.

4.4.3 Decentralization

Decentralization is the opposite of centralization. Decentralization – is when the authority to make decisions is dispersed by extensive delegation throughout all the levels of management. Centralization – when the authority to make decisions is concentrated at the top levels of the organization. In the case of centralization, decision-making authority is concentrated in a few hands at the top. While, in the case of decentralization greater number of important decisions are made at lower levels.

Factors to be considered to the amount or degree of centralization or decentralization are:

a. ***Size and complexity of the organization***

The larger the size of the enterprise, the more authority the central manager is forced to delegate. The smaller the size the need to decentralize authority decreases. For example,. If the firm has numerous separate businesses, the limitations of the capacity and/or expertise of the manager will usually lead to decentralization of authority to the respective units.

b. Dispersion of the organization activities

If the organization is highly geographically dispersed, it is very evident that a greater degree of decentralization must occur. For example, Ministry of Education which has many corporations under it may be best example of decentralization because of the size and geographical location.

c. competency of personnel available

A real shortage of managerial talent in the organization would limit the extent of decentralization of authority. If we are to decentralize or disperse authority we assume that there are trained managers to make good decisions. If the subordinates have managerial talent, right decentralizing certain authority will be logical. Similarly, if there is adequate supply of competent managers, right decentralization is necessary.

d. ***Degree of repetitiveness and standardization of activities as well as adequacy of the communication system***

If activities are standardized and if there is improved and adequate communication system there will be of less need to decentralize authority, i.e., the extent we decentralize will reduce. If there is repetition and standardization of operations, it is advisable to centralize some authority to control operations. If there is improved and adequate communication it is better to centralize and if there is delays in communication it is better to decentralize authority to improve communication. Generally, manager has to be obtain the best possible mix of centralization and decentralization on all decisions and functions to maximize returns. Neither decentralization nor centralization should be allowed to go to practice. We must have necessary balance or equilibrium between them.

4.5. Organizational Relationships and Behaviour

4.5.1 Formal and Informal Organizations

Many management people distinguish organizations as formal and informal ones.

Formal Organization

An organization is "formal" when the activities of two or more persons were consciously organized toward a given objective. It is drafted by the top management. It is a consciously drafted and coordinated programme. Unity of objective and organizational efficiency should be kept in mind when we create effective formal organization. The organization structure must contribute to the attainment of the goal of the enterprise, and help the people to meet the objectives with minimum effort.

The formal organization has the following important features:

1. It is consciously brought into existence for predetermined objectives, i.e., it is intentional and deliberate structure of roles, it is not as such haphazardly formed organization.

2. Authority and responsibility are defined. There is a clear line of authority in which an individual exercises or executes his duties.
3. The line of communication is also formalized. Communication follows the chain of command established by an organizations hierarchy.
4. The relationship of the superior and the subordinate is fixed.
5. It exists in a written form.

Informal organization

Informal organization Is a network of personal and social relations not established consciously, but arising and spontaneously as people interact one another. Informal organizations result through the bonds of personal relationships. The main point to be noted is that no conscious attempt is made to create an informal organization.

Informal organizations' relationships do not appear in the organization chart. It doesn't exist in a written form. Informal organizations come into being due to friendship, mutual regard, intimacy and close contact formed with relationship. For example, people can contact out side their official activities in places like coffees shops, lunch hour meetings, social gatherings, while playing chess, tennis during rest time may become good friends creating informal group. People who work on the same floor (2nd floor of the organization) may form an informal group. i.e. Even though they don't have formally written relationship between them, but due to some contact they create it.

In the informal organization there are no specific nor written rules of authority and responsibility. They are decided by the individual status, personnel behaviour, degree of friend ship, similarity etc. There is no formal line of communication in between the members and there is no formal sanction of authority. The authority here is earned not granted. The leader in informal organization emerges out by the strength of his personality, competence, age and other individual traits. They've a powerful influence on attainment of a goal. It develops within the formal organization. It contributes to the attainment of the joint results (objectives). For example, it is easier to ask for help for an organization's problem form a person you know, and who may even be in a different department than form a person you know only as a name on an organization chart. It brings convenience to the formal organization and helps to remove the deficiencies of the formal organization. Competent managers are aware of its importance and avoid antagonizing it.

Communication is faster in informal organization than in the formal organization. Here information passes through rumour or grapevine it doesn't follow the formal structure, it is informally distributed. For example, if we assume in a classroom. there are about 50 students which may contain several informal groups that constitute the informal organization with in the formal class known by the college or university. These groups may be formed because of in dorm residence, project work teams, seating arrangements, or during dinning time. These two types of organizations are integrally related.

4.6. The Organization Structure, Chart and Manual

The Organization Structure

The concept of organization structure is somewhat abstract and illusive. The organization structure, being abstract, is not visible in the same way as biological or mechanical structure, though it can be inferred form that actual operations and behaviour of the organization.

Organization structure is the pattern in which various parts or components are interrelated and interconnected. Thus, organization structure is the established pattern of relationships and components or parts of the organization. It is the relationship among various positions and activities. Since the positions are held by individuals, the structure is the relationship among people. Organization structure is a management tool for achieving the objectives of an organization. High productivity depends on both resources and structure being appropriate to the task at hand. The result of organizing is the creation of an organization structure.

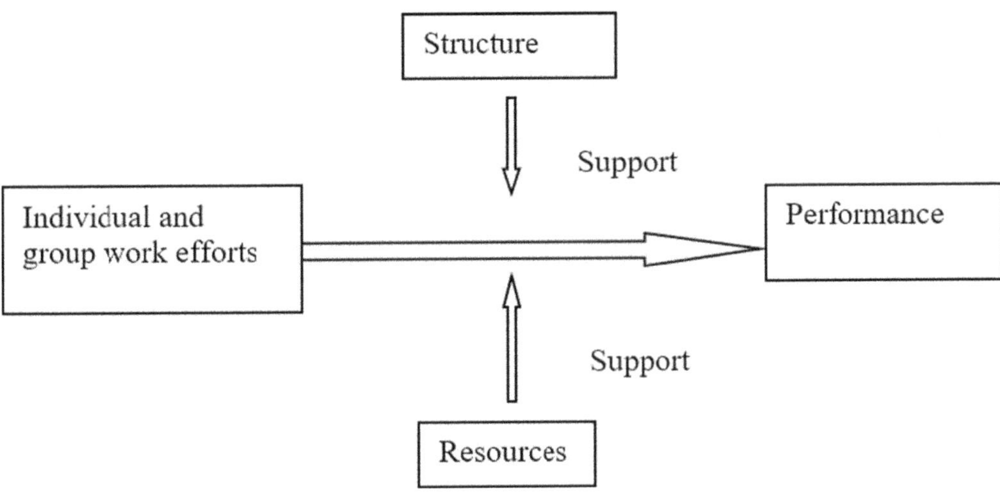

Figure 4.10 Organization Chart.

Organization Chart

An organization chart is a diagram that describes the basic arrangement of work positions within an organization. Or it is a diagrammatical form, which shows important aspects of an organization including the major functions and the respective authority of each employee. It is a graphical representation of the chain of command and relationships among jobs and units. Essentially, the chart can be compared to a skeleton diagram of the human body. It shows how parts are interconnected.

All organization charts show formal organizations. It is a useful static model of showing both the horizontal and vertical dimensions of the organization structure.

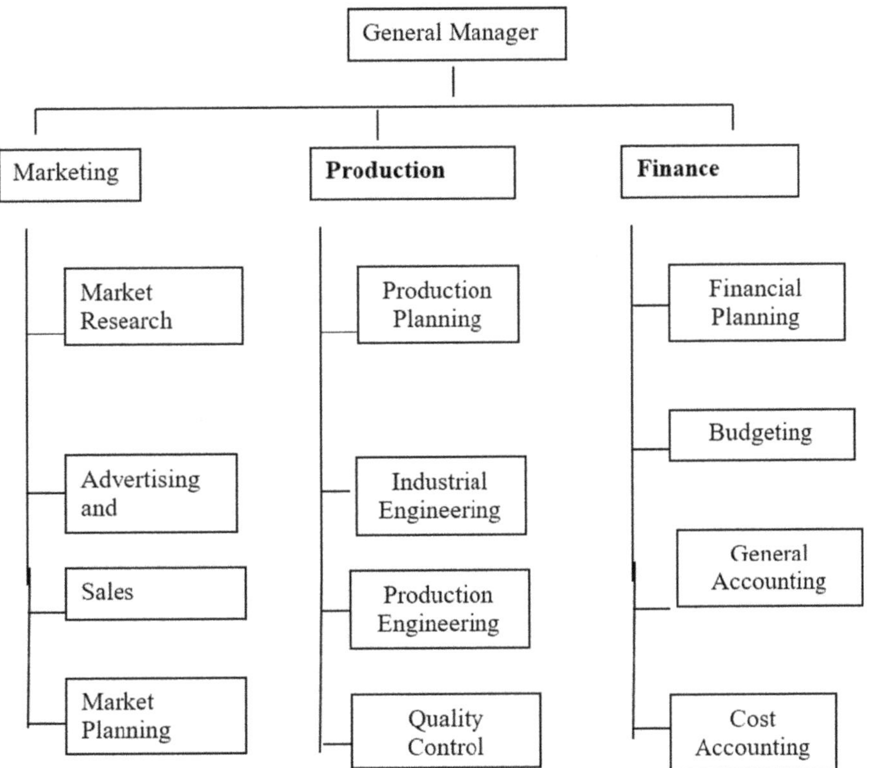

Figure 4.11 The horizontal and vertical dimensions of the organization structure.
Source: Daft, Richard L., and Dorothy Marcic. *Understanding management*. Cengage Learning, 2016.

Organizational Manual

It is the description of the organizational chart. It is designed to promote understanding of the basic organization structure. It contains useful information's such as organization chart, a brief description of the overall organizational objectives, policies, practices and procedures. It is usually prepared in the form of a book or booklet.

Forms of Organization Structure

The type of an organization structure is ordinarily determined by the nature and size of the organization. These could be no hard and fast rules about it. However, some of the most important alternatives are the following:

1. Line (military) organization

This form of organization structure is the easiest and simplest form of organization in which each position has general authority over lower positions.

Line organization is the basic framework for the whole organization. A pure line organization would consist of people who are directly involved in the fulfilment of the primary mission of the organization. It is a form of structure where authority is passed down from top management to middle managers and from middle down to lower level managers. It points out direct vertical relationships (superior-subordinate relationship) The relationships form a chain of command or a hierarchy of authority in the organization. Authority flows through the primary chain of command, according to the scalar principle.

Line managers are those in the organization directly responsible for achieving the goals of the organization. It is represented by the standard chain of command starting with the board of directors and extending down through the various levels in the hierarchy to the point where the basic activities of the organization are carried out.

Line executives are directly involved in the basic activities of an enterprise. They are the doers, the people who do and make things happen. For this reason they constitute the backbone of an organization. Line organization is the backbone of the organizational hierarchy.

In this type organization there is a vertical line of authority for this reason it is given the name "*line organization*", and because till recently the army used to be organized on this same pattern, it is also called "*military organization*". In university, for example, teaching, research and typing tests are line activities.

Line and Staff Organization

Staff functions are functions that are supposed to help and assist the line functions. They give advisory service to the line managers. Staff activities support line activities. Staff functions indirectly influence line activities through advice, recommendation, and research and technical expertise.

Functional authority without a right to command and decide is called staff. It is regarded as auxiliary in nature. The staff manager can only advise a line manager. The line manager can either take the advice or ignore it. The line manager is free either to accept or reject the advice. Line executives have direct control over the subordinates under them, but staff executives have no such authority. Rather, they are meant to aid and advice line managers at the same level. It is often said that "staff thinks while the line acts". Line and staff organization is a result of primary functional differentiation down ward (line) plus secondary functional differentiation out ward (staff). It utilizes the advantages of both pure line organization and staff organization. Staff personnel don't have formal authority and he/she is not in the chain of command.

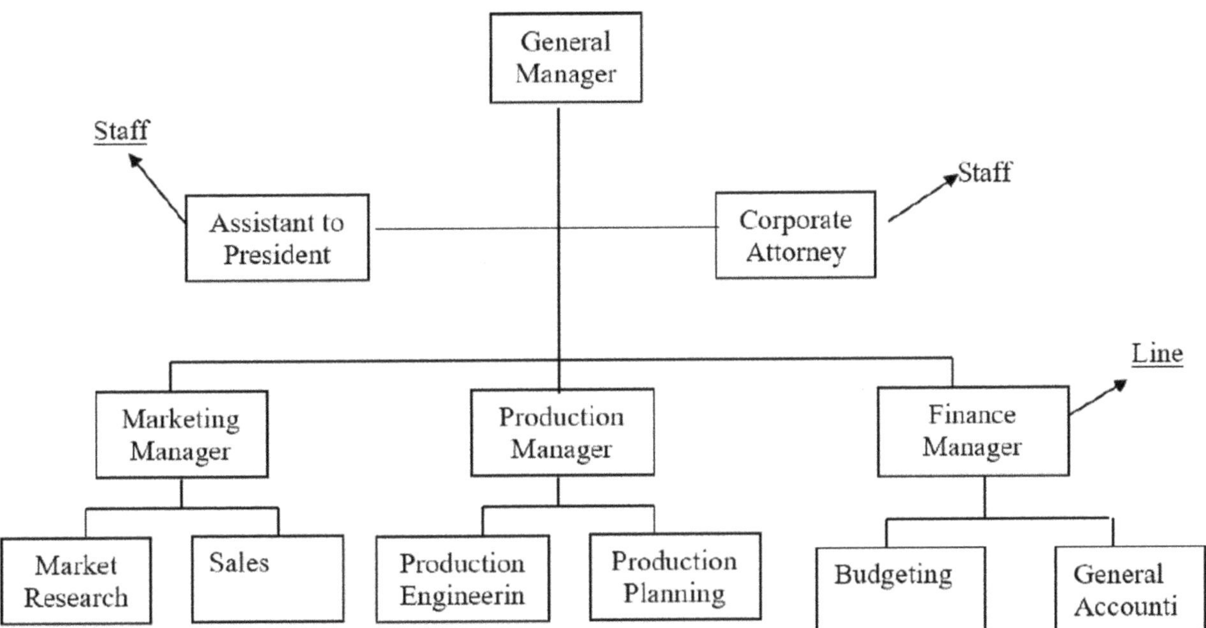

Figure 4.12 Line and Staff Organization.
Source: Daft, Richard L., and Dorothy Marcic. *Understanding management*. Cengage Learning, 2016.

3. Functional Organization

In this organization, the line executive, besides receiving orders from his immediate line boss, also receives directions from one or more specialists, i.e., other persons or units lying outside the formal chain of command (staff) make relation with the line ones. This will break the unity of command and a person may have two bosses. Of course, functional authority is only for and specified activities

Functional authority is the right and power of one department to issue orders and instructions to one, several or other departments in an organization But staff authority is the right to give an advice to line executives either to be accepted or rejected, but in formal authority the line executive is obliged to accept the instruction and be accountable for it.

Functional authority should be granted only when it is essential, because, extensive grant of functional authority may seriously damage the basis of line authority, viz, unity of command. It has developed from the increasing complexity of operations in an enterprise (specially in production department) and the need to have specialists to aid line executives. Under it, a specialist in a given area is allowed to aid and direct the line executive, although this is done within a limited and clearly defined scope of authority.

It typically rests on specialized experts or the possession of technical information and extends only over matters to which these knowledge can apply. Managers affiliated with such technical departments as accounting, personnel, legal, finance, and engineering frequently use functional authority to full fill their roles in an organization's division of labour.

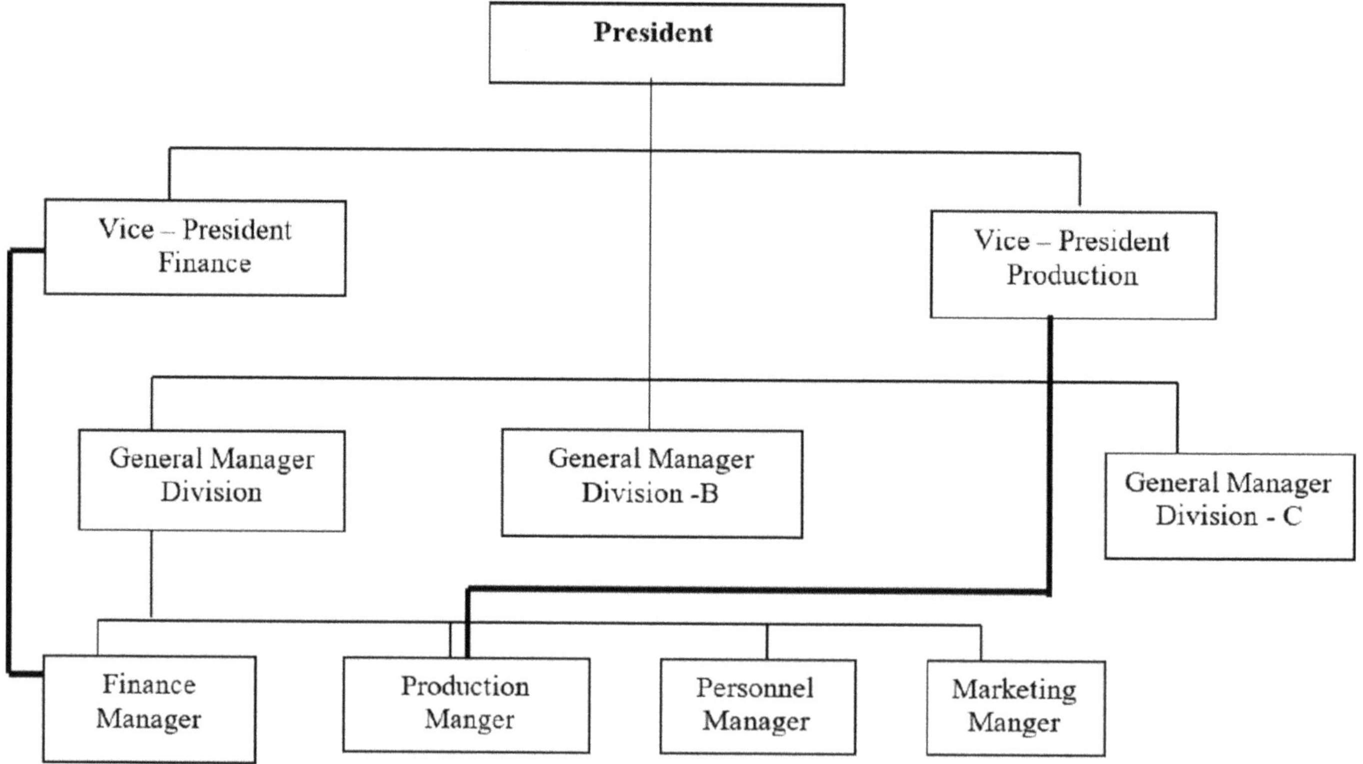

Figure 4.13 Functional and line authority.
Source: Daft, Richard L., and Dorothy Marcic. *Understanding management*. Cengage Learning, 2016.

Review Questions

1. What is organizing?
2. Discuss the basic concepts in organizing.
3. Discuss the various bases of departmentation including their respective advantages and disadvantages.
4. Which type of departmentation technique do you commonly know in many organizations?
5. What is the span of management? Discuss wide span and narrow span of management.
6. What is delegation? What are the processes of delegation? What are the obstacles of delegation?
7. Discuss decentralization vis-à-vis centralization? Which one do you favour? Why?
8. What is the difference between line and staff authorities? When do managers have functional authority?
9. What is the difference between line position and staff position?
10. How do you differentiate organizational structure, organizational chart and organizational manual?

CHAPTER FIVE

STAFFING

     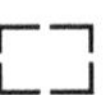 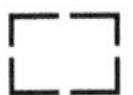

LEARNING OBJECTIVES

after studying this chapter, you will be able to:

1. Understand the meaning of staffing.
2. Develop an understanding of recruitment, selection, training, and development.
3. Describe the steps in the staffing process
4. Understand the process of employee training
5. Develop a staffing strategy plan at an organization.

Overview

This chapter covers the concepts and theories associated with human resource staffing. The chapter is exploring the recruitment, selection, training, the steps in the staffing process, employee training you, staffing strategy plan, all these topics to enable the readers to have a comprehensive idea and understanding.

5.1 Meaning of Staffing

The most important resources of an organization are its human resources, the people who supply the organization with their work, talent, creativity, and drive.

Staffing is filling and keeping filled positions in the organization structure. It is the process of filling jobs with appropriate persons. Staffing is closely linked to organizing. When the organizations lines have been drawn the organization has a skeleton, the process of staffing seeks to fill in the body around the skeleton. Staffing involves filling the positions needed in the organization structure by appointing competent and qualified persons for the jobs.

5.2 The Staffing Process

In order the organization to be supplied with the right people in the right positions at the right time the steps to be followed are:

5.2.1 Human resources planning (manpower planning)

Manpower planning or personnel planning is important to ensure that the personnel (human resource) needs of the organization will be constantly and appropriately met. This is made through the analysis of:

a) ***Internal factors*** – current and expected skill needs. Managers have to analyse the current supply of employees (their skills and abilities)

  - basic strategies and goals of the organization
  - vacancies and
  - departmental expansions and reductions

External factors – labour market, i.e., the availability of skilled manpower as required.

Future demand is projected for several reasons. First, this information is useful in planning the company's development efforts. For example, if a firm forecasted that it would need 250 new first level managers in the next five years, a management development program could be designed to train current personnel for such positions. Second, the information would be important in planning for recruitment efforts. If a need for 150 mechanical engineers were projected for the organization in the next three years, but only 50 were currently employed, plans would be required to recruit 100 additional engineers during this time.

Also effective human resource planning may help an organization avoid layoffs. This can sometimes be accomplished by not over hiring and by using attrition (not replacing employees when they leave the organization).

Before it comes into practice, it has to consider the organization's plan – basic strategy and detailed goals, for example, expansion or acquisition potential change in the external environment of the organization, for example, change in market, etc.

The organizational internal environment (such as its strategic plan) as well as its external environmental will broadly define for managers the limits with in which their human resource plans must operate. Once the broad limits have been established, managers can begin to compare their future personnel needs against the existing personnel situation in order to determine what recruitment, training and development procedures they will need to follow. The fact that the internal and external environments of an organization change means that managers must monitor these environments to keep their human resource plan up to date.

The central elements in human resources planning are:

a) ***Forecasting*** – attempts to assess the future personnel needs of the organization. It is forecasting the supply of human resources. Forecasters try to determine the number, type and quantity of people they will need to perform specific duties at a certain point in time.

   It involves estimating additional employment of people over a given period adjusting it against the internal human resource available.

Forecasting period usually extends from 6 months to 5 years. For instance, employment in specific category of 'A' can be described as follows:

1.	Required period	2016–2021	
2.	Departmental increase (it could be because expansion)	70	
3.	Retirements and turn over	30	
4.	Total additional needs for employment	100	—— Forecasting
5.	Internal resources (promotable staff in to category A from other levels)	40	—— Human Resource audit
6.	Total outside recurrent needs	100–40 = 60	

Therefore, over the period 1995 – 2000, we will require a total of additional 100 staff members of department A. This pool of 100 employees/managers will represent two streams:

1.	Recruitment of additional persons from outside (new entries)	60
2.	Additional persons through promotion from within –	40
	Total personnel needs	100

b. ***Human resources audit*** – once forecasts are completed the next step is to obtain information about the organization's present personnel. It is making an inventory of present manpower with their strengths and weaknesses, which helps mangers plan promotions to the vacant positions. Here, the skills and performance of each individual is evaluated and ranked according to the quality of their work.

The information thus obtained will give upper level managers an idea of the effectiveness of staff in each department. It assesses the organization's current human resource.

There are four basic steps in human resource planning:

a. Planning for future needs. How many people with what abilities will the organization need to remain in operation for the foreseeable future?

b. Planning for future balance. How many people presently employed can be expected to stay with the organization? The difference between this number and the number the organization will need leads to the next step.

c. Planning for recruiting and selecting or for lay off. How can the organization attain the number of people it will need?

d. Planning for development. How should the training and movement of individuals within the organization be managed so that the organization will be assured of a continuing life?

5.2.2 Recruitment

Once the forecast or manpower plan is made, the next step is to search the needed human resource. It is concerned with developing a pool of job candidates in line with the human resources plan. Its purpose is to provide a large group of candidates, pool of job candidates so that the organization will be able to select the qualified employees it needs.

Recruitment is attracting qualified employee candidates to the organization. It is the search for quality employees either inside or outside the organization to fill vacant positions.

Recruitment is an attempt of attracting interested applicants and then choosing the best of these for the available jobs, i.e., it is an attempt of providing a pool of perspective employees so that we can select the right person for the right job from this pool. Hence, recruitment precedes the selection process

Sources of Recruitment

The sources of recruitment can be broadly classified as:

a. Internal sources and
b. External sources

a. Internal sources

Refer to the employees currently working in an enterprise. Thus when there is a vacant position, someone working in the organization is transferred, promoted or demoted to it. Before looking to the external sources of recruitment, internal source should be exhausted. To fill the vacant position, here, the organization may have its own training program to prepare current personnel for certain positions.

Advantage:

- It is usually less expensive to recruit or promote from within than to hire from outside the organization.
- It may faster loyalty and inspire greater effort among organization members.
- Individuals will already be acclaimed to the organization and may therefore need less initial training and orientation.

Disadvantage:

- It limits the pool of talent available to the organization.

b) External Sources

The most commonly used external sources of recruitment are:

i) ***Advertisements*** – Through newspapers, magazines, television, radio and so on.

ii) ***Public employment agencies*** – They register the names of job seekers and pass them on to employers who fit the vacancies. They serve as a bridge between job seekers and the organization with a vacancy which requires qualified persons.

iii) ***Educational institutions*** – High schools, colleges, universities provide employers to recruit job candidates.

iv) ***Jobbers and contractors /direct hiring/*** – for positions requiring unskilled workers, the service of jobbers and contractors is very common.

5.2.3 Selection

Is the process of choosing the best person or persons among job candidates. It is the process of choosing from a pool of candidates who best meets job specifications of the organization. This step is very important since decision is to be made by both parties:

- the organization decides to offer the job to the applicant.
- the applicant decides whether the job offer will fit his aim and satisfies him.

Selection process will include the following steps:

i. ***Application form*** – is a fundamental media through which information is gathered about the applicant.

   It summarizes the applicants personal history and qualifications. These forms can elicit more factual information about the applicant. Also an applicant may be required to attach character testimonials and other references such as name, address, age, education, experiences, place of residence, sex, etc.

ii. ***Initial screening interview*** – to eliminate obviously unfit or unqualified employees. It is a quick evaluation of the applicant's suitability for a particular job. This is the first screening test for undesirable candidates.

iii. ***Thorough testing*** – used to judge the capacity of the candidate to learn on the job, to evaluate applicants' knowledge and skill, intelligence and abilities that are important to job performance, e.g. aptitude tests, intelligence tests, mechanical tests, character tests etc.

iv. ***Background investigation*** – the truthfulness of a candidate's application form will be checked. References may be made to the previous employer or to the university or college who gave him a certificate.

v. ***In depth selection interview*** – Conducted by the immediate manager

   to whom the applicant will report, to find out more information about the applicant as an individual, such as special interest of the individual other than the legal documents he submitted.

vi. ***Physical examination*** – to make medical examination by a recognized medical centre or qualified doctor. And transmitted by the doctor to the employer office, where by its purpose is to make sure that he can perform duties properly and to protect other employees against contagious diseases.

vii. ***Selection and placement*** – offering of the job to the applicant, who successfully passed through selection stages, i.e., fill a job vacancy or position to the individual who best fits the vacant position.

5.2.4 Induction and Orientation

New comers are introduced with their colleagues. New employees are provided with information about the organization, the job, and expected behaviours. They are made familiar with the company's policy objectives, rules and regulations, pay day, hours of work, opportunities, promotions, etc.

5.2.5 Training and Development

The aim of training and development is to increase the ability and skills of individuals and groups to contribute to the organizational effectiveness. Training is designed to improve job-related skills. Development programmes are designed to educate employees beyond the requirement of their existing jobs so that they will be prepared for promotion

Change is required of every one in every organization. To help adapt to change, organizations spend millions of USD annually in training and development to enhance employees' skills. Employees must maintain up–to–date skills so that they can continue to perform well as their jobs change.

Employees also must acquire new skills to gain promotions and undertake new jobs. Training programmes focus on giving employees' additional knowledge, behaviours and skills relating to their current jobs. Development programmes focus on helping managers improve their conceptual and interpersonal relations skills for future jobs.

In other words, training enables the employee improve his skills, adapt changes and become efficient and effective in the existing job, whereas development improves his personnel skill that enables him to perform beyond the existing job.

5.2.6 Performance Appraisal

This step compares an individual's job performance against standards or objectives developed for the individual's position. If performance is high, the individual is likely to be rewarded. If performance is low, some corrective action might be arranged to bring the performance back in line with desired standards. Performance appraisal is the systematic evaluation of the individual with respect to his performance on the job.

Performance appraisal reveals strengths and weaknesses of an employee. It depicts whether the employee has the ability to assume responsibility and can be promoted to higher position. It is the systematic process of evaluating each employee's job related strengths and weaknesses as well as determining ways to improve performance. Performance appraisal helps managers to distinguish between good and poor performers.

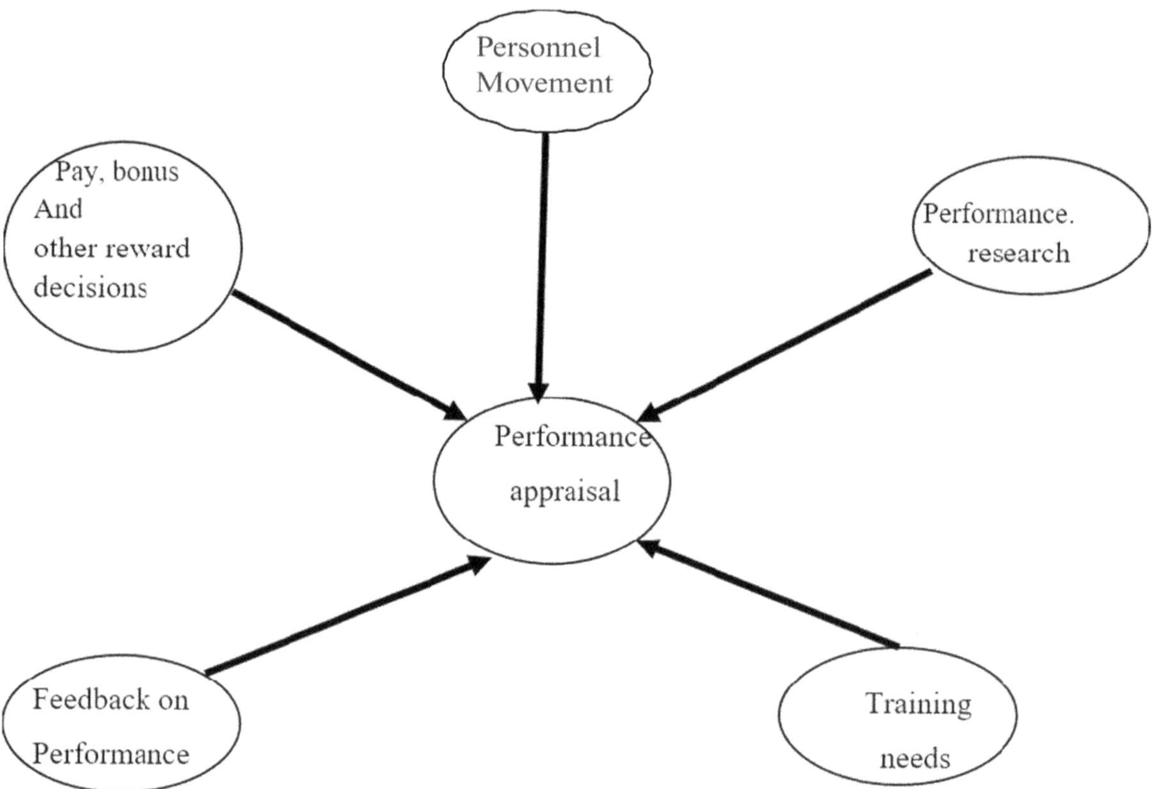

Figure 5.1 Performance Appraisal.
source: adopted from: Meyer, Herbert H., Emanuel Kay, and John RP French. "Split roles in performance appraisal." Psychology and Industrial Productivity. Palgrave Macmillan, London, 1981. 70-84.

The following are some of the important ways that managers use performance appraisal information:

a. ***Reward decisions*** – most organizations try to motivate employees by raising pay, bonuses, and other financial rewards on performance. For instance, if a factory becomes more profitable, it usually gives a bonus of employee's one-month salary freely, e.g., Mekelle –Temben –Adwa road construction employees, received a bonus of one-month salary while it was under construction.

b. ***Personnel movement*** – performance appraisal helps mangers make decisions regarding personnel movement. Who should receive a promotion? who should be transferred, demoted, or terminated?

c. ***Feedback on performance*** – a primary purpose of performance appraisal system is motivating employees to improve job performance. It provides feedback about their specific strengths and weaknesses, as well as guidelines for how to perform better.

d. ***Training needs*** – by identifying areas of poor performance, the manager can suggest training programmes to improve certain skills.

e. ***Personnel research*** – performance appraisals provide criteria for personnel research. For example, many organizations study voluntary and involuntary turnover rates to determine their impact on the organization. Whether turnover is high among poor performers and low among good performers, management can take advantage of turnover by replacing poor performers with potentially good performers.

5.2.7 Transfer, Promotion and Demotion

Transfer is a shift of a person from one job, organizational level, or location to another. It refers to changes in jobs that involve little or no change in status, responsibility and pay. It is the movement of an employee from one job or position to another within the organization without involving any significant change in the employment and status, responsibility or payment. Transfer is the movement of a person to a different job at the same or similar level of responsibility in the organization. Job transfers can be growth opportunities for the persons involved. They offer chances to broaden one's work experience, learn new skills and become more familiar with other parts of the organization. Mangers can also use transfers to get rid of a poor performing employees.

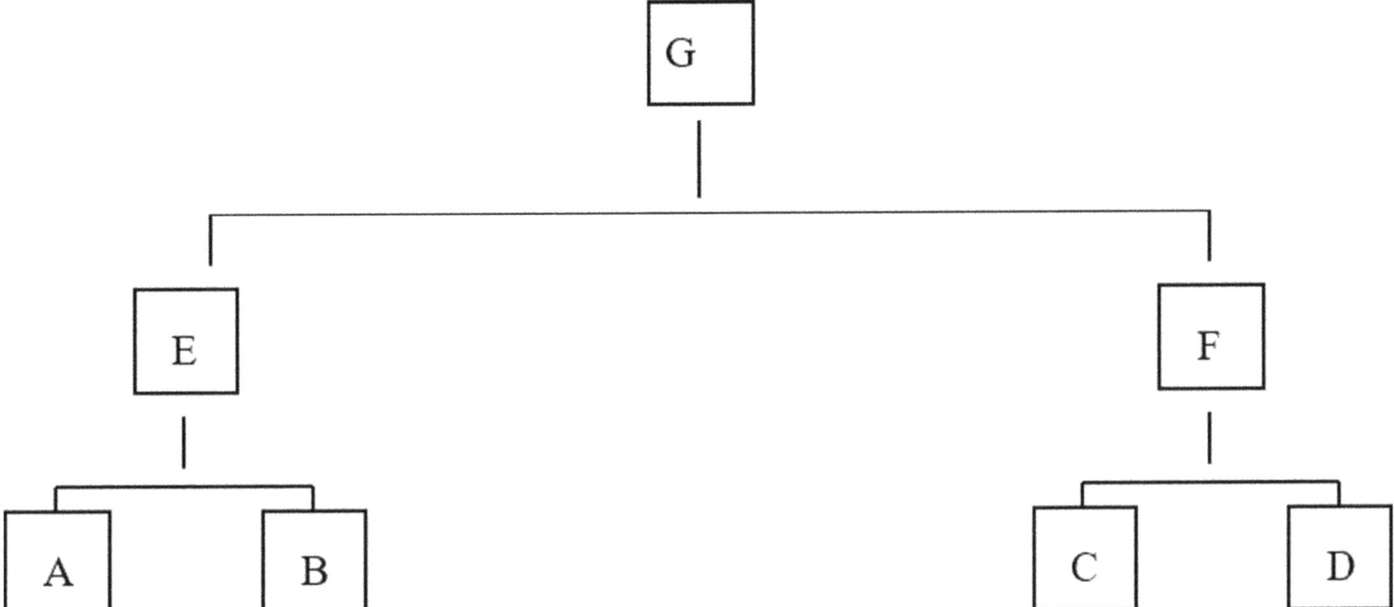

Figure 5.2 Transfer, Promotion and Demotion
Source: Bright DS, Cortes AH, Hartmann E, Parboteeah KP, Pierce JL, Reece M, Shah A, Terjesen S, Weiss J, White MA, Gardner DG. Principles of management. OpenStax; 2019 Mar 20.

i) ***Promotion***– refers to a shift for advancement of an employee to a higher job with more payment and prestige, higher status and higher responsibility. It is the movement of the person to a higher-level position within the organization. It is the advancement of an employee to better job – better in terms of responsibilities, more prestige or status, greater skill, higher grade, salary and increased privileges also.

   Every organization should have a properly devised promotion policy, so that when vacancy arises not only it can avoid the possible difficulties but it can also execute it properly. Otherwise, the process of promotion may be done in a haphazard manner resulting in many undesirable consequences.

   A sound promotion policy should be based on factors:

   1. Merit – appraisal of current and past performance (efficiency and effectiveness of the worker to accomplish assigned task).
   2. Seniority – length of service or experience of the employee.
   3. Ability – perceived capacity to perform higher level work.

ii) ***Movement Demotion***– refers to a shift of an employee to a lower position in the hierarchy due to inefficiency and incompetence to fulfil assigned tasks. It is the reverse of promotion.

If A and D interchange their positions we call it lateral transfer and if A is, placed on E, it is called promotion and if E is place at A's position it is called demotion.

5.2.8 Separations

Involves to those factors that bring the termination or ceasing to the relationship between the organization and the workers. The term separation includes resignations, layoffs, dismissals, and retirements or discharges.

Separations – arise for a variety of reasons as desire to live in another part of the country, competitive job offers at increased salary, or more challenging work, etc. Layoffs are temporary separations resulting from business slowdowns due to reduced sales, plant conversions, or physical relocation of facilities. Dismissals are separations initiated by the organization, generally as a result of poor performance or flagrant and repeated violations of rules. A major cause of separation is retirement.

In general, the contemporary recruitment, selection and placement procedures are systematic, professional and technical in character and they are designed not only to place the right man on the right job but also to see that there is enduring employee and employer relationship.

Review Questions

1. What is staffing?
2. What are the processes of staffing?
3. How do organizations attract a pool of candidates for recruitment?
4. What are the methods of recruitment?
5. What are the reasons for training?
6. Discuss the advantages of train the staff?
7. What are the benefits of performance appraisal?
8. How do organizations train their employees?
9. What are the reasons for separation in most of the Ethiopian organizations?

Short Case:

You are working for manufacturing company located in Ethiopia, the company producing a variety of products and serving a different type of client with different requirements and classes, your company looking for customer service officer to serve a high class customers. Therefore, the company determined the conditions and requirements that should be available on the candidate. outlines the steps should be incorporated in selection process.

CHAPTER SIX

DIRECTING (LEADING)

     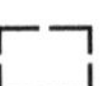 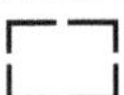

LEARNING OBJECTIVES

After studying this chapter, you should be able to:

1. Explain directing (leading) and its importance for business and life.
2. describe the characteristics of effective leaders.
3. Discuss the different types of leadership and its characteristics.
4. explain the sources of leader power and how leaders influence others.
5. Explain the contemporary leadership styles and related issues

Overview:

This chapter explores the topic of directing (leading) as one of most important topics in management. The chapter discuss the core concepts of directing, elements of directing, motivational factors, theories of Motivation, leadership styles characteristics, advantages of each style and disadvantages and consider how leaders influence others to get things done. also, this chapter discusses servant leadership and moral leadership.

6.1 Definition

All the managerial functions accomplish little if managers do not know how to lead people and to understand the human factor in their operations in such a way as to produce results. Directing is the part of the management function, which actuates the organization members to work efficiently and effectively for the attainment of organization's objectives. It constitutes the life – spark of the enterprise, which like electric power sets into motion. Planning, organizing, staffing are merely preparations for doing the work. The work actually starts when the managers start performing the directing function.

Directing is the interpersonal aspect of management, which deals directly with influencing, guiding, supervising and motivating the subordinates for the accomplishment of pre-determined objectives. Directing is a very difficult function because it deals with the complex human element of the organization, represents a complex of forces about which not much is known. It offers tremendous challenges with human beings. A person's belief, behaviour, satisfaction, and interaction with other persons are involved in the directing process. Leading is the most visible aspect of management. Even though leadership is the most visible part of the manager's job, it is still one of the least understood and agreed upon – no doubt because it deals so much with people. A variety of names for the term leading as actuating, initiating, directing, guiding, commanding and inspiring are usually frequently used.

Leading and being a manager are not one and the same thing to be a manager means to act effectively in the comprehensive sense of planning, organizing, leading and controlling. Leadership success is a necessary but not sufficient condition for managerial success. A good manager is always a good leader, but a good leader is not necessarily a good manager.

Directing is an interpersonal aspect of management, which deals with influencing and motivating or causing people to perform certain tasks intended to achieve the specified objectives. Directing is the manager's use of power to influence the behaviour of other persons in the work setting. *Power* in turn is the ability to get someone else to do something you want done.

There is a predominant feeling that directing is more of an art than it is a science. A capacity to enlist full measures of energy, enthusiasm, and ability of all employees toward a given objective is the vital mark of a successful manager. Directing function deals with the human factor, so it is a very delicate as well as difficult function.

6.2 Elements of Directing

Directing function consists of three elements. These are:

1. Motivation
2. Leadership, and
3. Communication

6.2.1 Motivation

The goal and mission of the organization can be achieved if the different departmental activities are directed to the common goal. This can be done if the manager knows what motivates people. If employees are not motivated, they will not perform effectively. Motivation is not the only factor that affects performance, but it is a major determinant of performance. Therefore, it is vital to the organization for manager to understand how to motivate employees.

What is Motivation?

It is difficult concept to define. A ***motive*** is an inner force that moves a person to behave in a certain way. A motive is a particular need or desire, a psychological force, inner force within our mind, setting us in motion to fulfil our need or desire. In essence motives or needs are the main springs of action. Motive implies action to satisfy a need. Motives are expressions of a person's needs. Motives are his/her inner drives.

Motivation is the process by which behaviour is energized and directed toward goal-oriented action. Motivation is the need or drive whit in an individual that drives him/her toward goal – oriented action. For example, a student may possess a strong need or want to perform well in a course, which will drive that student to study diligently to receive the goal of an A grade.

A *motive* "is an inner state that energizes, activates, or moves and that directs or channels behaviour toward goals. In other words, motivation is a general term applying to the entire class of drives, desires, needs, wishes and similar forces. To say that managers motivate their subordinates is to say that they do those things which they hope will satisfy these drives and desires and induce subordinates to act in a desired manner.

Motivators are things, which induce an individual to perform. A motivator is something that influences an individual's behaviour. Motivators are the identified rewards, incentives or things that sharpen the drive to satisfy these wants. A manager can do much to sharpen motives by establishing an environment conducive to certain drives. That is, a manager can enhance the drives by creating favourable condition in the working environment.

People can often satisfy their wants in a variety of ways. What a manager must do, of course, is to use those motivators, which will lend people to perform effectively for the enterprise. Therefore, a manager has to discover the needs and desires of the workers and through them he can motivate them as a result performance will be increased.

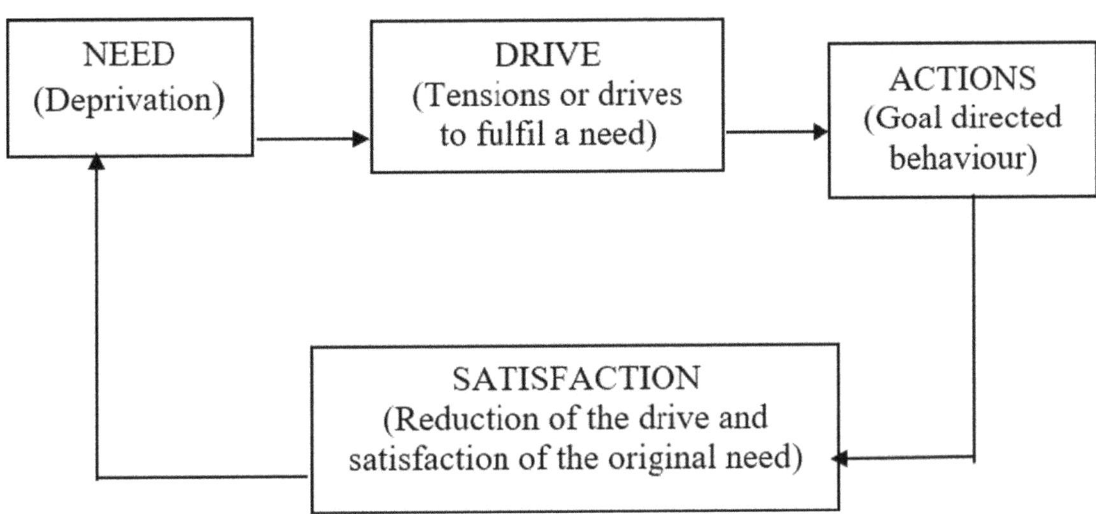

Figure 6.1 Model of Motivation.
Source: Bright DS, Cortes AH, Hartmann E, Parboteeah KP, Pierce JL, Reece M, Shah A, Terjesen S, Weiss J, White MA, Gardner DG. Principles of management. OpenStax; 2019 Mar 20.

If managers are to motivate subordinates they have to understand the factors within individuals that motivate them and cause them to act in a desired way. Every manager has to attempt to answer questions as: what needs do people try to satisfy? What impels them to action? Individuals have inner needs that they are motivated to reduce or fulfil. That is, individuals will act or behave in ways that will lead to the satisfaction of their needs.

Major Theories of Motivation

Abraham H. Maslow's Hierarchy of Needs Theory

One of the most widely used models for studying motivation within organizations is Abraham Maslow's hierarchy – of – needs. A psychologist, Maslow suggested that people have a complex set of needs. He arranged these needs (placed by Maslow)in order of importance, as illustrated below. Maslow theorized that people are driven by several needs, not just one. These can be categorized into five hierarchies of needs. The basic human needs (placed by Maslow) in an ascending order of importance as illustrated below. Maslow theorized that people are driven by several needs, not just one. The basic human needs as identified by Maslow arranged in an ascending order of importance are the following.

1. **Physiological needs** – are the basic needs for sustaining human life itself – food, water, clothing, shelter, sleep, and sexual satisfaction. Until these needs are satisfied to the degree necessary to maintain (preserve) life, other needs will not motivate people. People try to satisfy physiological needs (physical needs) first. For example, the primary motivation of a very hungry person is to obtain food, before attempting to meet higher order needs.

   A hungry person thinks of food and dream about food and is restless till this basic want is reasonably satisfied. Managers seeking to motivate subordinates by addressing physiological needs assume that people work primarily for money, which allows them to obtain food and shelter for themselves (and their dependents). Many people, especially in Third World Countries, are deprived of the means to satisfy these basic needs. A manager can motivate people through these needs by offering adequate wages and salary, and other economic incentives.

2. **Security or safety needs** – These are the needs to be free of physical danger and the fear of loss of a job, property, food or shelter. These are the needs for safety and stability as well as an absence of pain, threat, or illness, the desire for a stable job with medical care. unemployment and retirement benefits etc. Manager can satisfy such needs by providing insurance, retirement benefits, unemployment compensation etc.

3. **Social or affiliation needs** – since people are social beings, they need to belong, to be accepted by others. These are the needs for belongingness, friendship, love, association etc. Social needs include the need to talk to others, to associate with others, to express feelings of friendship, to accept and be accepted. When an organization doesn't meet affiliation needs, an employee's dissatisfaction may take the form of frequent absenteeism, low productivity, high levels of stress, and even emotional breakdown. Managers who recognize when subordinates are striving to satisfy affiliated needs may act in supportive ways. They may encourage co-workers to accept one another and to participate in company – organized social activities such as company sports programs and picnics. By fostering social relations, the organization satisfies affiliation needs within the work group. Also by allowing coffee breaks, providing lunch facilities and offering recreational activities.

4. **Esteem needs** – are the needs for self-respect a sense of personal achievement, and recognition from others. This kind of need produces such satisfaction as power, prestige, status and self-confidence. In satisfying these needs, people seek opportunities for achievement, promotion prestige and status that will provide recognition of their competence and worth.

   Managers who wish to motivate employees through esteem needs, they may publicly reward achievement with published performance lists, bonuses, pats on the back, lapel pins, and articles in the company paper. These and other forms of recognition help to promote employee pride. Also by providing job titles, privileged parking, private secretaries, promotions, opportunities for achievement etc.

5. **Self-actualisation needs** – is the highest needed in the hierarchy of needs. It is the desire to become what one is capable of becoming. It is the stage of realizing one's full potential. Doing what one wants to do with one's life is called self-actualisation.

   Managers who wish to motivate such individuals may make the individuals to discover the growth opportunities inherent in their jobs, involving employees in the decision making process, restructuring jobs, or offering special assignments that call for special skills.

2. Herzberg's Two – Factor Motivation Theory

Maslow's need theory has been considerably modified by Frederick Herzberg and his associates. Herzberg's research purports to find a two-factor explanation of motivation. It is also called dual – factor theory and the motivation hygiene theory of motivation. His original study was based on intensive interviews with 200 engineers and accountants. As a result of his interviews two groups of factors influence workers' feelings about their jobs: ***motivators*** and ***hygiene***.

i. Hygiene factors or "job context" factors.

Company policy and administration, technical supervision, salary working conditions, interpersonal relations, status, security, and personal life. These were found by Herzberg and his associates to be only "***dissatisfiers***" and not motivators. If they exist in sufficient or in high quantity and quality, they yield no dissatisfaction. Their existence doesn't motivate in the sense of yielding satisfaction; their lack of existence would, however, result in dissatisfaction.

Dissatisfaction is not simply the opposite of satisfaction or motivation, i.e., a person who is not dissatisfied is not necessarily motivated, but simply a neutral feeling. Their adequate availability do not produce high motivation. Improvements in hygiene factors can prevent and /or help eliminate job dissatisfaction; they will not improve job satisfaction, i.e., job satisfaction and job dissatisfaction are two separate dimensions.

ii. The satisfiers (motivators) or "job content factors"

Include factors such as achievement, recognition, challenging work, advancement and growth in the job. Their existence will yield feelings of satisfaction. Improvements in satisfier factors can increase job satisfaction. Manager's goal should be to correct poor hygiene to eliminate any sources of job dissatisfaction and to build satisfiers to maximize opportunities for job satisfaction or motivation.

To generalize

Motivators (job content factors)

a. When absent, prevent both satisfaction and motivation.
b. When present, lead to satisfaction and motivation.

Hygiene (job context) factors

a. When absent, increase dissatisfaction with the job.
b. When present, prevent dissatisfaction but don't increase their satisfaction or motivation.

MC Gregor's Theory X and Theory Y

Douglas McGregor identified two styles of management, theory –X (autocratic), and theory – y (participative). Douglas Mc Gregor postulates two sets of beliefs, popularly referred to as Theory X and Theory Y that leaders may have regarding subordinates. According to McGregor, the beliefs as assumptions that a manager or leader makes about people can be described as follows.

Theory – X manager

Theory – X manager assumes

1. The typical (average) employees dislike work and will avoid it if they can. Because they dislike work, most subordinates must be controlled, or threatened with punishment to get them exert effort toward the achievement of the goal.
2. Average human beings prefer to be directed and be led than to lead to avoid the instances of being irresponsible and less ambitious.
3. People by their very nature are lacking ambition.
4. People by their very nature are irresponsible

Since, theory – X visualizes the workers as inherently lazy, passive and unambitious, they have to be strictly handled, supervised and controlled. Subordinates shouldn't be left themselves to carry out their jobs. Leaders autocratically have to lead and push subordinates to have an effective work.

Theory- Y manager assumes that

1. Average people are naturally willing to work.
2. Average people are willing to accept responsibility. Under proper condition, they are not only willing to accept but also seek responsibility.
3. Average employees who are committed to the company's objectives will exercise self-direction and self-control.
4. Average people are capable of imagination, ingenuity, and creativity towards the solution of organizational problems. They have capacity to exercise relatively high degree of imagination, ingenuity and creativity in the solution of organizational problems, that management can't monopolize initiative ness and creativity.

Therefore, managers have to allow subordinates to participate in decision-making process. They have to permit more participation, freedom and responsibility in their work. Democratic leaders encourage their employees to participate in the decision making process, emphasis is shifted from punishment to reward. Communication flows openly from both leader and subordinate while in theory – X, it flows from superior to subordinate.

6.2.2 Leadership

Leadership is the art or process of influencing people so that they will strive willingly and enthusiastically toward the achievement of group goals. Leadership is an ability to influence, inspire, and direct the actions of a person or group toward attaining desired objective. Leadership is the process of influencing group activities toward the setting and achievement of goals. Ideally, people should be encouraged to develop not only willingness to work but also willingness to work with zeal and confidence.

Nature of Leadership

The characteristics of leadership are:

1. Leadership is a process of influence exercised by the leader on group members. Successful leaders are able to influence the behaviour, attitude and beliefs of their followers. Leaders must have followers, i.e., one can't be a leader unless there are people to be led. Leaders have to have power to influence followers than followers have to influence the leaders. Leaders have to be able to change the behaviours of the led.
2. Leadership is related to a particular situation at a given point and time.
3. A successful leader has to be able to subordinate the individual interests of the followers to the general interest of the group.
4. A leader is a representative of his group and works to protect the interest of its members. He shares information, experience with subordinates.

Leadership Levels

The leadership levels is based on Jim Collins, et al., 2001.five level of leadership were identified the critical importance of what Collins calls Level 5 leadership in transforming companies from merely good to truly great organizations.

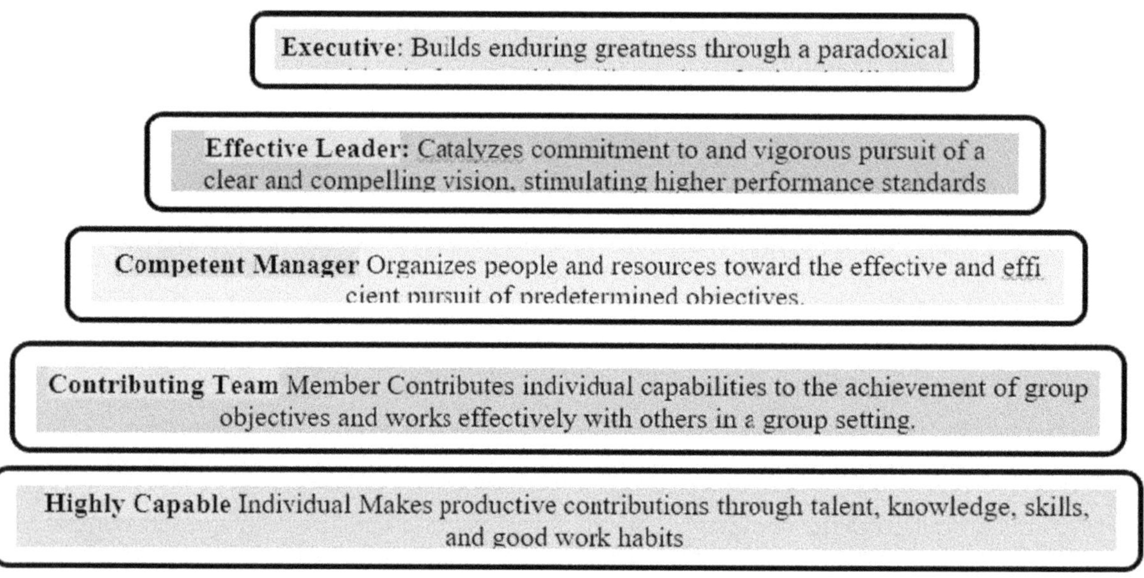

Figure 6.2 Leadership Levels.
Source: **Adapted from:** Jim Collins, Good to Great: Why Some Companies Make the Leap... and Others Don't (New York: Harper Collins, 2001)

Theories of Leadership

There are three basic approaches to leadership

1. Trait theories of leadership
2. Followers theories of leadership
3. Situational (contingency) theories of leadership

1. Trait Theory of Leadership

This is the traditional theory of leadership. It believes that a leader possesses certain in born special traits, which are inherited rather than acquired. It explains leadership in terms of personal or physical qualities (characteristics). They view that leaders are born not made, is in fact still popular among lay persons. Leaders as a group have been found to be brighter, more extroverted, self-confident than non-leaders. They also tend to be taller. However, although millions of people have these traits, most of them obviously will never attain leadership position.

Physical attributes may be helpful in the physical performance of some jobs (such as the police or military), but effective leadership rarely depends in a person's height and weight. In general, this approach has not been a very fruitful approach in explaining leadership. Not all leaders possess all the traits, and many non-leaders may possess most or all of them. Also, it doesn't give any guidance as to how much of any trait a person should have. This approach is based on the assumption that certain identifiable physical, social and personal characteristics are inherent in leaders. That is, the presence or absence of these characteristics (traits) distinguished leaders from non-leaders.

2. The follower's Theory of Leadership

It maintains that leaders are chosen by the group for their ability to help solve the group tasks. It believes that leadership is a function of acceptance from followers. It states that if the leader is able to develop and mountain a group, the leader is able to give them supportive relationships, and the leader is capable of motivating them, then he is a good leader.

The major emphasis is an acceptance by the group (followers), i.e., a leader here is a means of achieving the goals of the group.

3. The Situational (Contingency) Theory of Leadership

Leadership is strongly affected by the situation from which a leader emerges and in which he works. There is no one best style of leadership universally applicable for the situations. Each leadership style is effective when used in the right situation. Therefore, a manager has to understand the situation to have a good match between the leadership style and the situation. Leadership is a function of the leader, the follower, and the situation. Successful leadership depends on matching the leader's style to the situation's demands.

Leadership Styles

Leadership style is the behavioural pattern in which a leader adopts. Leadership style in a particular situation is determined by the leader's personality experience, nature of followers and the environment. Leader's personalities refers to the traits of a leader such as brave, more aggressive more decisive and more articulate, intelligence, their self-confidence, extroversion, judgment, etc. for example, intelligence and verbal ability are important traits for an English teacher. Leadership style – is the typical or consistent behaviour that a leader tends to use while interacting with subordinates (the led). Broadly speaking, there are three basic styles of leadership

1. Autocratic or Dictatorial leadership (I-approach)

The autocratic leader gives orders, which he insists shall be obeyed, i.e., employees are expected to follow orders. An autocratic leader determines policies for the group without consulting the subordinates and believes in "carrot and stick" rule to motivate the subordinates. The autocratic leader was seen as one who commands and expects compliance, who is dogmatic and positive and who leads by the ability to withhold or give rewards and punishment. He/she assumes full responsibility for all actions. He/she determines plans and policies. He/she freely uses threats of punishment and penalty for motivation and obedience. It may work in the short run, e.g., in emergency or war. When we have untrained, undisciplined, illiterate and unorganised labour, it may also be effective.

Here, subordinates have no scope to influence the decision of the leader. It demoralizes them, retards their growth, and lowers the quality of performance. There is no scope to develop managers; it only creates messengers. An autocratic, non-participative leadership is apparently most effective (especially if benevolent) when decisions are routine, there are standard procedures and rules, and subordinates don't feel an urge to participate.

2. Democratic or Participative Leadership – We Approach

The democratic leader allows the group members to participate in decision-making process. Members are considered as very important entities. There is sharing of ideas, information and decision making activities with subordinates. The leader believes in maintaining good human relations with subordinates and encourages participation in all levels. A leader draws ideas and suggestions from his groups by discussion, consultation, and participation.

Participation in decision-making assures better labour management relations, higher morale, greater job satisfaction and reduced dependence in the leader. We have two-way flow of communication. Under democratic leadership

- There is greater employee and group cooperation.
- There is greater employee and group employee and group satisfaction
- Higher employee morale
- Improved decision making, planning and organization
- Recognition of human relations
- Highest personal growth and development of employees.

Democratic leadership can win easily confidence, cooperation, loyalty as well as initiative of the group. Supportive participative leadership is apparently more effective when decisions are nor routine, information and rules for decision-making are not standardized, and subordinates feel the need and urge for independence, initiative and self-expression, and their participation is legitimate. When supportive leadership is combined with efficient managerial functions, we have both high productivity and high satisfaction.

3. Laissez – Faire or Free – rein Leadership (Abdicative or They approach)

The leader uses his/her power very little, if at all, giving subordinates a high degree of independence, or "free rein" in their operations. The leader depends entirely on his subordinates to establish their goals and the means to achieve them. He lets them plan, organize and proceed. The leader becomes just another member of the group. He becomes merely an information booth. He is on the position of a leader just to supply information, materials etc with minimum control. This is also known as permissive style of leadership, where there is least intervention by the leader.

Free – rein leadership is suitable for highly trained and professional staff. They are creative, self-motivated, require minimum guidance and control. Such leaders perceive their roles as one of facilitating the operations of followers by furnishing them information and acting primarily as a contract with the group's external environment.

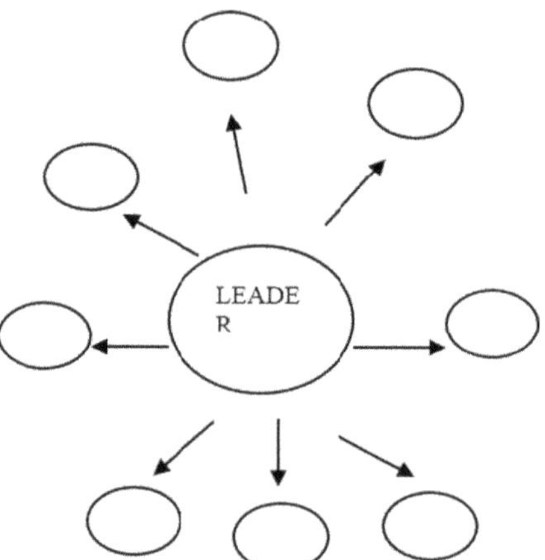

Figure 6.3 Autocratic leadership (Down ward communication only).

Summary points about the types of leadership

Features of autocratic leadership

1. Issues of orders to subordinates

2. Leader – decision maker
3. One – way communication
4. Implicit obedience
5. Emphasis on negative incentives - fear – punishment
6. "I" style

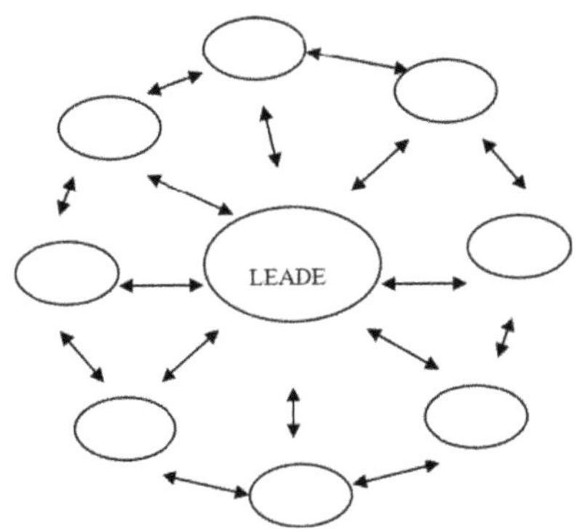

Figure 6.4 Participative leadership (Multidirectional Communication).

Features of participative leadership

1. Interchange of ideas and two – way communication Fig.6.4
2. Participation in decision making process
3. Emphasis on satisfaction of Egoistic (psychic) wants
4. Scope for use of human creativity and initiative
5. Recognition of human values "We" style

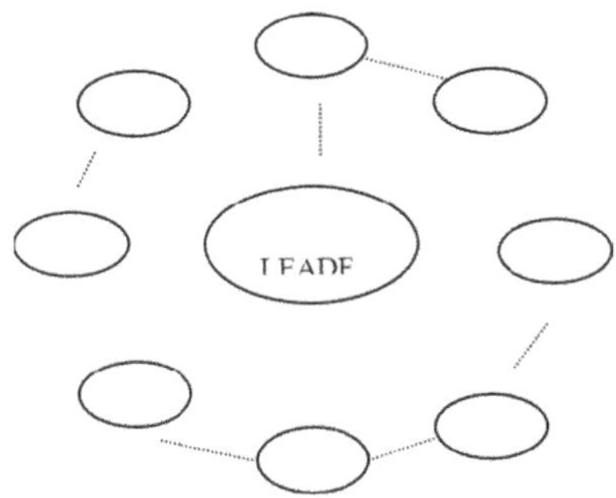

Figure 6.5 Laissez faire leadership (Information, material supplied when needed).

Features of laissez faire leadership

1. Complete freedom for group or individual decision
2. Leader furnishes leadership when asked
3. Leader - information supplies when asked
4. Complete non participation by leader in determining tasks and companions
5. No appraisal, control, etc.
6. "You" style

Leadership is a relationship existing and affected by:

(1) The leader – his/her personality
(2) The led – the group of followers with their problems, needs and attitudes.
(3) The situation in which the leader and the led react with one another.

Review questions

1. What is leading or directing?
2. Leading is considered to be the most challenging management function. Explain.
3. What are the elements of leading?
4. What is motivation? How do managers motivate their subordinates? Discuss by explaining the theories of motivation.
5. What is leadership? What are the types of leadership styles? Which style do you prefer? Why?

6.2.3 Communication

Learning Objective:

1. Understand the concept, scope and significance of the communication.
2. understand the principles & techniques of business communication.

3. Develop the skills effective and real time communication.
4. discuss the different elements and steps of communication.

Overview

This section covers the nature and scope of communication Meaning, Significance for business, communication process, Types of Communication, elements of Communication, and importance of communication.

Communication concept

Communication is the exchange of information between two or more people in a way that creates understanding. It is the transfer of information from the sender to the receiver with the information being understood by the receiver. Communication is an exchange of facts, opinions, ideas or emotions between two or more persons. Communication is the process by which people attempt to share meaning via the transmission of symbolic messages. Communication promotes managerial efficiency and performance. Communication helps to gain acceptance of organizational rules, policies by subordinates. Communication helps in bringing harmony between the management and subordinates. It brings in cooperation of others to the organization. Communication helps to have a clear understanding of ideas, instructions by the subordinates. It can bring the desired change in performance by criticizing mistakes, by introducing new methods of performance and being communicated to the subordinates the organization can obtain the desired performance. In general, communication is the life – blood of an organization (Bovee, 2011).

The Communication Process

Communication takes place in the relationship between a sender and a receiver. It can flow in one direction and ends there.

A model of the communication process:

1. **People** – play the role of
   - ***Sender*** (encoder) – is the source of information and the initiator of the idea or message. The sender encodes the message
   - *Encoding* is translating thoughts, ideas or feelings into a series of symbols for communication. For example, you may want your letter to convey certain ideas and impressions and to explain why you are interested in that company. You also want to provide background information about your qualifications for the job and how you believe the job will further your career. When you transfer these ideas to paper, you are encoding your message. Encoding is necessary because information can only be transferred from one person to another through representations or symbols usually in the form of words, gestures that the sender believes to have the meaning for the receiver.
   - ***Receiver*** (decoder) – the person who perceive the sender's message or the person who reads, listens or observes the senders message or idea.
   - "Decoder" – translates the message of the receiver into a form that has meaning to the receiver.
   - *Decoding – is the process by which the receiver interprets the message and translates it into meaningful information.*

Receive Transmit

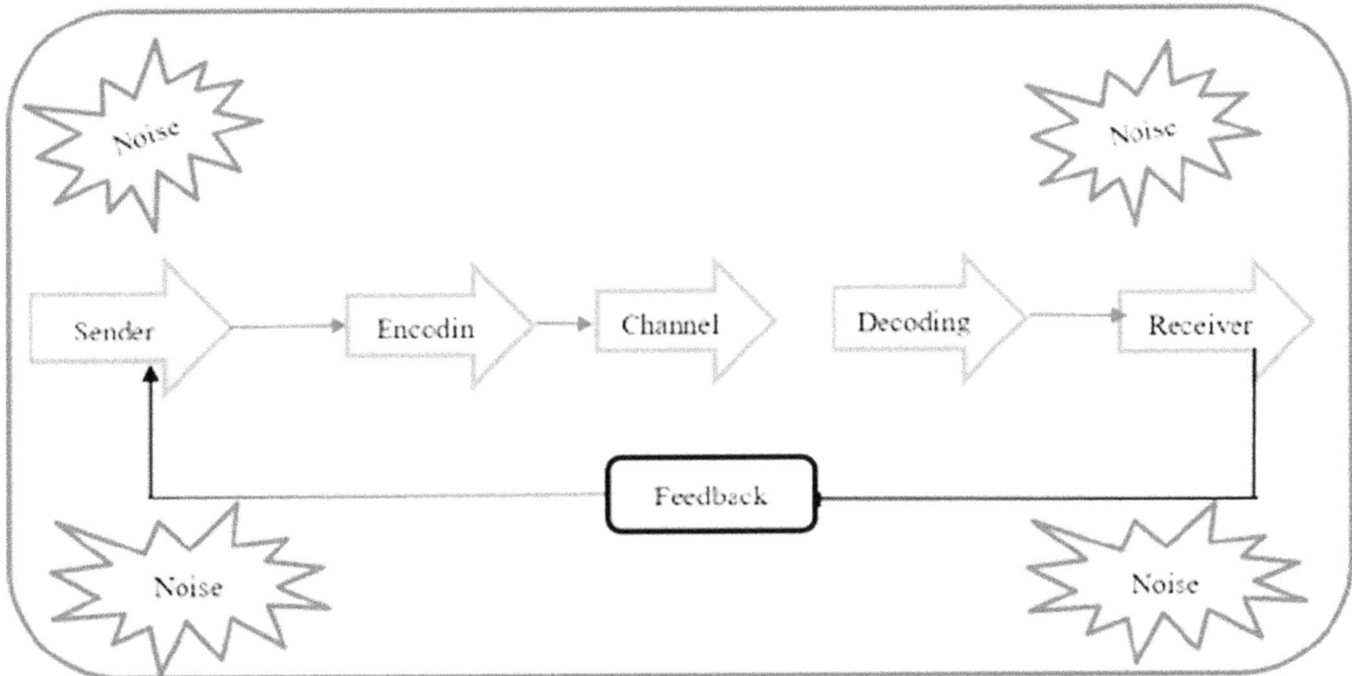

Figure 6.6 Elements of communication process.
Source: adopted from: Lillico, T. Michael. Managerial communication. Elsevier, 2016.

It is a twostep process; the receiver must first perceive the message then interpret it.

2. **The message** – the encoded information sent by the sender to the receiver. Message is the physical form into which the sender encodes. Messages could be:
   - ***Verbal symbols***
     - written – letters, books, periodicals, circulars, manuals, newspapers, posters, advertisements, suggestion schemes, etc.
     - Oral – telephone, radio, face – to face communication, interviews, meetings, conferences and seminars are conducted orally.
   - ***Non-verbal messages***
     All messages that are not spoken or written are nonverbal messages – gestures, facial expressions (smile, red face), nodding a head, eye contact, coming early, staying later in the office etc.
     For instance for something to do, you glance around the room – and at the other end of your row (student) an attractive student of the opposite sex is staring at you.
     - You look away
     - The other looks away quickly
     - You glance back
     - The other glances back
     - You smile faintly
     - You incline your head toward the professor and roll your eyes.

- The other smiles wider and nodes once.
- You glance toward the door.
- The other looks at you, then at the clock, then at the door.

3. **Channels** – is the path a message flows from the sender to the receiver, such as air for spoken words and paper for letters.

   For communication to be effective and efficient the channel must be appropriate for the message. When a phone conversation would be an unsuitable channel for transmitting a complex engineering diagram, express – mail might be more appropriate.

4. **Feedback** – is the receiver's response to the sender's message. It is the receiver's reaction to the message sending back to the sender. It is the reversal of communication process in which a reaction to the sender's communication is expressed. Since the receiver has become the sender, feedback goes through the same steps as the original communication. It is the best way to demonstrate that a message has been received and whether it has been understood.

5. **Noise** – is any element or activity that disturbs, confuses, or makes communication process more difficult. It is an interference with the flow of a message that hinders the message from being understood clearly and accurately. For example radio signals may be distorted by bad weather. Rain may disturb communication bad handwriting hinders from being understood the message. Therefore, if your handwriting is not legible, you need to recognize that you are placing a noise that hinders communication. The noise can be in the sender, in the channel or in the receiver.

   Managers must attempt to reduce noise whenever and wherever possible to improve the quality and accuracy of the message.

Types of communication

1. Based on the relationship between the sender and the receiver
   i. Formal communication channels – the communication flows following the structure of the organization.
   ii. Informal communication channels – the communication does not follow the formal structure or goes in the form of grapevine. Grapevine is the organization's informal communication system. Grapevine carries information (messages) based on social interaction. It is a rumour gossip talk or hearsay
2. Based on the flow of information
   i. Down – ward communication – It is sending of message to lower organizational levels like orders, instructions, directives, information, counselling interviews, lectures, conferences etc.
   ii. Up – ward communication – transmission of information (message) from subordinates to supervisors like reports, ideas, suggestions, complaints, grievances, protests, etc.
   iii. Side way Communication
      a. Horizontal – lateral communication or it occurs among persons working at the same level in the hierarchy of authority.
      b. Diagonal – communication with persons at different levels who have no direct reporting relationships.
3. On the basis of the methods used
   i. Verbal – oral and written
   ii. Non-verbal – gestures, body movements, etc.

Importance of Effective Communication

Effective communication is important to managers for three primary reasons.

- Communication provides a common thread for the management processes of planning, organizing, leading, and controlling.

- Effective communications skills can enable managers to draw on the vast array of talents available in the multicultural world of organizations.
- Managers spend a great deal of time by communicating face-to face, electronic or telephone communication with employees, supervisors, suppliers or customers (Markaki., Sakas, and Chadjipantelis., 2013).

Review questions

1. What is communication? What is its importance to a manager?
2. Discuss the processes of communication.
3. Discuss the types of communication.
4. Mention four (4) advantages of effective communication in a business firm.
5. Today's business depends mainly on technology, and among what technology has provided is email as mean for communication. Mention three (3) justification of why or why not agree with this statement.
6. Discuss the challenges of communication in working environment today.
7. Describe how managers can improve communication in their organizations.
8. How can you describe the impact of social media on communication within the organization?

Short Project:

1. Visit a service company locating close to you or the company that you are working for and conduct a simple analysis of an communication directions (upward and downward) analyse the means of information exchange, also analyse informal communication and which is more applied (formal or informal communication).

Short Case:

Maria is managing a medium-size company offering a consultation service. She is a hard worker with good experience. However, many of Maria's clients started to complain because of some issues related to the consultation reports; Maria directly reported that to the responsible person in the company, the head of report and support but, he refused to accept what Maria reported in front of the other staff members and some clients. How do you assess the way of communication and the response?

CHAPTER SEVEN

CONTROLLING

      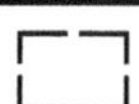

LEARNING OBJECTIVES

After studying this chapter, you should be able to:

1. Explain the meaning of controlling.
2. Explain the steps in the process of controlling.
3. Define organizational control, and identify the main output and behavior controls managers use to coordinate and motivate employee.

Overview

The objectives of this lesson are to enable to define management; to describe the nature and scope of management; to know the difference between management and administration; to understand various levels of management; and to describe the various skills that are necessary for successful managers.

7.1 The Nature of Control

Of all the management functions discussed previously, controlling comes last because it applies to each of the others. Without some way to monitor the execution of plans, managers would not know whether their work was effective or efficient. People and processes must be monitored to prevent, detect, and correct unacceptable differences between managers' expectations and actual results.

In its most basic form, *Controlling* is the management function in which managers set and communicate performance standards for people, processes, and devices. A *standard* is any guideline or benchmark established as the basis for the measurement of capacity, quantity, content, value, cost, quality, or performance. Whether quantitative or qualitative, standards must be precise, explicit, and formal statements of the expected result. Once those who must abide by standards understand and can apply them, standards serve as mechanisms to prevent and detect unacceptable deviations from plans. Standards may be applied to people and processes before, during, and after work is performed.

This chapter will examine the need for controls, the control process, general types and characteristics of controls, and methods for making controls effective and efficient.

In the series of managerial functions, planning is the first function and controlling is the last. Success in business is very often proportionate to the astuteness of its planning and the skill with which it is controlled. Plans can be effectively achieved in most organizations only with good controls, and planning is always pre-requisite for controlling. Planning seeks to set goals and programs and control seek to secure performance in accordance with plans.

Definition

a. According to Koontze and O'donnell (1998), "The managerial function of control is the measurement and correction of the performance of activities of subordinates in order to make sure that enterprise objectives and the plans devised to attain them are being accomplished. It's thus the function of every manager, from the chief executive to the Forman."

b. Controlling is also defined as the process by which management sees if what did happen was what was supposed to happen. If not, necessary adjustments are made.

An analysis of the foregoing statements regarding control brings out the controlling function of management.

i) Planning is the foundation of control:

Planning sets the course, control observes deviations from the course, and takes corrective action.

ii) Action's the essence of control:

Control terminates in taking corrective action where there is a deviation in performance from the desired goals.

iii) Delegation is the key to control:

Control is exercised by taking action, and action can be taken within the authority delegated. Accountability must be within the authority given to the manager.

iv) Information is the guide to control:

Control exercised by a manager on the basis of the information and reports from those actively doing the job. Such reports and information may be described as "feed-back" from subordinates. Feedback enables the manager to determine how far the operations.

7.2 Controlling and the other management functions

As Bittel (1989) noted: "Controlling is the function that brings the management cycle full circle. It is the steering mechanism that links all the preceding functions or organizing staffing, and directing to the goals of planning. "The planning process determines the objectives that eventually become the foundation for controls. As the first function, planning is at the heart of all the others. The strategic objectives and plans made at the top level in an organization are derived from the organization's purpose and mission. From these plans flow the goals to be achieved by successively lower levels of management. As these plans flow the goals to be achieved by successively lower levels of management. As these plans and goals are developed, managers must establish controls to monitor progress toward them. The feedback from these controls should tell managers how each level of the organization indeed, each individual – is progressing toward the relevant goals. The feedback may indicate that progress is proceeding as planned. If progress falls short of the plan, however, the feedback should indicate that managers need to change the plan (Odiorne, 1980).

When Cadillac, a division of General Motors, introduced the all-new 1992 Sevile and EL Dorado models, demand quickly exceeded initial estimates. Managers changed the production schedule so dealers had the supply to meet the demand. Shifts in production were possible because a control mechanism allowed for feedback from dealers about customer demand.

Budgets are both plans and controls. Budgets forecast the sources and amounts of funds that will flow into an organization over a period of time and allocate funds to various activities. Equally important, budgets help guarantee that funds are received and spent as planned. a brief look at an example illustrates how important controlling is and how it affects and is affected by the other four management functions.

Planning and Controlling: Based on market research, Procter and Gamble develops a plan to create and market a new soap. The plan calls for a 15% profit and a 10% share of the soap market. Along with these plans and goals, managers design and establish controls to provide feedback about profits, costs, sales, and market penetration. The company budgets for the added processes, facilities, supplies, training, and personnel required to produce the product and bring it to market. It must also monitor the sales of its other brands of soap to determine if the new brand is capturing sales from existing products rather than from competitors.

Organizing and Controlling To accomplish its plans, Procter and Gamble modifies its organizational structure by adding a product team to launch the new soap. Senior managers delegate authority to the product–team manager, arrange to manufacture the soap in existing production facilities, and defined and delegate authority to those who will assist the new team. They create controls to monitor production and determine whether the allocation of resources and authority has been appropriate to the job.

Staffing and Controlling: To accomplish its plans, Procter and Gamble must acquire workers at all levels and place them in the new positions. (Recruitment can occur inside and outside the organization.) Managers must establish a chain of command and a compensation plan for the new team. In addition, the new team members must be trained. As part of the staffing process, a mangers create controls to evaluate the effectiveness of the recruiting, hiring, compensation, and training of the new product team and those who assist the team in manufacturing and support positions.

Directing and Controlling: Employees in many different units– production, product team, sales, customer service, and advertising, for example–must work together to accomplish the goals established by the plan and within the means specified by the budget. Managers establish controls to ensure smooth work flow and progress toward goals. In addition, managers establish controls to enforce standards. For example, managers must evaluate workers and be evaluated themselves. Each employee must receive feedback in regard to his or her performance. Managers must reward success and take corrective action when appropriate. Managers must also establish methods of monitoring rewards and corrective actions.

In addition to its relationship to the other four functions, controlling meets a very practical need. Organizations have limited resources. The successful acquisition and use of these resources determine a firm's survival. No person or organization should expend resources to achieve a goal without arranging to monitor their use.

7.3 Controls in an Organization

At every level in an organization, managers need controls to prevent problems, to monitor activities and to provide feedback about processes and people, the following couple of statements display the four primary types of controls, which monitor personnel, financial informational, and operational activity.

Personnel Controls: Managers use various tools to control human resources. Human resource inventories, job descriptions, job specifications, and performance appraisals are but a few. Statistics can also be control measures. Statistics about absenteeism, lateness, safety, and costs provide managers with valuable information about personnel.

Financial Controls: Financial controls focus on income, expenditures, cash flow, asset mix, and the acquisition and investment of funds. Financial controls are among an organizations most useful tools. They help ensure access to sufficient funding, without which no organization can achieve, its goals.

Informational Controls: These controls help managers and others get the information they need to make timely and intelligent decisions. Many organizations operate management information systems that rely heavily on electronics to collect, process, disseminate, and store information. Information must be gathered from a variety of sources, inside and outside an organization. Every individual and group must determine what information is needed. Then the individual or group must ensure that the information is received, at the right time and place, in suitable quantity, quality, and format.

Operational Controls: The fourth type of control, the operational controls, monitors anything that is not being monitored by a personnel, financial, or informational control. In general, this means that operational controls monitor the use of physical resources by every individual and group within an organization.

- Policies are adequate
- Procedures (for such activities as purchasing, payroll, maintenance, and selling) are in place, communicated properly, and effective.
- Inventories are adequate and secure
- Plans are effective
- Products and services meet internal and external customers' needs and expectations.

7.4 The Control Process

You are now ready to examine the four steps of the control process. As fig 7.1 shows, the steps are (1) establishing performance standards, (2) measuring performance, (3) comparing measured performance to established standards, and (4) taking corrective action.

7.4.1 Establishing Performance Standards

As you know, a standard is a quantitative or qualitative measuring device designed to monitor people, money, capital goods, or processes. The exact nature of a standard depends on

- Who designs, works with, and receives the output from controls
- What is being monitored
- What is to be achieved through monitoring
- Where monitoring efforts will take place (location and functional area)
- When controls will be used (before, during, or after operations)
- What resources are available to expend on the controls

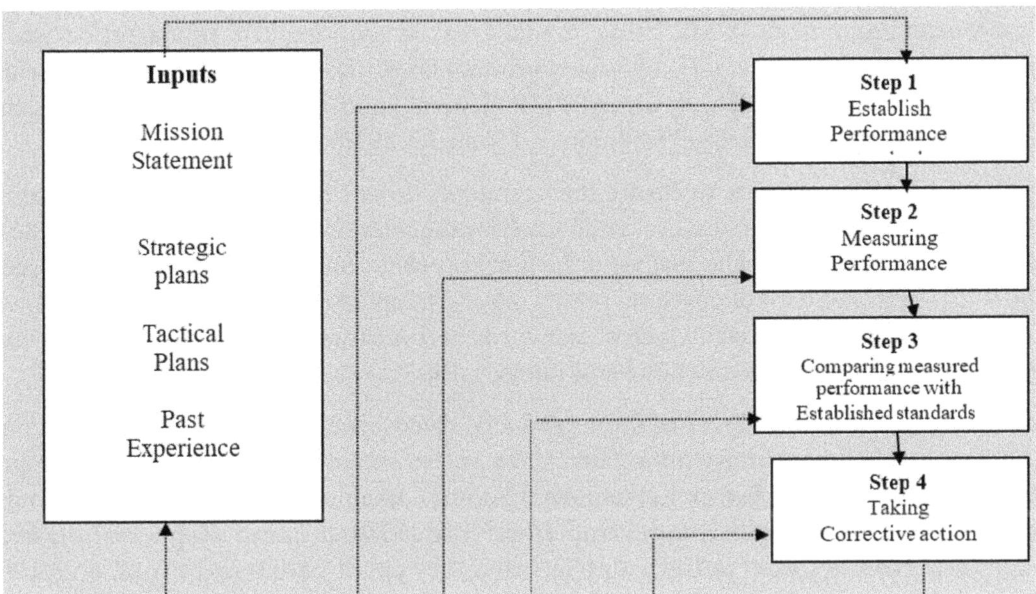

Figure 7.1 Steps in the control process there seems something missing in the diagram!
Source: Kinicki A, Williams BK, Scott-Ladd BD, Perry M. Management: A practical introduction. McGraw-Hill Irwin; 2011.

Standards and controls deal with time, costs, quality, productivity, or behaviours. Once set, standards must be continually re-evaluated to ensure that they are still necessary and valid.

Time: The goal of standards that deal with time is usually to ensure sufficient time to achieve tasks. Standards for handling inventory ensure that goods are products be delivered at a time convenient for customers. Standards about feedback ensure that information reaches decision-makers in time for them to make meaningful improvements to operations.

Time standards determine priorities, schedules, and sequences of events. Remember that to an organization, time is money. By controlling time, an organization can help control its finances.

Costs: Money is a finite resource; few organizations ever seem to have enough of it. Budgets are created on the basis of what is needed and what is available. Many projects and product ideas are cancelled for lack of funding or because they will cost more than the anticipated benefits are worth. Managers must use only the budgeted amount for each budgeted activity or less, if possible. Like time, costs must be managed to get the most from each dollar.

Quality: Quality can be defined as how well the features and characteristics of a product or service satisfy customers' needs. Quality should be designed into processes, products, and services from their inception. The commitment to quality must be part of an organization's culture, and it must start with top managers. The top managers should involve everyone (including suppliers) in the quest for quality and use feedback from customers as one aspect of the quality control system. Thomas J. Barry (1991) of the American Society for Quality Control wrote:

[3]To control quality, companies create quality assurance (QA) systems, "a validation process to ensure measurement accuracy and standardization. The QA system focuses on constant incremental quality improvement measurement and result" (Barry, 1991). Many organizations rely heavily on quantitative, statistical measures to ensure quality.

Productivity: Productivity is the amount of output achieved from a given set of inputs. Improvements in productivity should lead to improvements in both quality and profits. Productivity can be measured quantitatively and qualitatively. Examples of quantitative measures of productivity include the number of customers served per hour and the total units produced per machine–hour of operation. Qualitative measures incorporate such factors as customer feedback–feedback about how well they were treated by a customer–service representative, for example. As Seidman and Skancke (1990) observed, "No job category is beyond measurement or evaluation. But remember, no single statistic that relates to worker effort should be regarded as an absolute measure of productivity."

Managers at General Foods decided to use a comprehensive approach to measuring productivity when they decided to become the nation's lowest–cost food producer. The company developed a sophisticated control system, the Plant wide Productivity Measurement Program, or PPMP. Using standard cost–accounting data, managers devised individual productivity indexes for each aspect of General Foods' many product lines. The component measures yielded an aggregate productivity index for each product or plan. By using PPMP, General Food's managers were able to identify production inefficiencies and meet cost–reduction targets (Seidman and Skancke, 1990).

Behaviors: Managers must take great care to ensure that standards do not encourage behaviours that compromise the organization's mission and goals, Salespersons evaluated solely by the sales revenue they generate may be tempted to treat all sales as equal rather than emphasize sales that yield the highest profits. Similarly, the division manager evaluated primarily against the short–term standard of quarterly profits may be tempted to ignore the long–term investment needed to ensure the organization's future survival. Control standards and measurements must seek to create comparability between individual and organizational goals (Bittel and Ramsey, 1985).

Top managers at ConAgra, a giant producer of food products, discovered that standards emphasizing decentralization had led to behaviours that were undermining efficiency and profitability. As Lubove (1992) reported, ConAgra was operating as "a decentralized patchwork to business fiefdoms, "unable to maximize its own potential. Each unit ordered packaging form different suppliers, for example, and made long–distance telephone calls over different networks. Each bought raw materials from outside suppliers that they could have bought from one another. New CEO

3 Measurement is the springboard to involvement, allowing the organization to initiate corrective action, set priorities, and evaluate progress. Standards and measures should reflect customer requirements and expectations. Each employee must be a partner in achieving quality goals. teamwork involves managers, supervisors, and employees in improving service delivery, solving systemic problems, and correcting errors in all parts of work processes.

Philip Fletcher set out to achieve closer cooperation among the subsidiaries, especially in purchasing and distribution. "I want us to buy as a $20–billion–;lus company but maintain [an] independent operating company culture" (Lubove, 1992).

7.4.2 Measuring Performance

After standards are established, managers must measure actual performance to determine variation from standard. the mechanisms for this purpose can be extremely sensitive, particularly in high–tech environments. Building modern airliners, for example requires extraordinarily refined measurement and control systems. Along with visual inspections, technicians induce electric current in the metal surfaces to create magnetic fields. Any distortion in the fields indicates a problem (*Business Week*, November 18, 1991).

Computers are becoming increasingly important as tools for measuring performance. They can monitor people and operations as they occur, and they can store data to be used later. Many retail stores use computerized scanning equipment that simultaneously accesses prices and tallies sales and then tracks inventory by department, vendor, and branch store. The computerized scanning systems can also track the sales personnel, recording transactions and sales-clerk activity. The displays and reports these systems produce often show current standards and actual performance measurements. Computerized systems of all kinds give managers the up–to–the–minute information they need to make sound decisions.

7.4.3 Comparing Measured Performance to Established Standards

The next step in the control process is to compare actual performance to the standards set for that performance. If deviations from the standards exist, the evaluator must decide if they are significant – if they require corrective action. If so, the evaluator must determine what is causing the variance.

To understand variance in regard to manufacturing consider an operation that mills a billet of titanium into a complex shape to be used as an engine part. The established tolerance, or standard of variance, for the part is plus or minus 1/1000 inch from the specified dimensions. Periodically throughout the milling process, the machinist measures the part to be sure that it remains within tolerance. Any part milled beyond the tolerance must be rejected. A search for the cause of the unacceptable variance begins.

The source of a deviation may lie beyond the employee who first discovers it. Suppliers may have shipped faulty materials. Previous operators may have been poorly trained, dishonest about results, or misinformed about applicable standards. If equipment is in poor condition, it may be incapable or producing output that meets the standards–no matter how hard the operator tries. Determining the cause of substandard performance involves going beyond an examination of task performance, however. It involves examining the standards being applied and the accuracy of the measurement and comparison processes. As Bittel and Ramsey (1985) explained, the control may be too loose or too tight:

> *If control is too loose, a deviation between actual and planned performance may result in poor coordination among organizational sub–units and the failure to respond in time to unforeseen problems or opportunities. Loose control may also reduce some of the incentives for managers to meet their pans. On the other hand, tighter control generally calls for additional data collection, information processing, and management reporting. The cost and inconvenience of the 'red tape' associated with tight control is likely to be resented by the persons being controlled. Tight control may restrict the ability of lower–level manager to exercise imagination and initiative in response to changed conditions.*

In the productivity – and quality–centred environment of today, workers and managers are often empowered to evaluate their own work for quality, productivity, and cost improvements. Individuals and groups throughout organizations are being given the responsibility to control their own behaviours and operations. By putting the authority to make decisions in the hands of those who are best equipped to make them, employees can respond almost instantly to substandard performance.

7.4.4 Taking Corrective Action

When an employee determines the cause, or causes, of a significant deviation from a standard, he or she must take corrective action on avoid repetition of the problem or defect. Policies and procedures may prescribe the actions. Such guidelines help shorten the time needed to react to deviations. Policies and procedures cannot be employed in all instances, however.

In some cases, pressures and controls imposed from outside an organization dictate the nature of corrective action. Equifax, a company that provides consumer credit reports, recently had to take action as a result of legal challenges. *Business week* (July 13, 1992) reported the extent to which Equifax executives decided to change company practices:

> *Equifax successfully avoided being sued when it agreed on June 30[1992] to revamp its methods. After talks with attorneys general of 18 states, Equifax announced it would go beyond federal law to ensure the accuracy of its credit reports and correct errors promptly. Equifax said it would continue with many of the steps it had already taken, including installing new software, providing a toll–free number for consumer questions, looking into disputes within 30 days, and providing free copies of reports to consumers denied requests for credit. The state attorneys extracted a similar agreement last year from TRW, another leading credit report company.*

Some corrective actions are automatic. Just as a thermostat can activate a heating or cooling system automatically, assembly operations with computer–guided equipment can sense deviations and take corrective actions without the need for human involvement. Managers must not overlook automatic controls when searching for the causes of substandard performance. even automatic controls can malfunction on occasion.

Some corrective actions call for exceptions to prescribed modes of behaviour to retain the goodwill of a valued customer, for example, a manager may authorize an exception to the firm's refund policy. Some hotel and restaurant chains empower customer–service employees of "do whatever it takes" to guarantee customer satisfaction. If managers direct employees to do whatever it takes, the managers must allow the employees to use their discretion and judgement. The employees will face problems for which no guidelines exist–problems that will demand unique and creative solutions. Procedures, rules, and policies should not be substitutes for good judgement and employee initiative.

7.5. Types Of Controls And Control Systems

This section will begin by discussing three types of controls: feed-forward controls, concurrent controls, and feedback controls. Each focuses on a different point of a process–before the process begins, during the process, or after it ceases. Most experts agree that controls "are most economic and effective when applied selectively at the crucial points most likely to determine the success or failure of an operation or activity" (Bittel, 1989). A restaurant must focus on controlling the quality of its ingredients, their proportion, and their presentation. All these control points are critical to the restaurant's safe and effective operation. Poor ingredients will yield a bad meal, as will poorly cooked food. Poor customer service will alienate diners. Figure 7.2 shows how the three types of controls apply to restaurant operations.

7.5.1 Feed-forward Controls

Controls that focus on operations before they begin are called **feed forward Controls**. (These controls are sometimes called preliminary, screening, or prevention controls.) Feed forward controls are intended to prevent defects and deviations from standards. Locks on doors and bars on windows, safety equipment and guidelines, employee–selection procedures, employee–training programs, and budgets are all feed-forward controls. When a manufacturer works closely with its suppliers to ensure that the suppliers deliver goods and services that meet standards, the manufacturer is implementing a feed-forward control. A maintenance procedure the keeps equipment in top–notch shape is also a feed-forward control.

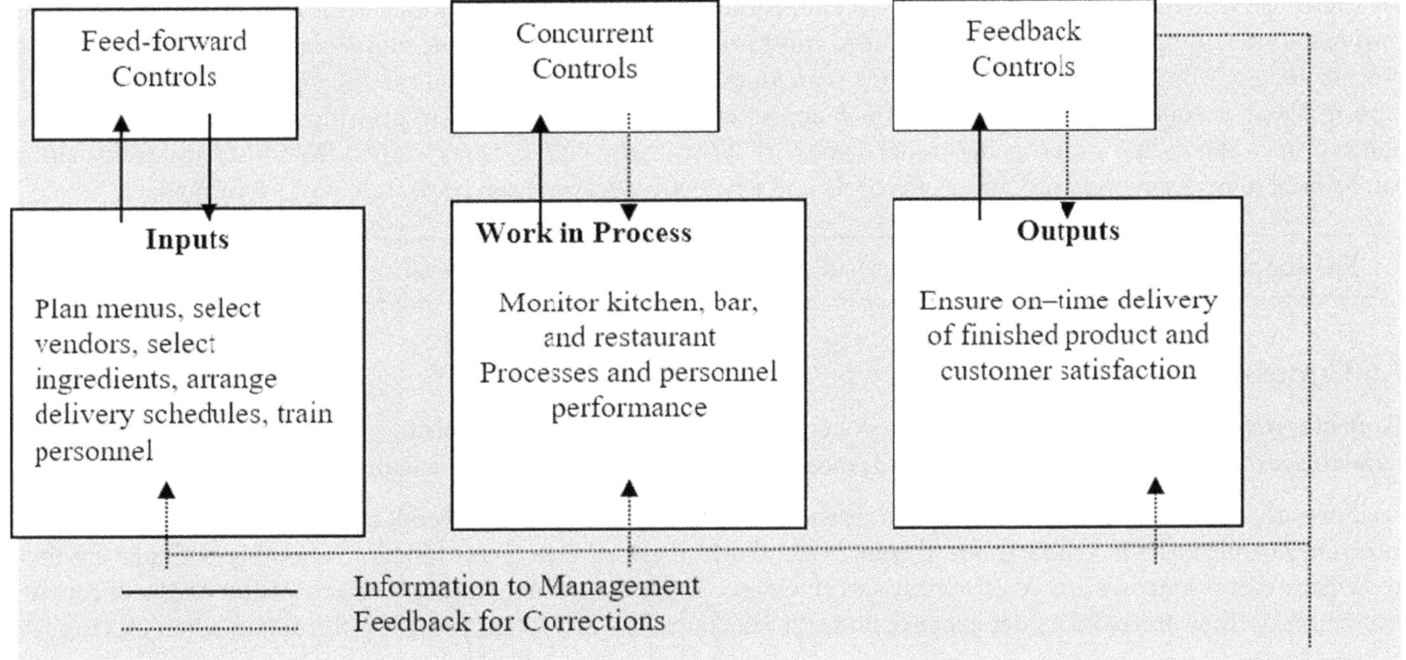

Figure 7.2 Three types of controls applied to restaurant operations.
Source: Okwachi SW, Miricho M, Maranga V. A Study Focus in to Hospitality Restaurant Operations in Regard to Food Security, Through Food Waste and Loss Control Mechanisms. EasyChair; 2018.

Feed-forward control A control that prevents defects and deviations from standards.

7.5.2 Concurrent Controls

Controls that apply to processes as they are happening are called Concurrent controls, or steering controls. Consider word processing software, which allows a writer to change a document on a video display terminal before storing or printing it. The software provides concurrent control. A word processor's spelling checker also provides concurrent control.

Some concurrent controls are designed to provide readouts or audible warnings. Most photocopiers and computer printers, for example, have display panels that alert their users to malfunctions during operation. Many of the devices on the dashboard of an automobile are concurrent controls. The odometer keeps track of miles traveled; the speedometer tracks the speed of the vehicle. Various warning lights alert the driver to impending or actual problems, such as low levels of fuel or oil and problems with the brakes or computerized systems. The steering wheel is a concurrent control that allows a driver to make adjustments in the course of the vehicle. If you try to exit a newly built automobile without turning off the headlights, you may be concurrently controlled by a warning device, perhaps even a gently scolding electronic voice.

The most important concurrent control in any undertaking is often the skilled and experienced operator, whose eyes, ears, and 'feel' for the operation give timely warnings that things are not as they should be. Recognizing the importance of experienced employees as control mechanisms, many companies are enhancing workers' power to affect operations.

Concurrent control: A control that applies to process as they are happening.

7.5.3 Feedback Controls

Controls that focus on the results of operations are called **feedback controls.** They are after-the-fact, or post performance, controls. They are called feedback controls because the information they provide is fed back into the process or to the controller, who must then make any necessary adjustments. "On a larger scale, however, measurements and comparisons made after an operation has been concluded (post performance) serve to guide future planning, goals, inputs, and process designs" (Bittel, 1989). At the end of the year, for example, a manager should carefully review the budget control report. Which accounts were overdrawn? Which accounts retained a surplus? Were priorities established through the budge proper and in line with organizational demands? Why or why not? Lessons learned from historical information can be used to perform every task more effectively and efficiently. Everyone can learn from past performance.

Feedback control: a control that focuses on the outputs or results of operations.

7.6 Control Systems

Control system: A system in which feedforward, concurrent, and feedback controls operate in harmony to ensure that standards are enforced, goals are reached, and resources are used effectively and efficiently.

Feedforward, concurrent, and feedback controls should be viewed as part of an overall **control system.** Able managers integrate suitable control combinations to enforce standards, make sure elements function smoothly with one another, and ensure that resources are used effectively and efficiently. Today companies are emphasizing feedforward and concurrent controls. They are avoiding dependence on feedback controls, which often provide information when it is too late to avoid losses.

7.7 Characteristics of Effective Controls

Controls at every level focus on inputs, processes, and outputs; but what characteristics make controls effective? Effective controls are focused on critical points and integrated into the corporate culture. They are timely and accepted by those who use them or abide by them. In addition, effective controls are economically feasible, accurate, and comprehensible.

Focus on Critical Points

Critical control points are all the operations that directly affect the survival of an organization and the success of its most essential activities. Critical control points exist in many areas of business activity-production, sales, customer service, and finance, for example. Controls should focus on those points at which failures cannot be tolerated and where time and money costs are greatest.

The objective is to apply controls to the essential aspects of a business, not the peripheral ones. Having a sales person report on all the activities undertaken during a long sales trip would be one way to control. The resulting report would probably obscure the important issues, however, and the task of writing it would burden the sales person. A simple report of actual sales calls and sales revenues would be far more relevant and effective.

Integration

Controls exhibit integration when the corporate culture supports and enforce them and when they work in harmony, not at cross-purposes. When controls and the need for them are consonant with the organization's values, the controls will be effective. Coordinated controls do not impede work; they function harmoniously to give people what they need to make informed judgements.

It is also realized that risk management/controlling would mean more than rules. It would require reforming the company's culture and instilling in individuals the commitment to act ethically and responsibly in all their undertakings.

When managers and employees trust each other and workers at all levels believe that the controls are necessary, employees can be relied on to implement the controls. When everyone accepts the organization's mission and culture, the corporate climate nourishes self-discipline and commitment. Work teams are self-policing and share values that are consistent with those of the organization. As workers enter these supportive environments, managers and co-workers take care to ensure that the newcomers "buy into" the culture (Walton, 1985).

Acceptability

People must agree that controls are necessary, that the particular kinds of controls in use are appropriate, and that the controls will not have negative impacts on individuals or their efforts to achieve personal goals. Controls that appear to be arbitrary, subjective, or an invasion or privacy will not elicit the support of those they affect. Likewise, controls that are redundant (except when necessary for health and safety) or too restrictive will go unsupported. In fact, such controls will stimulate covert and overt opposition. Too many controls, confusing controls, and too few controls create stress and resistance. Frustration, fear, and loss of motivation and initiative can result.

Timeliness

Controls must ensure that information reaches those who need it *when they need it:* only then can a meaningful response follow. One reason for setting deadlines is to ensure that information flows promptly. If deadlines are treated casually or unrealistically (if the manager always wants things yesterday), people will soon come to ignore them. In such a case, deadlines are totally ineffective as controls.

Ensuring timely flow is one goal of management information systems. Kmart employs modern technology to link its stores to headquarters and vendors. Among the sophisticated equipment the organization uses are point-of-sale devices that, via satellite, transmit merchandise information to buyers and vendors. The devices can also provide instant credit authorization to speed customer checkout. These tools saved enough money to pay for the satellite system in less than two years (Comins, 1992)

Economic Feasibility

The costs of a control system must be weighed against its benefits. If the resources expended on the controls do not return an equal or greater value, the controls are better left unimplemented. Suppose a costly security system includes highly trained personnel, sophisticated electronic surveillance equipment, and fingerprint scanning. Such a system is suitable for valuable capital equipment and facilities, but not the office supply cabinet.

Sometimes controls must be costly and redundant. Jet aircraft, nuclear power plants, hospital operating and intensive care facilities, and the space shuttle need redundant systems, or backup systems, to allow them to overcome a potentially life-threatening failure of the primary system. NASA will not launch the space shuttle if one of the three main computers on board is malfunctioning. Redundant and expensive controls are often required to prevent problems that, if they occur, would mean irrecoverable loss or irreparable damage far more costly than the controls.

Accuracy

Information is useful if it is accurate. Accuracy relates particularly to concurrent controls used to diagnose deviations from standards. Controls that offer inaccurate assessments feed decision makers the wrong input, which causes them to give inappropriate responses. When a project manager reports that production is two weeks behind schedule because of poor team attendance, her boss begins an investigation. It turns out that, though several people have been absent, they were not key to production. The delay was actually caused by the failure to properly plan the flow of work and set meaningful deadlines.

Comprehensibility

The more complex a control becomes, the more likely it is to create confusion. The simpler the control, the easier it will be to communicate and apply. Anyone who has struggled with assembly instructions for a hobby kit knows first-hand how rare well-written instructions are. Controls in the form of instructions are often complex because more than one person created, implemented, or interpreted them. Complexity can also result when control users lose sight of the purposes of the control.

Too many controls can lead to confusion. (The notion that if one control is good, two must be better, is common but incorrect.) Refinements in reporting procedures often lead to the proliferation of controls. The result can be a profusion of data that side-tracks control efforts.

Computers are reducing complexity and confusion in many environments. Bar codes attached to inventory items of materials moving along an assembly line simplify the process of tracking. Some computer software allows voice commands–even commands in a foreign language–to activate or access processes. Machines that use symbols rather than words further overcome language barriers. "Smart" software and a few keystrokes or flicks of a light pen can get things on track. All these innovations enhance communication by keeping it simple.

Review Questions

1. Discuss the meaning of controlling?
2. Outline the processes of control.
3. Discuss the relationship between controlling and other management functions.
4. Discuss the types of control.
5. What are the characteristics of control?
6. Identify the benefits the company will derive from a good control system.
7. What are the problems faced by the organisation in implementing an effective control system?
8. Discuss the relationship between planning and controlling.

Short Case:

Addis Ababa rose Ltd is a company exporting fresh flowers for international markets in Europe. After a long period of high performance and profitability, but lastly started to face trouble with market share due to growing competition and the capabilities of the new rivals from Latin America and Asia besides the dissatisfaction of customers because of price and quality problems. Therefore the company started to develop a solution; one of the solutions is the controlling process.

Questions:

1. Determine the advantages of a sound control system.
2. How can you find a relationship between planning and controlling to ensure that plan is achieved.
3. develop a controlling process for Addis Ababa company to overcomes the problems that facing

CHAPTER EIGHT

CONTEMPORARY ISSUES

     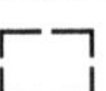 

8.1. Technology and Innovation Management

LEARNING OBJECTIVES

- Explaining the main technological innovations nowadays and their influence on tourism.
- Being aware of some experiences of technological innovation and its implementation in the tourism industry.
- Emphasizing the opportunities and benefits of incorporating new technological advances in tourism.

Overview

management practices help organizations several ways, the innovation role of the top management team cannot be understated in terms of product and process improvement, which in turn significantly improve profitability, this section presents a comprehensive overview on technology and innovation management and the effect of management on technology and vice versa, besides the practices, operations, issues and trends.

History moves through periods characterized by many features and characteristics related to life in its social aspect, business, politics, and economics, which stimulate the search for explanations, justifications, and theories to understand or deal with them. Therefore, new trends and methods develop based on the new developments. (Freeman and Hagedoorn 1994). These new methods and methods were represented by technology, globalization of markets, corporate migration to Asia and other changes (Freeman and Hagedoorn, 1994). The new technologies related to advanced manufacturing techniques and mass production techniques, along with the technology and techniques of communication and social interaction, as well as alliances and trade blocs.

Innovation is essential for commercial companies. For Drucker (1973), this, along with marketing, is one of the two most important issues.

Innovation is also an essential determinant of macroeconomic growth and an "engine" for growth (Freeman, 1982). The success of local SMEs in the local and international markets leads to the successful performance of the overall national economy.

Innovations and technology affect various areas of business such as processes, materials, technologies, aerospace, computers, communications, and biotechnology, as they have become one of the dominant forces in the international economy and trade. From the managerial perspective, the technology management process is relatively new, as it represents a driving force from within and outside the organization, which means that technology must be managed as an internal capacity and as an institutional or national structure in addition to being a competitive tool for competitors (Levi Jaksic et al., 2012).

8.1.1. Definition of Technology and innovation management

Technology "refers to the theoretical and practical knowledge, skills and artifacts that can be used to develop products and services as well as their production and delivery systems

Innovation is the development or implementation of a new or significantly improved thing (good or service), process, new marketing method, new way of doing business, workplace organization or external relations (OECD, 2005)

Innovation is defined as the adoption of an idea or behaviour, whether a system, policy, program, device, process, product or service, that is new to organization" (Damanpour, 1992, p. 376)

innovation management

It is not easy to find a single or agreed-upon definition of innovation management and technology management. The concept of MI refers to new traditions and structures on the cutting edge of technology, showing that it does not have a global model.

While other researchers see MI as something new to a company and adapted from another context, perhaps from peer companies

MI is also referred to as new management practices aimed at improving company performance.

Innovation management includes many things such like:

- learning to find the most appropriate solution
- to the problem of consistently managing aforestated process
- finding the most effective ways and practices.
- managing the process of learning from the lessons and obstacles

Objectives of Innovation Management

- To reap in the economic benefits of new technological inventions by commercializing them on time
- To integrate technology into overall strategic objective of the organization.
- To get into and out of the technologies faster and more efficiently.
- To accomplish technology transfer.
- To reduce new product development time.
- To manage large,complex & interdisciplinary projects and systems.

Challenges of Managing Innovation

1. Why Change?
   - Only innovation matters.
2. What to Change?
   - Ranging from changes in product & service to the ways(i.e. process innovation).
3. Understanding Innovation.
   - Understanding common problems associated with partial views of innovation.
4. Building an Innovation Culture.
   - Managing Innovation is all about creating firm specific ways of doing things (practices, behavior) which define its approach to the problem.
5. Continuous Learning
   - Firms constantly needs to develop their routines to deal with the environmental challenges.
6. High Involvement Innovation
   - Higher level of participations in innovation represents a competitive advantage.

Innovation Management Dimensions

There are many dimensions associated with innovation from practices and behavior point of view: innovation strategy, management systems, innovation culture, creativity, exct..

Innovation and management level:

In all profitable companies and non-profit organizations, there is a structural hierarchy that determines the levels of management in terms of thinking, planning, implementation and control. We do not find that there are three levels of management

- strategic level
- Tactical level
- operational level

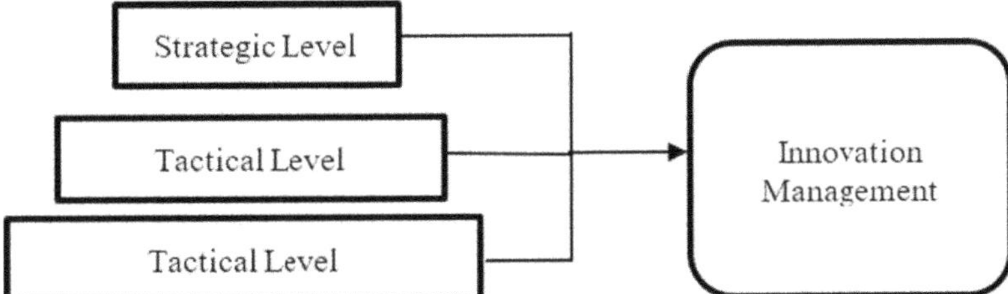

Figure 8.1 Innovation and management levels. Source: Developed by the authors;

Strategic level

According to the levels of management, innovation management at the strategic level is based on determining the company's basic and strategic directions, taking into account the contextual conditions, expected changes and conditions of uncertainty, as well as customers and their needs.

This level should focus on long-term goals, technology, the level of innovation and innovation, tools and methods of development, as well as mechanisms for implementing innovation.

Tactical Level

At the tactical level of management, innovation is dealt with at the level of planning activities in terms of the effectiveness that innovation will bring at the level of activities through the procedures and means that are used in addition to simplification and facilitation in work can achieve cost savings.

Operational level

Innovation management is dealt with at the operational level through the control of production processes that allow for maximum utilization of resources and capabilities, talent and expertise of employees in innovation and development of new solutions to problems.

The management of innovation at this level is based on simplifying activities and procedures, which in turn will lead to the achievement of various positive results.

8.2. Diversity Management

Learning Objectives

1. Discuss the nature of diversity and distinguish between diversity management and equal employment opportunity.
2. Identify and describe the major dimensions of diversity in organizations.
3. Discuss the primary impact of diversity on organizations.
4. Describe individual and organizational strategies and approaches to coping with diversity and discuss the multicultural organization.
5. Discuss the basic issues in managing the knowledge function in organizations.
6. Relate human resource management and social issues.

8.2.1. Introduction

The diversity management approach has emerged to keep pace with organizational development policies and to maximize the importance of using And rationalizing the performance of human resources in organizations, and considering it one of the effective tools of sustaining business growth and profitability, Which supports the company status in the market particularly these days because of hyper competition and global business issues.

Workforce diversity is a natural and common occurrence in all organizations. diversity is receiving increasing attention at present due to the increasing demands for equality, tolerance and acceptance of the other on the one hand. Where diversity is of great importance in the process of innovation and the development of ideas that lead the organization to growth and development, as the management of diversity helps to employ it better and generate significant benefits from it to help the organization stimulate creativity and improve organizational performance. Furthermore, as economies become global and open, many companies are expanding their operations beyond local boundaries, which requires a better understanding of the methods used to maximize the benefits of diversity.

Diversity has been used since 1970 to refer to minorities and women in power. It has long been familiar to managers that diversity in the workplace is increased gender equality, national and ethnic representation in the workforce.

Diversity management should be based on building, developing and maintaining diversity in the organization because the organization is a broad framework that includes many different components culturally, sexually or cognitively where they are accepted because of competence regardless of the differences between them, and a multicultural organization is an organization in which races and cultures mix There is also another, deeper dimension to diversity in organizations. Diversity management means opening the organization to become more inclusive, wider culture, and more creative that respects the uniqueness and diversity of personalities.

8.2.2. Concept of diversity management

There is sometimes confusion between diversity management and parity, but diversity management does not address multiple issues, just as it differs from parity. Not for the benefit of any group.

Diversity management can be defined as the different cultural and social identities of individuals who work together in the work environment. While it is defined as the differences between individuals in the social and historical background that cause different powers and privileges inside and outside organizations.

It is the application of effective management practices that recognize human and social diversity in the workforce and customers and the difference between them, and the management of these differences in terms of gender, origin, age, culture, language, disability, religion, sexual orientation, and any other characteristics that shape the opinions and orientations of individuals in organizations to take advantage of the benefits of diversity in increasing the effectiveness of Business and organizations, achieving justice among all workers in organizations, and impartiality to one group at the expense of another.

Advantages of Diversity Management

1. Increase skill diversity and improve organizational reputation
2. Reducing the intensity of organizational conflict in the organization.
3. Improving human relations.
4. Reducing the individual's feeling of job alienation
5. decreas the turnover
6. increase the organizational flexibility

Diversity management dimensions

Diversity management has been classified into several types based on two groups, the first of which includes the primary dimensions of age, origin, ethnicity, gender, physical abilities, and sexual orientations, while the second group includes secondary dimensions, which are work experience, income, marital status, military experience, religious beliefs, place of residence, parental status, and education.

Diversity Management Process

The diversity management process is complex and requires clear planning and following a systematic step that help in achieving diversity management objective. Many steps can be follows in managing diversity, including:

- Set diversity management objectives
- Make the necessary changes to maintain diversity.
- Ensure that all policies are compatible with diversity management
- Avoid allowing bias in HR.
- Develop strong equality policies and communicate them to all employees.
- Disseminate the culture of respect, tolerance, patience, and cooperation issue appropriate penalties for those who offend the system and practice racism and discrimination.
- Conduct a cultural review and develop strategies for intervention.
- Develop guidelines for identifying and addressing social issues affecting workers.

8.3. Total Quality Management

Learning Outcomes:

You should be able to:

1. Explain The concept and principles of quality management (QM)
2. Understand the processes of Quality Assurance, and Control
3. Apply QM principles
4. Describe the total quality management steps.

8.3.1. Introduction

Quality has recently aroused great interest among business institutions and academicians due to the increasing competitiveness of companies, producers, and service providers, which made customers more capable and could choose the best options.

Therefore, every company must be distinguished through high levels of Quality determined according to the characteristics of customers and the needs that will be satisfied.

Quality is of strategic and vital importance for both the customer and the producer, regardless of the type and size of products or services, because the Quality of the product plays a pivotal role in the company's competitive strategy at the business level and in the local, regional and international markets. The failure of the product to meet the needs and desires of the business cannot be compensated by any marketing effort or selling effort. Quality helps to build and improve good relations between the company and its stakeholders (the organization, customers, competitors and society) and helps in improving the competitive position, facing the challenges of severe competition in the business environment and obtaining a Competitive Advantage in the markets because Quality is considered one of the determinants of sustainability and continuity because it is linked to the demand for The company's products and the continuity of customers, and therefore it is a guarantee for the survival and continuity of the company.

8.3.2. Quality Concept

To clarify the concept of quality, we will focus on three main entrances to the definition: quality reflects the benefit achieved by one of these three parties: the producer, the customer, and the society. The benefit achieved by the product is reflected in the design and meeting consumer's desires and objectives. From the customer perspective, quality is a value, that is, how a good product can achieve its intended purpose and at an acceptable cost. Finally, the benefit achieved by the consumer is manifested in the extent to which his needs and desires are satisfied. Many studies shows that quality directly affects profit. A company that has a small market share and produces low products achieves an average of 7% return on investment, while a similar company that produces high-quality products achieves 20% return on investment. If we make the obvious assumption that quality increases market share, that return on investment will jump from just 7% to 29%. In Japan, it was estimated that the companies that received the Deming Prize made, on average, twice the average industrial profit. Pignanelli., & Csillag,. (2008).

From a societal perspective, the product should not harming society by offering products that are harmful to health, the environment or life in general

8.3.3. Total Quality Management

Total quality management refer to a philosophy that involves everyone in an organization in a continual effort to improve quality and achieve customer satisfaction.

Total Quality Management means that the organization's culture is defined by and supports the constant attainment of customer satisfaction through an integrated system of tools, techniques, and training. This involves the continuous improvement of organizational processes, resulting in high quality products and services.

The application and practice of total quality management within the company requires the availability of several foundations and principles that are commensurate and complement each other to achieve the organization's direct and indirect goals in the short and long term, which is to improve the level of performance within the organization (managers, employees and outside the public dealing with it) (Evans, 2007.), these principles as follow:

- planning,
- top management support,
- human resource development,
- facts based decision making.

TQM is a dynamic process because it already contains a several principles that make up the management philosophy. Therefore, your quest for the success of TQM is not as easy as teaching employees the techniques of assertive communication. A clear understanding of the existing principles. As there is no one-size-fits-all in TQM, in other words, the success of TQM may represent a challenge that requires patience and commitment.

Total quality management is considered as a dynamic process because it contains a set of principles around twelve principles or more that reflect the management's aspect of quality. Therefore, your quest for the success of total quality management is not as easy as teaching employees the techniques of assertive communication, and any application of total quality management but its need to modify the methods and tools; it depends on a clear understanding of the principles. As there is no one-size-fits-all in TQM, in other words, the success of TQM implementation facing a challenge that requires patience and commitment (Stevenson, 2007).

Steps of applying total quality

1. Evaluate the Company's Culture:

To implement TQM, the company needs to evaluate its organizational culture. The culture of the company can be evaluated through:

- Continuous improvement measurement.
- Authority equals responsibility.
- Rewards for results.
- Teamwork and collaborative work.
- Job security.
- Justice

2. Training and learning:

the company must educate and train the staff through various forms of practical or executive training so that employees can apply quality according to the principles and requirements of total quality.

3. Quality board:

The company should establish a quality board or committee for a variety of reasons. Members must represent all levels in the company, including senior management, middle management, and employees. This great diversity of experiences and capabilities may help encourage cooperation between the team members.

4. Information dissemination:

One of the responsibilities and tasks of the Quality Council is to disseminate and share information with all employees and to ensure the effectiveness of the communication process.

5. System Integration

The consolidation process demonstrates how the tools, techniques, techniques and training of TQM should be integrated into a company, although there is no specific formula for defining which system or to what extent these three elements should be integrated. (Talib., Rahman., & Qureshi, 2013)

Review Questions

1. explain the philosophies of quality management.
2. Describe total quality management process.
3. Discuss the steps total quality management implementation.
4. Describe the quality systems components

Reference Books

Anderson DR, Sweeney DJ, Williams TA, Camm JD, Cochran JJ. An introduction to management science: quantitative approach. Cengage learning; 2018.

Boone, Louis E. and Kurtz, Dauid L., Principles of Management, Random House Inc, 2nd ed., Toronto, 1981.

Bose DC. Principles of management and administration. PHI Learning Pvt. Ltd.; 2012 Mar 9.

Bovee,C. and Thill, J.V."Business Communication Today",11thedition,Prentice Hall, 201.

Bright DS, Cortes AH, Hartmann E, Parboteeah KP, Pierce JL, Reece M, Shah A, Terjesen S, Weiss J, White MA, Gardner DG. Principles of management. OpenStax; 2019 Mar 20.

Brooklyn M. Cole, Manjula S. Salimath. Diversity Identity Management: An Organizational Perspective. Journal of business ethics (2013).

Carpenter, M. A., Bauer, T., Erdogan, B., & Short, J. Principles of management. Washington, DC: Flat World Knowledge, 2012.

Daft, R.L. and Marcic, D. Understanding management. Cengage Learning. 2016.

Daft Richard, L. New Era of management. Australia: South Western-Cengage Learning, 2010.

Damanpour, Fariborz. "Organizational size and innovation." Organization studies 13.3 1992: 375–402.

Dan Groszkiewicz and Brent Warren, "Alcoa's Michigan Casting Centre Runs the Business from the Bottom Up," Journal of Organizational Excellence (Spring 2006): 13–23. (used with permission).

Darr, Kurt. "Introduction to management and leadership concepts, principles." Essentials of management and leadership in public health 7 (2011).

David R. Hampton. Contemporary Management, McGraw- Hill Inc. New York, 1981

Drucker, Peter F. "Managing the public service institution." The public interest 33 (1973): 43.

Drucker, Peter. The practice of management. Routledge, 2012.

Earnest, Dale. Management: Theory and Practice, McGraw- Hill Inc. New York, 1981.

J. Timms. Introduction to business and management. University of London International Programmes Publications Office, London, united Kingdom, 2011.

Jakšić ML, Marinković S, Kojić J. Technology and innovation management education in Serbia. In Innovative Management and Firm Performance 2014 (pp. 37–67). Palgrave Macmillan, London.

James, A.F. Stooner and R. Edvead. Freeman, Management prentice – Hall, 4th, New Delhi., 1989.

Collins J. Level 5 leadership: The triumph of humility and fierce resolve. Managing Innovation and Change. 2006 Aug 30;234.

Hillier, Frederick S. Introduction to management science: a modeling and case studies approach with spreadsheets. McGraw-Hill College, 2007.

Joharis M. The effect of leadership, organizational culture, work motivation and job satisfaction on teacher organizational commitment at senior high school in Medan. International Journal of Business and Management Invention. 2016;5(10):1–8.

Jones, Gareth R., and Jennifer M. George."Contemporary Management. 4th ed. New York, NY: McGraw-Hill Irwin. 2006.

Karmakar A. Principles and practices of management and business communication. Pearson Education India; 2011.

Kinicki, Angelo, et al. Management: A practical introduction. McGraw-Hill Irwin, 2011.

Kinard, Jery, Management, D.C. Heath and Company, Toronto, 1988.

Koontz H, Weihrich H, Cannice MV. Essentials of Management-An International, Innovation and Leadership Perspective|. McGraw-Hill Education; 2020.

Koontz, Harold, and Weihrich Heinz: Management; McGraw Hill Book Co., 9th ed., New York, 1988.

Koontz, Harold, Cryil O'Donnel and Weihrich Heinz: Management ; McGraw Hill International New York, 1980.

Lillico, T. Michael. Managerial communication. Elsevier, 2016.

Markaki EN, Sakas DP, Chadjipantelis T. Communication management in business. The latent power for career development. Procedia-Social and Behavioral Sciences. 2013 Feb 27;73:319–26.

Merrill, Harwood F., Classics In Management: Tera Prevala publishing Industries., India, 1980.

Meyer, Herbert H., Emanuel Kay, and John RP French. "Split roles in performance appraisal." Psychology and Industrial Productivity. Palgrave Macmillan, London, 1981. 70–84.

OECD. Oslo Manual - Guidelines for Collecting and Interpreting Innovation Data, 2005.

Onsongo EN, Maina ZR. Employee attitudes towards organizational diversity on business performance; perspectives from the small and medium enterprises employees in Kisii Town. Review of Contemporary Business Research. 2013;2(1):30-40.

Prasad, L. M. Principles and practice of management. Sultan Chand & Sons, 2020.

Peter F. Drucker. Management: Task and Responsibility, Haper and Row, New York, 1973.

Plunket, Warren R. and Attner, Raymong F. Management, 6th Ed., South-Western College Publishing; 1997

Levi-Jakšić M, editor. Proceedings of the XIII International Symposium SymOrg 2012: Innovative Management and Business Performance. University of Belgrade, Faculty of Organizational Sciences; 2012 Jun 3.

Relation between Secondary School Administrators' Transformational and Transactional Leadership Style and Skills to Diversity Management in the School. Educational Sciences: Theory & Practice (2014).

Robbins SP, Coulter MK. Management. Pearson Education India; 2009.

Robbins SP, Coulter M. Management 13E. Pearson India; 2017.

Robbins SP, Coulter M. Management. New Jersey: Prentice Hall; 2012.

Robbins, S.P. and Coulter, M. Management (Vol. 470). New Jersey: Prentice Hall, 2012.

Samuel C. Certo. Principles of Modern and Management, Allyn and Bacon Inc., Boston.1986.

Swansburg, Russell C., and Richard J. Swansburg. Introduction to management and leadership for nurse managers. Jones & Bartlett Learning, 2002.

Sisk, Henery. Management and Organization, South Western Publishing Co., Chicago, 1982.

Terry, George R. and Franklin, Stephen G., Principles of Management, Richard D. Irwin Inc., 8th ed., Homewood, 1988.

Lester, David. "Measuring Maslow's hierarchy of needs." Psychological reports 113.1 2013: 15–17.

Okwachi SW, Miricho M, Maranga V. A Study Focus in to Hospitality Restaurant Operations in Regard to Food Security, Through Food Waste and Loss Control Mechanisms. EasyChair; 2018.

www.ingramcontent.com/pod-product-compliance
Ingram Content Group UK Ltd.
Pitfield, Milton Keynes, MK11 3LW, UK
UKHW061706190726
13853UKWH00008B/2439